C000133176

Switching to Goddess

Humanity's Ticket into the Future

First published by O Books, 2008
O Books is an imprint of John Hunt Publishing Ltd., The Bothy, Deershot Lodge, Park Lane, Ropley,
Hants, SO24 0BE, UK
office1@o-books.net
www.o-books.net

Distribution in:	
	South Africa
	Alternative Books
UK and Europe	altbook@peterhyde.co.za
Orca Book Services	Tel: 021 555 4027 Fax: 021 447 1430
orders@orcabookservices.co.uk	
Tel: 01202 665432 Fax: 01202 666219	Text copyright Jeri L. Studebaker 2008
Int. code (44)	
	Design: Stuart Davies
USA and Canada	
NBN	ISBN: 978 1 84694 134 4
custserv@nbnbooks.com	
Tel: 1 800 462 6420 Fax: 1 800 338 4550	All rights reserved. Except for brief quotations in critical articles or reviews, no part of this book may be reproduced in any manner without prior written permission from the publishers.
Australia and New Zealand	
Brumby Books	
sales@brumbybooks.com.au	
Tel: 61 3 9761 5535 Fax: 61 3 9761 7095	The rights of Jeri L. Studebaker as author have been asserted in accordance with the Copyright, Designs and Patents Act 1988.
Far East (offices in Singapore, Thailand, Hong Kong, Taiwan)	
Pansing Distribution Pte Ltd	
kemal@pansing.com	A CIP catalogue record for this book is available
Tel: 65 6319 9939 Fax: 65 6462 5761	from the British Library.

Printed and Bound by Digital Book Print Ltd
www.digitalbookprint.com

O Books operates a distinctive and ethical publishing philosophy in
all areas of its business, from its global network of authors to
production and worldwide distribution.
This book is produced on FSC certified stock, within ISO14001
standards. The printer plants sufficient trees each year through
the Woodland Trust to absorb the level of emitted carbon in
its production.

Switching
to Goddess
Humanity's Ticket
into the Future

Jeri L. Studebaker

BOOKS

Winchester, UK
Washington, USA

Contents

3. Good Times

7. Fight

8. The Fix

Figures

Acknowledgments

I'd like to give thanks to the following:

To Debbie Fleming, for putting aside work on her own books to read the manuscript for this one, for making exceptionally thoughtful written suggestions throughout the entire manuscript, for her encouragement and enthusiasm for the book, and for her skill at snagging my misplaced modifiers and missing commas.

To Clarke Owens for reading the manuscript, making copious notes and comments, and playing the best Devil's advocate a woman could ever want.

To Gloria Mallet, who introduced me to the Goddess years ago and then told me I could and should write a book about Her.

To Gina Hoffses for reading the manuscript from her perspective as an archaeologist and anthropologist, for tagging places I needed to strengthen and elaborate, and for offering generous amounts of enthusiastic encouragement.

To my "blood sister" from second grade, Kathy Brown, who also put aside work on her own books to read the manuscript and make suggestions.

To Morgaine Swann at The-Goddess and Goddess minister and author Karen Tate for their inspiration, ideas and encouragement. To all my online Goddess buddies — especially Ann Johnson, Terri Joburg, and Paul at "Evoking the Goddess."

To Jan Schrock, without whose consistent and unflagging encouragement this book might never have been written. Thanks go to Jan for sharing her fabulously creative ideas, for reading the manuscript not once but twice, for slipping me pertinent and timely articles from *The Nation* and other sources all along the way, and for her vociferous and unqualified enthusiasm for the book throughout the entire writing process.

To my mother for being there for me, even though she doesn't agree with or understand everything I write about the Sacred Feminine; she is one of the world's top moms, a role model not just for me but for many.

Thanks also to all the librarians who worked to feed me information, especially those at the Walker Memorial Library, Westbrook, Maine: Karen Valley, Jennifer Leo, Lisa Wojcik, and Dori Hawxwell.

Thanks also to the librarians at the Burbank Branch Library, Portland, Maine; the Bates College Library, Lewiston, Maine; the Bowdoin College Library, Brunswick, Maine; and the Colby College Library, Waterville, Maine.

Special thanks to Lynn Bivens, Reference Librarian at the Walker Memorial Library, who never grew tired of searching out the rarely read and obscure reference books I called in to him on a regular basis.

Introduction

My father's was a god family, my mothers' a family of the Goddess. It was enough to drive a kid crazy.

My father's family were early converts to a tiny Christian sect akin to the Amish and Mennonites, and in 1736 fled to America to practice their faith. Every Sunday my parents, brothers and sister and I would hop into the family station wagon and Dad would drive us from the city deep into farm country for church services. In Dad's church the women managed the music. Cousin Virginia Funderburg played the piano, Cousin Nancy Skillings the organ, and Mother sang in the choir with Aunt Francis and various cousins.

Although we were a small congregation, when we sang the sound swept over us like the rise and fall of a mighty sea. My otherwise reserved grandmother contributed a lusty alto refrain to "Onward Christian Soldiers" and "The Battle Hymn of the Republic" while my Aunt Esther smiled at the congregation and pumped her arm in a cross-shaped motion, beating out four-quarter time to keep us on the same note at the same time. Once during Sunday church services Mother and I sang "When I Fall on My Knees in Front of the Lord." Over and over during practice we sang "face" in place of "knees" and then burst into fits of nervous giggling. Mother's family — a 180-degree turn from Dad's — was prone to fits of uncontrollable laughter; more on them later.

While women tackled the music in Dad's church, men tackled everything else. Men were the deacons, ministers and ushers. Before Sunday worship service cousin Glen Funderburg trudged up to the balcony where the teens sat, to pass out two-by-three-inch illustrated pamphlets on the evils of alcohol, playing cards, and motion pictures. During the service, men collected money, waiting patiently at the end of each pew for people to plunk their bills and coins into the offering plate and pass it on.

Every summer the church heated up to boiling and dozens of donated funeral-home paper fans appeared in the sanctuary like battalions of butterflies. The heat made the varnish on the wooden pews sticky. One Sunday I stuck to a balcony pew and escaped only by sacrificing to the pew the nap of my pink-checked seersucker skirt. This could have been the same pew Aunt Vernona Skillings hauled up in the 1940s and carried out all by herself when the church caught fire. Even though the men still talk with pride about Aunt Vernona, she was nevertheless a woman, and so her role on Sundays naturally narrowed to handling music.

Dad's church circled around the War God Jehovah. Undoubtedly at least one of our ministers at some point read Exodus chapter fifteen verse three to the congregation: "The Lord is a warrior; the Lord is his name...." By the time I was five, the phrases "Battle Hymn," "Mighty Fortress," and "burnt offering" were standard fare in my vocabulary. By six I could decline verbs like stone (to death) and smite (smiteth, smote, smitten). All our ministers spoke non-stop about Father, Son and Holy Ghost, never about Mother, Daughter and Holy Grandmother.

For Sunday dinner Grandma always killed a couple of hens. Lying on a white platter with their four-toed orange feet still attached and surrounded by the tiny orange egg yolks they'd been carrying at death, the stewed hens dominated the dining-room table. But it was the men who "said grace" and otherwise dominated the meal. Across the hens and over the heads of the rest of us their voices boomed — about religion, politics, economics and so on. The women said things like "Please pass the succotash" and "Dougy, don't dribble on your clean shirt."

The men on my mother's side of the family said the prayers too — but no one listened much. Instead of church, Mother's family revolved around picnics in the park and holiday parties. This family sailed to America a hundred years earlier than Dad's — in the 1630s when Indians still practiced their old ways. Anyone in America as early as the 1630s had a lot of work done on them by the Great-Mother loving Native Americans, which could be why in Mother's family, the women were as much the movers and the shakers as the men were.

After church on Easter, instead of Grandma Studebaker's for dinner we always opted for Mother's family, who held Easter in the Lawrenceville Community Center. Crossing the threshold of the Community Center's large double doors we'd step into a whirlwind of sound and color: a babble of chatter, flushed faces, dishes clattering in the kitchen, laughter, boys drumming a basketball on the wooden-plank court at the east end of the Center, lacy festoons of Easter pinks, lime greens and daffodil yellows bedecking the women, who wound in and out among the dark-suited men. The aroma of pipe tobacco and hot coffee. More laughter. The table opposite the basketball court groaned under food heavily laced with sugar, cream and butter: Great Aunt Lucille's homemade biscuits and egg noodles; Grandma Ramsey's Waldorf Astoria $300/£192 red cake, fried chicken; fifteen kinds of pies including Great Grandma Davis' sugar pie; and so forth.

Mother's was a fun-and-games family. The grownups were more like kids than the kids, and the kids were consulted on all important issues. After dinner the men and younger people played cards, the women chatted, and Grandma and her five sisters (often called "The Sisters" by the rest of us) sat together in the southwest corner of the Center. At this point a few of us sneaked out back and hid candy for the Easter-egg hunt.

The Sisters got more excited by the egg hunt than the rest of us did. Flushed with pride and excitement they'd carefully lead toddlers out to the grass — babies bedecked in frilly pastel dresses or tiny bow ties and suit jackets. The Sisters would hover as the babies teetered forward, dragging their Easter baskets with puzzled frowns on their faces and no idea what they were supposed to be doing in the grass. Crouching in the sun with cameras, mothers dotted the yard, shooting film as if chronicling the pope stumbling upon the Holy Grail.

My mother's family didn't really worship goddesses. They did, however, live the old Goddess ways far more than my father's family did. And Mother's family illustrates an important point: some of the healthy old ways of our goddess-revering ancestors still linger with us today, even though over the past 6000 years goddesses have been mostly forced underground. But you have to go back a ways to get to the healthy times I'm talking about — before, for example, the new Johnny-come-lately war gods forced Hera, Venus, Inanna and the others into becoming their wives and concubines, and before these gods threw Athena, Bellona, Inanna, Minerva and hundreds of other goddesses down on the ground, sat on them, and made them promise to become war gods too. In fact these so-called war goddesses are merely mealy-mouthed makeovers of the real goddesses who came before them.

Jehovah, Indra, Allah, Mars, Ares, Odin and the other war gods are the new kids on the block. For the first 1.89 million of the 1.90 million years we humans have stomped around on planet earth, we survived quite nicely, thank you, without war gods. It was only about 6000 years ago, in places like Mesopotamia and ancient Egypt that these gods first reared their ugly heads, pounding around all over the place with names like Ninurta, Imdugud, Menthu and Wepwawet. Sometimes we don't even know their names, but it's clear from their pictures what they are; archaeologists call them things like "thunder god" and "conqueror god" (Frankfort 1939).

Before the war gods drove into town in their fiery war chariots and with their social hierarchy and sun worship, there's good evidence that much of the world revolved around healthy female deity. For almost 40,000 years before the war gods hit town, if people made anything that looked like deity, it was not male but female. What's more, during this time most of the world knew little if any war, violence, or social hierarchy. Compared to what followed, the era before the war gods was an actual Never-Never land of adventure and excitement mixed with little if any human-caused large-scale pain or ugliness.

Although this book is an exposé on how the war gods overthrew us and on the awful things they've done to us since then, it's also about how we can — and must — pitch them out on their ears and make a beeline back to the last real religious system we had: the system of the Goddess. Anthropologists all agree that humans need "supernormal" religion (why, is something we'll get to later). But the war gods are political-control machines and not really religions at all. As a result, the world's been religion-starved ever since they rolled into town. The goddesses, on the other hand, and especially the mother goddesses, worked for us: they jacked us up into smart, creative, non-violent, egalitarian, democratic, rich, sensual, playful, courageous risk-takers.

The old goddesses have never abandoned us. They bubble up regularly from their subterranean hideaways — but in disguise. King Arthur and Robin Hood for example are men of the Goddess. Cinderella, Sleeping Beauty and many of our old fairy tales are tales of the Goddess. By unmasking the Goddess in these tales and rubbing the war-god tarnish off Her, we can get important clues about the exact nature of our healthy old Goddess way of life.

Whether you imagine Goddess as an actual supra-rational being or as a "myth to live by" doesn't matter: when we switch back to Her we'll cure most of what ails us. Although the switch must be international I'll dissect it in this book mostly from a Western perspective, adding a bit about Japan and her ancient guiding goddesses as we go along. Before the war gods hit, however, people all across the globe were scoring big with their own guiding mother goddesses — in Australia, Africa, the Americas, China and the rest of Asia too. When they're ready, in other words, most of the peoples in the world today have their own ancient pre-war goddesses to slide home to.

If we ditch our war gods and open the doors to our old guiding goddesses it is my firm belief that we can transform ourselves from unloved waifs wallowing in cinders, into the royal heirs and heiresses we were meant to be — as healthy as the offspring of the world's healthiest mothers. Evidence for this comes from archaeology, anthropology, linguistics, biology, chemistry, history, and other disciplines. If all this sounds like heaven to you please read on.

1

War Gods, or, We Are What We Worship

We Are What We Worship.
If we worship gods who solve problems through teaching people instead of punishing them, we too will solve problems through teaching. If we worship a universal life force that loves us just because we exist and not because of how blindly obedient we are (or how successful), then we can expect our family, friends, spouses and lovers to love us just because we exist and not because of our svelte physiques, our finely featured faces, our fame, or our fat bank accounts. And if when our lives are threatened, our deities are willing to risk their lives to save us, then we feel safe. If we worship gods at home with the human body and all its natural functions, then we too will feel comfortable with and celebrate our senses of touch, smell, taste, sight and hearing.

I'm not alone in my thinking, here. In *The Myth of the Goddess*, Anne Baring and Jules Cashford remind us that although "it may seem a lot to claim that mythic images are so important to all areas of human experience ... the discoveries of depth psychology have shown how radically we are influenced and

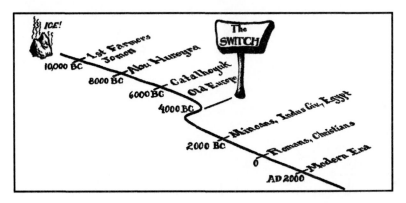

motivated by impulses below the threshold of consciousness, both in our personal and in our collective life as members of the human race" (Baring and Cashford 1991: xiv).

It is my belief that the world is jammed in a mess today because few of us do follow gods like the ones I've described above. Instead, most of us follow creatures who solve problems through slaughtering, massacring and butchering human beings, and through stoning them to death for crimes as scandalous as being stubborn or working on Sunday (Deuteronomy 21.18-21; Exodus 35.2). Most of us hold up as ideal, creatures who frown at our bodies. Most of us love deities who "love" us only on condition that we slavishly obey them — even when we're ordered to burn our children alive (just to see if we'll do it — check out Genesis 22) — or on condition that we aren't physically disabled.

Of course those of us worshipping these gods say, "It's not my god causing the world mess. The mess comes from the greed, lust and violence we're all born with. You think things are bad now — without my god, we'd be slimy, slanderous, slobbering, slathering, incestuous, cannibalistic slitherers slinking across the landscape from one point to another."

I don't think so. For one thing, through time thousands of human societies have existed — and quite nicely I might add — without help from dictator father gods, war gods or sky gods. Most of these societies haven't lacked for food, shelter, warmth, entertainment, or fun and games. What's more, most of the time their children play nicely together and adults get along with each other too. Some of these societies have existed for possibly up to thousands of years without one peep from a war, daddy, or sky god. Unfortunately the current plague of planetary war gods has obliterated many if not most of these fine folk.

Not only that, there's evidence that before about 4000 BC, much of the world turned not around war, sky and father gods, but around peaceful, earth-based, mother goddesses. What's

8

more, when it did so, our best evidence shows that war was mostly absent from the human landscape. Also seemingly rare were interpersonal violence; totalitarianism; social-class snobbery; me-first scrooge-ism; the low boot-licking the "high and mighty"; slavery; poverty; stuffed-shirt boors; and sexually uptight sweeties with two left feet. If we're born greedy and grabby, it's Goddess apparently and not gods who helps us curb our appetites.

Love No Matter What
It only makes sense: healthy mothers love their children unconditionally, no strings attached, and if Mother is our overarching role model, then chances are good everyone's going to look at everyone else through Mother's rosy, positive-regard eye glasses. People are going to look at you and see you the way mom sees you (especially if mom's psychologically healthy): as a pretty sharp cookie who's hunky dorrie almost all of the time. Of course she's going to bark at you if you don't perform up to standards — the ones she knows you can meet — and so will other people in this goddess-based world I'm speaking about. It's not like it's all a free ride. But in general, Mom and therefore everyone else is going to love the socks off of you, no matter if you're two-feet high, have curly hair sprouting out your ears, and the breath of a bear just breaking out of hibernation.

In their article "What Is This Thing Called Love?" in *New Scientist*, Anderson and Middleton say it best: "Of all the forms of love, none seems as deep, strong, selfless or enduring as the love of a mother for her child, nor is any other bond so ubiquitous in the animal kingdom" (Anderson and Middleton 2006: 32). With this kind of love as our model, how could we miss?

Alice in Opposite Land
Unfortunately, somehow over the past 6000 years we lost our pre-4000 BC wonderland world. Like Alice stepping through the

looking glass, we now live in its mirror opposite. Instead of egalitarian, courageous risk-takers, most of us are snooty, sniveling, bully-wimps who look down our noses at those "below" us, and kowtow to those "above." Instead of democratic, peaceful, creative paragons, most of us lick the boots of the rich — "Big Money" for short. Big Money owns our media and our leaders, and is busily infecting our air, water, soil and food. Big Money drags us into war after war, and we don't know what we're dying for, but we know we love it (The flag flying over the battlefield … And the rocket's red glare … Achilles' heel! Helen of Troy! G.I. Joe! War spies … and the caissons go rolling along …. Give him a hearty welcome then … and so forth).

It's all what one might expect from people who hold up a warrior god to their children and say, "Kiddies, here is the highest rung." This is as good as it gets. An absent, untouchable sky god, a father god when "father" in nature is often an unknown quantity. In most of nature, if father is present at all, he loves you with strings attached.

Unlike daddy birds, daddies in most of our closest animal cousins the great apes do not hunt for and help feed baby. As a matter of fact if they're not watched carefully, chimp and gorilla males — like males in many species — kill and eat their own babies for breakfast. According to primatologist Frans de Waal, "Doubt about whether infanticide" by males "is a real phenomenon in wild animals has largely subsided. It is now known to occur in a wide range of species, from lions to prairie dogs, and from mice to gorillas. Current estimates of infanticide … are astonishing: 35 percent in grey langurs, 37 percent in mountain gorillas; 43 percent in red howler monkeys; and 39 percent in blue monkeys" (de Waal and Lanting 1997: 118).

Interestingly however, one of our closest cousins, a fairly newly discovered primate called the bonobo, is a rare bird in that bonobo males do not seem to kill newborns. Although we're not sure what makes the bonobo so unique here, my bets are all on the fact that bonobo males and females share the power. If a male tries to get sassy with a female, the female simply grabs a few friends and they all stand up to the dude like a well-oiled machine. My guess is if any male tried to harm a hair on junior's head, this 'machine' would have a meltdown.

"How did bonobos escape this curse" of baby-battering daddies, asks Frans de Waal. "Are infanticidal tendencies simply absent in the bonobo male, or did females evolve effective counterstrategies? Perhaps both are true: when females find a way of protecting themselves against infanticide, the tendency may disappear in males" (de Waal and Lanting 1997: 119).

More on these fascinating cousins later (turns out one reason we don't know more about them is they spend tons of time enjoying various and sundry kinds of paramouric encounters and they just, well, made researchers *blush*...).

The Lucky Sex Is Born That Way

While human fathers don't as a general rule kill their offspring, they don't seem to have the direct pipeline to unconditional love that mothers have, either. Even fathers who haven't flown the coop (and many of course do just that) don't always love you unconditionally. Many fathers love you only if you make the honor roll, the soccer team, make it into a good college, or win gold in the Winter Olympics. Then there are those millions of dads who *do* love their kids unconditionally. It's my feeling, however, that those dads aren't born that way. They have to learn it. And who do they learn it from? Mothers. Their wives, their own mothers, grandmothers and aunts, teachers and neighbors.

Among humans and all life on earth, it's mothers and mothers alone whose unconditional love is as natural as breathing. We've all heard the stories of mothers who single-handedly lift 2-ton trucks when their kiddy's caught underneath. "The mother's drive to protect her children is the most powerful heroic instinct we know. Cindy Parolin showed no hesitation when she leapt to

11

the defense of her 6-year-old son. Attacked by a cougar, Steven was saved by his mother's incredible bravery as she wrestled with the animal for hours while he was dragged to safety by his brother and sister." ("Natural Born Heroes," BBC).

I'm not saying all women are perfect. Bad mothers are a dime a dozen, and some even abuse and murder their own children. Some of you've had fab dads and mucky mothers. Others have been sabotaged by women and saved by men. What I am saying is, in general the evidence points to the metasymbol of the healthy mother and not the healthy father as the role model most likely to succeed in leading us to the world we all want to live in.

And I'm not talking here about a mealy-mouthed, simpy world, but one in which we're all just as on-the-spot plucky and powerful as the parent who lifts the 2-ton truck off the child. It just so happens this parent is not a father but a mother. Go figure. This isn't putting men down; it's just a simple fact of nature that while mothers come biologically equipped to lift trucks off kids, dads don't. This doesn't mean there's no place for men in the new world we need to get to — far, far from it.

Although some of you, men and women alike may think of this as an attack on men, it's certainly not. Failing to use the right role model to guide our behavior has brought us to the brink of obliteration. In my opinion, we no longer have time or energy to lug the male ego around on our backs; it weighs us down in an era when men and women alike need all the energy and strength we can muster to keep the planet going. In other words, y'all, please lighten up and get a grip.

Whomped by War Gods

Today over half the world — a whopping 53 percent of us — worship the god of Abraham, a war god known variously as Yahweh, Allah and Jehovah, "YAJ" for short, and according to Oxford University professor Richard Dawkins "the Old Testament psychotic delinquent" (Appendix F; World Religions;

Dawkins 2006: 38). In Exodus 15.3, YAJ just comes right out and says it: he's a warrior. "The Lord is a warrior, the Lord is his name" (KJV) or "The Lord is a man of war; the Lord is his name" (ESV). What's more, depending on what version of the Bible you're holding, the words "war" and "warrior" appear 250 to 300 times (Strong 1996; BibleGateway.com), while according to *Strong's Exhaustive Concordance of the Bible* "armies," "arms" and "weapons" appear another 176 times (Strong 1996). Oh sure, "peace" is in the Bible a few hundred times too, but that doesn't make us peaceful — only schizophrenic and liable to do peace half the time and war the other half.

In addition to YAJ, Jehovah followers also worship the being Jesus. Jesus really doesn't help the situation much. He died "for" us — but only because in his mind we're so mucky that all that would scrub us clean was his pitifully painful death. Talk about your guilt trip. Even though Christians call Jesus "prince of peace," he comes right out and says he's not: "Do not suppose that I have come to bring peace to the earth. I did not come to bring peace, but a sword" (Matthew 10.34). And even if some do think of him as a peace prince, he's still stuffed into the same rule book as YAJ, the self-ID'd warrior. If you think stuffing "war" and "peace" into the same rulebook 300 times makes for big-time schizophrenia, try stuffing a war- and a hyped-up peace god together and watch the squirrelly behavior double or triple. Who do people follow? Whichever is convenient at the time, of course. If all's hunky dorrie, they follow a meek and mild Jesus Christ. If someone's threatening their home heating oil, they (conveniently) switch to the war god.

In addition to the 54 percent of us worshipping YAJ, another 13 percent of the world worships a host of Hindu gods, two of whom — Indra and Karttikeya — are war gods. And although until recently China's one-fifth of humanity (Fishman 2005: 2) has been barred from practicing religion, when they did they too worshipped war gods — Huangdi, Chi You, and Kan'u among others, with Huangdi surviving "in today's popular culture" (Leeming 2005: 73). In Japan, Shinto war gods include Hachiman and Bishamon (also known as Bishamonten and Tamonten) and even today many Japanese worship their old Shinto deities (Levinson 1998: 216).

Although it's not generally known, Buddhism too has its violent gods. One is the "protector" Dorje Shugden, the "lightning-breathing terror with three bloodshot eyes, wreathed in the smoke of burning human flesh." In India as we speak, Dorje is triggering monk-upon-monk violence. For example in 1997 in Dharamsala India a Shugden monk knifed an anti-Shugden monk in a "ritual stabbing" (Van Biema 1998: 70). Another little-known fact is that in World War II Buddhism helped inspire Japanese suicidal violence (Harris 2004: 233).

Interestingly, moderates of all religious stripes claim their particular religion is completely and perfectly stuffed full of peace. For instance Christian moderates loudly and proudly proclaim that Christianity circles around the "Prince of Peace." You have to wrinkle your forehead and wonder what in the world they think about Jesus ordering them to kill heretics (John 15.6) or about the same orders bubbling forth from the hoary and hallowed Old Testament (Deuteronomy 17.2 and 13.12-16).

And if you can pin them down, how do they explain the fact that their peace religion resulted in hundreds of thousands being butchered by the Christian Inquisition in a centuries-long tirade that fizzled out only a few hundred years ago? What do they say about the fact that as recently as 70 years ago Christianity produced anti-Semitism and other anti-isms (against gypsies, homosexuals, the disabled, and so forth) so rabid they resulted in the death of millions (Harris 2004: 101)? How do they explain the fact that even today "peaceful" Christians are murdering others ("bad" children, "bad" abortionists) in the name of their holy book? Politically active and well-funded American Christian Reconstructionists as we speak are publicly calling for the death penalty for juvenile delinquents, adulterers, those pushing "false" religions, and others of like ilk (Boston 2001: 1 of 11). If this is what a peace religion looks like, give me your war religion any day.

If you're a Christian moderate saying to yourself, "Oh, no one takes seriously anymore that stuff in the Bible about stoning people to death," think again. As you read this, American "Reconstructionists," also known as "Dominionists" are calling for the actual murder of those who according to your Bible are unfit to live: "gays, ... blasphemers, heretics, apostate Christians, people who cursed or struck their parents, females guilty of 'unchastity before marriage,' 'incorrigible' juvenile delinquents, adulterers…, (probably) telephone psychics,… and those guilty of raping married women or 'betrothed virgins.' Adulterers, among others, might meet their doom by being publicly stoned" (Olson 1998: 1-3). And if you think Reconstructionists are just running around in la la land, you'd be twice mistaken:

> It would be easy to dismiss the Reconstructionists as the lunatic fringe…. But, in fact, they have rather extraordinary entree and influence with top-tier Religious Right leaders and institutions. James Dobson's *Focus on the Family* is now selling DeMar's book, *America's Christian Heritage*…. TV preacher Robertson has … hired Reconstructionists as professors at Regent University. Jerry Falwell employs Reconstructionists to teach at Liberty University… (Sugg 2006).

For a variety of reasons in America today the Christian Right is looking more every day like a branch of the U.S. military. Best-selling author Chris Hedges, graduate of Harvard Divinity School and foreign correspondent for the *New York Times* and other publications, warns that "shadowy" Christian paramilitary organizations are springing up all over the U.S. like poison toadstools in an enchanted forest. "American Veterans in

Domestic Defense" in Texas, "Christian Identity" (they believe they're going to fight a religious war in the near future), "The Faith Force Multiplier" (its leader says Christians will defeat Muslims — but "only if we come against them in the name of Jesus"), and "BattleCry," a youth movement full of colorful war language and military pictures, are all recently-sprouted Christian groups hungry for war or violence — or both.

My favorite is probably BattleCry. In big cities all across the US, this sterling organization holds Christian rock concerts for the youth of America. But garden-variety rock concerts these are not. At these concerts, war holds center stage. As rock bands blast out war songs, the words to each song are thrown up on a giant screen so the audience (up to 25,000 at a time) can sing along: "We're an army of God and we're ready to die…. Let's paint this big ol' town red…. We see nothing but the blood of Jesus…."

Then the grand wizard of the organization, one Ron Luce, leaps up onto the stage, grabs a mike and booms "'This is war! And Jesus invites us to get into the action, telling us that the violent — the 'forceful' ones — will lay hold of the kingdom!'" Unbelievably, Hummers (based on the military Humvee vehicle) and "ranks" of Navy SEALs parade proudly throughout the whole shebang.

Meanwhile, American televangelist Pat Robertson (and Jerry Falwell while he was still living) has "sanctioned" the use of preemptive nuclear-weapons strikes on the "enemies of God." If your reaction at this point is "Get ooout!" just wait a minute — it gets better: According to the Christian Right, Jesus is not the "He Loves the Little Children of the World" saint you sang about in Sunday School, but a strapping bloke with bulging muscles waving a sword in the air. Likewise, Christian men are pictured as macho warriors.

The language pouring out of the mouths of the Right is lush with "metaphors about the use of excessive force and violence against God's enemies," says Hedges. "Jesus, like God, has to be a real man, a man who dominates through force." Hedges goes on to say that the Right's "holy-war" rhetoric both "terrifies and delights" its followers. The "yearning" for the final battle, the Battle of Armageddon, ripples through the Christian Right "like an electric current." War is "the final aesthetic of the movement."

"But this is just the fringe," you say. "There can't be more than a handful of lunatics like these in the Land of the Free and the Brave." Wrong. The hard-core Christian Right — those who want to make not only the U.S. but the world a theocratic state — form 7 to 12.6 percent of the American population. Furthermore, says Hedges, "The potency of this radical movement far exceeds its numbers." For one, they're "taking over the machinery of U.S. state and religious institutions." And just as their god Jehovah commands, they're panting not after figurative, but literal Christian world domination and empire (Hedges 2006: 27-35, 79).

Richard Dawkins thinks there might be some kind of connection between the sad facts above and his own list of personality defects of the Christian god Jehovah: "… a vindictive, bloodthirsty …, misogynistic, homophobic, racist, infanticidal, genocidal, filicidal, pestilential, megalomaniacal, sadomasochistic, capriciously malevolent bully." Dawkins adds: "Those of us schooled from infancy" in Jehovah's ways "can become desensitized to their horror" (Dawkins 2006: 31).

Like their Christian cousins, Muslim moderates too are sure theirs is a religion of peace. "[T]he violence we see in the Muslim world" they tell us "is the product of politics and economics, not faith." And yet "on almost every page the Koran instructs … Muslims to despise non-believers." What's more, the Islamic doctrine is "undeniable: convert, subjugate, or kill unbelievers; kill apostates; and conquer the world." If they martyr themselves for Allah, men are promised any and everything — all the way from their own private heaven harem, to the right to heave-ho 70 people up to heaven with them. In other words, murder for Papa Allah and he'll shoot you straight up to heaven along with tons of sex for fun, and for comfort your entire extended family (Harris 2004: 31, 113, 123, 233).

The Moderate Menace

The problem with the world's state-sanctioned war-god religions — and almost all state religions are war-god religions — is not their fundamentalists but their moderates. In general it's moderates not fundamentalists who have the wealth, power and training to lead societies. Who cares if moderates promise they'd never act on the barbarisms in their holy books? By blessing these books, they're blessing everything in them, from "an eye for an eye" to the death penalty for "cursing a parent." And in the process they've left the door wide open for Reconstructionists to shove a giant toe in.

Writing for *Church & State*, Rob Boston notes that Recons are now firm fixtures in the American political system: "leaders have made three forays into Washington DC since July 2000, meeting with members of Congress and their staffs." And in the 2000 US presidential election, Christian Reconstructionist Howard Phillips, running on the Recon's Constitution Party platform, garnered a full 98,020 votes nationwide (Boston 2001: 2, 10 of 11).

Sam Harris, author of the award-winning *New York Times* bestseller *The End of Faith*, also says it's moderates who are the problem. You're dangerous because you feel the path to peace is through religious tolerance, that once we learn to respect all faiths, world peace will be a shoe-in. According to Sam this is not only baloney — it's strychnine-laced baloney: "... the very ideal of religious tolerance — born of the notion that every human being should be free to believe whatever he wants about God — is one of the principal forces driving us toward the abyss" (Harris 2004: 14-15).

The Bible is a bomb loaded with yellow-cake uranium and ready to blow when conditions are ripe. For centuries moderates — the best and brightest among us — have endorsed with gusto this encyclopedia of sickness. Today slick-tongued weasels are waving it in the air and pointing with grimy fingers to Biblical verdicts about who should die for crimes such as not being a virgin on the wedding night (Deuteronomy 22.13-21) and teasing a bald man (2 Kings 2.23-24). Unfortunately Americans at least are now living in a climate of fear so thick it's blinding many into empty headedness.

This fear fog is likely to thicken before it thins. Along with Sam Harris I ask you to "Imagine what it would be like for your descendants to experience the fall of civilization. Imagine failures of reasonableness so total that our largest bombs finally fall upon our largest cities in defense of our religious differences. What would it be like for the unlucky survivors of such a holocaust to look back upon the hurtling career of human stupidity that led them over the precipice?" (Harris 2004: 224).

How Do War Gods Lead to War?

Not long ago a friend of mine said "Jesus not Jehovah is the god in my denomination. Jehovah is just a funny old guy you don't take seriously." My friend seems to believe both he and the Methodist Church consider Jehovah about as weighty as a circus clown. But this doesn't square with the facts. First, Jesus (who my friend IDs as his god), takes Jehovah seriously — and warns his followers to, too. Second, by definition the father of a god is a god, snapping Jehovah into deity status and therefore — it would seem — making him a force to be reckoned with. Third, considering how often it mentions him, the Methodist holy book (the Bible) certainly takes Jehovah seriously. Jehovah stands out as the central actor in the Old Testament. If he's so trivial, why is he chugging around in every other verse in the larger of the two books comprising the Methodist guide for living?

Even though my friend may not realize it, I believe he does take Jehovah seriously — not consciously obviously, but below the consciousness level. Although we're still not exactly sure how it works, no serious thinker today doubts the existence of the unconscious mind. Neither does anyone doubt that this hidden part of the mind influences our behavior. Why are our minds divided into conscious and unconscious chambers? According to Harvard University Johnstone Professor of Psychology Steven Pinker, one theory is this: If it had to register every little jot and tittle it came across, your mind would soon dump into burnout. So it registers only those things that seem most important in "updating an understanding of the world and figuring out what to do next." Everything else gets bumped into an X File — your unconscious mind — for future reference on an as-needed basis (Pinker 2007).

At any rate, beginning in childhood those of us living in war-god societies periodically bump into info about one or all of the war god's favorite pastimes: mass killings, mass death, and massive wars of destruction. If you don't believe the Bible isn't jam packed with this stuff, turn to Appendix J, "Cruelty in the Bible: Short List." Deuteronomy alone bristles with cases of Father Jehovah brutalizing his "children":

"And we took all his cities at that time, and utterly destroyed the men, and the women, and the little ones, of every city, we left none to remain." — 2.34

"And we utterly destroyed them, ... utterly destroying the men, women, and children, of every city." — 3.6

"And when the Lord thy God shall deliver them before thee; thou shalt smite them, and utterly destroy them; thou shalt make no covenant with them, nor shew mercy unto them." — 7.2

"And thou shalt consume all the people which the Lord thy God shall deliver thee; thine eye shall have no pity upon them." — 7.16

"Thou shalt surely smite the inhabitants of that city with the edge of the sword, destroying it utterly, and all that is therein, and the cattle thereof, with the edge of the sword." — 13.15

"And when the Lord thy God hath delivered it into thine

hands, thou shalt smite every male thereof with the edge of the sword: But the women ... shalt thou take unto thyself." — 20.13-14

"But of the cities of these people, which the Lord thy God doth give thee for an inheritance, thou shalt save alive nothing that breatheth." — 20.16-17

You might have heard verses like these in church, you might have picked up a Bible and stumbled across them, you might have heard a television preacher honking on about them, or an English lit teacher might have read a few out loud. And in America, if you haven't sung it yourself, more than once in your life you've undoubtedly heard "The Battle Hymn of the Republic" — in school, in church, or if nothing else at televised state funerals.

Unfortunately, children rarely witness adults reacting with disgust to Jehovah's, Yahweh's or Allah's lust for combat, carnage and cruelty. As a rule, adults seem almost bored by the Lord and "his terrible swift sword." The result? On a conscious level the info fails to make a big impression on children. As adults, kids rarely remember the first — or any time — they heard about Daddy War Lord's mass killings and wars of destruction.

All this info, however, lodges in the unconscious (as does any stimulus your brain runs into but doesn't register consciously). And when your country declares war, your unconscious whispers in your third ear, "Hey! God does it — it's cool." You might not rush out and enlist in the military, but you find it hard to join war protests — or even to ring up your government reps to register dismay.

So how do war gods help lead a society to war? In part through an unconscious process that spins along in the minds of the members of the society. And just as individuals in psychotherapy are healed by raising information from the unconscious to the conscious mind, so might we help heal our societies by lifting the mass cruelty of our war gods from unconscious to conscious levels.

Pitching the Baby with the Bathwater

But why have deities or religion at all? In *The End of Faith,* Sam Harris says no to both. Although he admits that "...spiritual experience, ethical behavior, and strong communities are essential to human happiness," he thinks our current religions are the worst way possible to meet these needs. As a matter of fact they're not just bad for meeting needs, they're actually leading us to "the abyss" and to the "fall of civilization" (Harris 2004: 221, 15, 224).

Harris, however, trots out nothing to replace the gods but meditation, a greater understanding of the "I," "selflessness," "experiments in consciousness," and "liberation from the illusion of the self" (Harris 2004: 204-221, 219, 215). In other words, the philosophy that hasn't helped the East anymore than western philosophy has helped the West. To one degree or another, both are based on blasting our bodies as bad, on blasting an entire sex as barely above notice, and on blasting Mother Earth along with everything She stands for: the miracle of our senses, our sexuality, our relationships to one another, and our connection to the earth and everything on it. Like western philosophy, eastern philosophy too is male-dominated and harbors a mistrust of the earth, nature, wealth, playfulness, creativity, sensuality and healthy human desire. Typically the emphasis is on disembodiment, energy and male mind contemplating its navel.

In contrast to religious faith, which is "irrational," Harris insists that anything replacing god religions must be "rational." The problem with this is there's "rational" evidence that humans aren't smart enough yet to cope without supra-rational answers to certain questions we have no rational answers for (where do we go after we die, why are we here, and so forth). Sure, science may answer these questions some day, but personally I can't wait for "some day" to roll around. I want answers now, bud.

After studying hundreds of human cultures for over a century now, anthropologists have failed to find even one that doesn't have a full-blown supra-rational religion. Take a peek sometime at George Peter Murdoch's *Ethnographic Atlas,* a world map of almost 1200 different world cultures and the essential traits of each. You'll notice that not one is missing a religion — an organized set of beliefs and practices revolving around *supra-normal* beings and forces. "Religion is about the relationship between human beings and the supernatural world," says anthropologist David Levinson. "Of the dozens of definitions of religion that have been suggested by theologians, historians, sociologists, anthropologists and others, this one cuts to what is common to all religious systems" (Levinson 1998: vii).

So supra-rational religion has been found in every known culture. Anthropologists use the term "cultural universal" for traits like religion. In anthropology it's a big-time rule that universals are either very old or very important — and usually both. Other universals include gender roles, myth, language, games, moral standards, the incest taboo, and cooking (which can unlock nutrients we don't get from raw food) (Aman 1999).

So how exactly is supra-rational religion so important to human functioning that all known human groups, past and present, have kept it hanging around? Well, as mentioned above, a biggie is it answers questions neither science nor anything else has answered well: where do we come from, why are we here, where do we go after we die, where did the universe come from, where and when does time end, and where does space end and begin, etc. Emile Durkheim, one of the early icons in both anthropology and sociology, said religion also provides us with social cohesion, psychological support, ethical education, and euphoria. This is a fancy way of saying it holds our social group together, gives us moral support when things get tough (not to mention financial support), tells us how to treat each other and why, and can sometimes make us feel like we're on cloud nine doing the rumba (Durkheim 1995).

Later sociologists haven't been as fuzzy-wuzzy about religion as Durkheim was, many of them seeing it more than anything else as a thorn in society's side. But when sociologists study religion, they study mostly industrialized state religions — in other words, the scruffy father-sky-war-god religions. Rarely do they bring into the picture the non sky-war-god religions of the indigenous cultures around the world. So when sociologists say religion is bad, what they're really saying is the war-god religions are bad. And I, of course, say huzza, huzza, huzza. Yes, yes, yes. The war gods are driving us crazy.

But let's not pitch the baby with the bathwater. Just because war gods are bad doesn't mean all religions are bad. Although few of us alive today on the planet have ever tried following a guiding mother goddess, as we've seen, it would appear logical that such a deity would have much to offer the world. Besides, I suspect most of those who've rejected the war gods have substituted the God Science in daddy's place. More on this later.

Like It or Not, Religion's Here to Stay

At any rate Marx was not totally but only partly wrong. Not all religion is bad. And even if it were, it's not something we can stamp out any more than we can stamp out thinking. At its core, religion is about answering the Big Questions — questions people are always going to think about. Where do we go after we die? How you answer that question — whether it's "to heaven/Hell" (God the Father); "back to the Great Mother's womb" (God the Mother); or "nowhere/to dust/I don't know" (God Science) — is a clue to what your religion is.

Stalin, Mao and Pol Pot outlawed religion, but if you think Russians, Chinese and Cambodians stopped believing in their gods (and whispering about them to their children), think again. Now that China's relaxed a bit about life, it's recognizing "...five religions ...: Buddhism, Daoism, Islam, Catholicism and Protestantism. Other religions are regarded as evil cults or feudal superstitions (folk religion)..." (Chan 2005: 6). These five male-god religions didn't just spring out of nowhere overnight; they've

24

been preserved over the long dark winter's night of religious repression in China. The ancient mother-goddess religions were shoved underground over most of the land millennia ago.

On the other hand, ancient beliefs in a guiding mother goddess by peoples such as the recently discovered and amazing Moso of Yongning Province, still exist above ground to some extent. The unbelievable Moso are the only known people in the world without marriage; your sexual partners come and go as they please, and even though jealousy happens, since the Moso hold taboos against it, it's a rare bird.

The Moso are also "...alone among their neighbors to have a guardian mother goddess rather than a patron warrior god" (Mathieu 2003: 399). This Mother Goddess is Segge Gamu, "the white lioness." Segge Gamu has many lovers, but Her special lover is the God Azhapula (Namu 2003: 101). Unfortunately, with the coming of China's new religion policy, the happy, healthy Moso and their mother goddess will be forced underground, while Jehovah, Allah and Buddha will have free rein in this country that's stomping around with a fifth of the world's population under its belt. More on the Moso too, later on.

The God Called Science

The well-known Oxford University scientist Richard Dawkins doesn't seem aware that religion can't be ditched. He says all religion should be pitched and replaced with science (Dawkins 2006: 347; 1997). One problem with this is, as much as Dawkins squawks it isn't (Dawkins 1997), much evidence shows that science itself is a religion. To see if science is a religion, let's check it against a popular definition of religion, one authored by the anthropologist Clifford Geertz. Although penned in 1973, this definition is still being used today by social scientists. For Geertz religion is "(1) a system of symbols which acts to (2) establish powerful, pervasive, and long-lasting moods and motivations in men by (3) formulating conceptions of a general order of

25

existence and (4) clothing these conceptions with such an aura of factuality that (5) the moods and motivations seem uniquely realistic" (Kipnis, 2001, quoting Geertz 1973: 90).

First, is science a "system of symbols"? You bet your sweet bippy it is! What's more symbol-y than science? Second, does science "establish powerful, pervasive, and long-lasting moods and motivations"? What? Have you ever seen scientists left to their own devices? Straggling out of their labs with a six day's growth of beard (at least the male ones), squinting into the sun, and simply awash in lack of hygiene? What do you think keeps them in that lab for six days straight without food, water, rest or exercise — except "powerful, pervasive, and long-lasting moods and motivations"?

Third, is science guilty of "formulating conceptions of a general order of existence"? In other words, does science answer the Big Questions we all expect religion to answer? Again: bingo: Where do we all come from? "We're all 32c/21p worth of chemicals." (May not be an answer you like, but it's an answer). Where do we go after we die? "Back to 32c/21p worth of chemicals." Why are we here? "To reveal, break apart and dissect the secrets of the universe."

Fourth, does science "clothe the above conception of the universe with an aura of factuality"? You're darn tootin' it does! Science doesn't say "Well, it's just a guess that we're 32c/21p worth of chemicals...." No siree it does not. This is fact, pure and simple. We ARE chemicals. Period. End of sentence. As Dawkins himself puts it, "Well, science is not religion and it doesn't just come down to faith.... *Science is based upon verifiable evidence*" (Dawkins 1997: 1; emphasis the author's).

Fifth, do "the moods and motivations" of science "seem uniquely realistic"? Well, you'd have to ask a science lover or a scientist about that. Why not ask the one who just stumbled out of his six-day stint in the lab? The bleary-eyed one with the beard stubble.

And finally, going back to Levinson's definition of religion, is science about our relationship to the supernatural world? Well, in my opinion, many of the phenomena science investigates certainly seem beyond the natural world to me: Black holes in space? Time travel? Or how about 'string theory,' which insists the universe is composed not of particles, but of strings?

My guess is that unbeknownst to themselves, most atheists are meeting their religious needs through the religion of science. In the West at least, this religion formed only recently — after the fires of the Christian Holy Inquisition had finally burned themselves out: "The Inquisition's excesses so disgusted 'men of intelligence' that they turned away from the church altogether ... to build a wholly secular world on the smoldering ashes of the 'holy fires' .... From those fires rose Francis Bacon ... calling for an aggressive attack on nature's 'secrets' — always a metaphor for female genitalia ... a scientific method that would allow men to 'interrogate Nature,' ... to put her 'on the rack' (Sjoo and Mor, 1991: 323).

A word of caution: I'm not saying we should replace science with religion — not by a long shot. Both have their place. The modern world depends greatly on science and science has brought us wonderful things. I am, however, cautioning against using science to fill religious needs, into turning science into something it's a dunce at — i.e. being a god. The ramifications of this are legion and would fill a second book.

Born Numskulls

One of the things setting humans apart from animals is that we have no instincts. Oh sure, you see the term "human instincts" bandied about all over the place, but it's the prevailing notion among scientists today that we humans were bypassed when the instincts were passed out. By "instinct" I mean a behavior package with many behaviors in it, all of which go together to form a unit. For example, the nest building of birds is an instinct since it involves many separate behaviors which all add up to a finished home for birds. Automatic courtship behavior in deer and other animals is another example. Bird migration is another. To qualify as an instinct, a behavior package must also be something you do automatically with no training; it must be irresistible to you; and it must be something everybody in your species does automatically without training.

Here's an example of an instinct clearly demonstrating that an instinct is not a single behavior, but a related pack of behaviors: Normally female rats are scared of everything — including (believe it or not) baby rats. But when females are injected with the hormones estrogen and oxytocin — the latter being the hormone that makes females in all species bond with their babies — these rats go into full-blown baby-being-born mode. Suddenly they're building nests. They grab any and all babies in sight and plop them into the new nests. They wash the babies. They defend the babies against all would-be intruders. And even though they have no milk to feed them, these females nonetheless snuggle down next to the little ones in baby-nursing posture (Moberg 2003: 67).

We humans on the other hand are born numskulls. We are born in a pitiful, pathetic state of knowing next to nothing about how to live life and stay alive doing it. We have to be taught almost everything, from how to build our "nests," to courtship behavior, to how to speak, and how to find food that's safe to eat (do you know how to tell the friendly mushrooms from the ones that'll put you six feet (1.8 meters) under in a trice?).

In other words, at birth we're like spanking new computers — minus software. Oh sure, the hardware's there, but what good is it without operating instructions? Other animals at birth get free software; we alone have to write our own. Three broad classes of possible operating software programs for humans are: God the Mother, God the Father, and God Science. Each of these software programs circles around a central force that is alternately female, male or neuter (science) and that shapes our behavior. How does the God Science stack up to Daddy and Mother? To find out, let's take a gander at how they all three answer the Big Questions.

First, where do we come from?

Jeri: "Mother, you first."

Mother: "You came from my womb, you sweet, lovable thing, you."

Jeri: "Daddy?"

Daddy: "From a long line of fathers, going all the way back to Adam."

Jeri: "And God Science, what's your take on this?"

God Science: "Thirty-two cents worth of chemicals."

Jeri: "Thank you all. Next Big Question: Where do we go after we die?"

Mother: "Right back to my warm, loving womb — and from there into your next life."

Daddy: "Depends. For most of you it's going to be pretty bad news."

God Science: "Back to 32c/21p worth of chemicals."

Jeri: "Okay. Why are we here? I mean, what's the purpose of my life?"

Mother: "To love everything I've made unconditionally, no strings attached."

Daddy: "Me. It's all about me. You're here to make me look good."

God Science: "You're here for one reason and one only: to dissect Mother Earth and learn Her secrets."

Jeri: "Science, are you serious? Where did you come from, dude?"

God Science: (No answer).

Jeri: "Jeesh, you're creeping me out, mister. Okay, next. What is sin?"

Mother: "Sin is when you fail to give unconditional regard to anything I've created — plants, animals, people. I mean you are to honor it all, sis."

Daddy (frowning in Mother's direction): "Wrong. Sin is when you don't love me best."

God Science: "Sin is emotion, which obscures rational thinking."

Jeri: "Okay. Interesting answers. Next, how do you — the Great Unknown — see me, a human being living on planet earth?"

Mother (a dreamy look on Her face): "You my dear were born unutterably lovable. From the minute I laid eyes upon you, you inspired profound love in me. Nothing you could ever do or become would make you unlovable in my eyes."

Jeri: "Mother, I like that. Daddy?"

Daddy: "Boy, were you born bad. I'll love you, but only on condition."

Jeri: "Condition? What condition?"

Daddy: "Oh no, not just *one* condition."

Jeri: "Okay which *conditions*?"

Daddy: "First when I say jump, you say …"

Jeri (sighs): "Yeah, yeah, yeah. 'How high.'"

Daddy: "Dang right, 'how high'!"

Jeri: "What else?"

Daddy: "On condition that you make me look good."

Jeri: "Are you still holding that D in geometry against me? I got that 20 years ago!"

Daddy: "And what have you done since then to make up for it? What kinda dad do you think that makes me look like?"

Jeri: "Jeesh! I'm moving on to God Science. God Science, how do you see me?"

God Science: (No answer)

Jeri: "Science? … God Science? Are you there?"

God Science: (Still no answer)

Jeri: "What does that mean? He won't answer…. What am I, dirt?!"

~ End of interviews ~

Pick Your Spectacles

Imagine putting on each of three sets of eye glasses in turn — Father God's, Science God's, and Mother God's. Each gives you wildly divergent views of yourself, others, the earth and the cosmos. First put on Daddy's glasses. Look in a mirror: what you see is someone only potentially lovable. Off in the distance high over the western horizon, you see a giant male figure — Daddy. He's frowning at you. "Look at you," he says. "You're a mess. Come back after you've worked on yourself. If you do, you might make it up to where my love is."

And you look again in the mirror and jeesh! You do look pretty ratty. It's depressing because you've tried to do the things Daddy wants. You've developed for example a nice, juicy sex complex, and you really have come to believe — as Father's told you many times — that you were born bad.

Keep Daddy's glasses on and look at the rest of the world. What do you see? Naturally the same thing you saw in the mirror: human beings as bad off as you are. In fact, they look so bad it's obvious to you they deserve to be robbed, cheated, discriminated against, evicted, abused, locked up, raped. It's all okay because they're bad, Father says so. Of course a few don't look so bad. As a matter of fact some look pretty prosperous. So prosperous in fact you feel a touch nasty toward them. Somehow they've won what you desperately want — Daddy's love.

Looking through Daddy's lenses it's fairly obvious your whole life is going to be taken up pretty much with trying to win Daddy's conditional love, which is always hanging, like the carrot on a stick, just out of reach. Your brothers and sisters too are panting for daddy's love, and all of you are scrambling frantically over each other to reach the top where — somewhere — Daddy's love lies.

Now take off the Father glasses and put on Mother's. As your eyes sweep over the dramatically altered landscape, you draw in a sharp breath. Look in the mirror though at yourself first. What do you see? No longer someone potentially lovable, but someone incredibly and unalterably lovable. Someone born radiating lovable qualities; no matter what you do, say, feel or look like, the world is stuck with loving you. The universe loves every dimple, every hair on your body. It can't help it. You inspire unutterable love, you *are* love. The cosmos can't help loving and cherishing you any more than mother can help cherishing baby.

Behind the vision of lovableness that is you is the awesome earth and universe. The Earth has long, wavy hair swaying in the wind and a pregnant belly — it's huge, much larger and more powerful than you — and this Earth loves you, is smiling at you, can't help it, because the earth and the universe and everything in it you don't understand is a Great Mother Goddess.

Now look out at the rest of the world. You see all humans the way you yourself are seen by the Mystery — as completely, unutterably lovable. You're all brothers and sisters, and you're all getting equal portions of the pie (love) from the Universe, the Unexplainable, The Power. No one has to scramble or perform tricks for love — it's all around, free as air.

No one's getting more than you, so no one arouses nasty feelings in you. And you don't feel a push to get more than others have — why waste the time? What meaning would it have? The only thing other humans inspire in you is mother-love. As a mother loves her child — cute as plums or plug ugly, healthy or sick, neurotic or sane, good or bad — so you react to the people in your life. Whether you're a man or woman, your great anthropomorphic model for behavior makes you an unconditional-lover of humans. This orientation floods your thinking, your seeing, your feeling, your speaking, your consciousness, your subconsciousness, your ego, your identity, your heart, your body, your soul and so forth.

What's more, as a child of the Mother Goddess, you don't love a schizophrenic or a paraplegic because the Mother told you to, or because you want to be "good" and win Her love — you already have that hands down, no sweat. Neither do you love them because you want to get to heaven or escape that Daddy War-Lord invention "Hell." On the contrary — you love schizophrenics simply because they are lovable ... draw the love right out of you. In other words, you don't manufacture this love; you don't have to work to produce it (or feel guilt because you can't). It's just there. Period. It exists. You overflow with it. Whether you want to or not. You can't help it. It comes with the Mother Goddess, with the Mother's set of spectacles. It's a "natural byproduct," so to speak.

32¢/21p Worth of Chemicals (or, The Jar on the Shelf)

Now change spectacles for the third and final time, to those of God Science. Before you look into the mirror this time though, prepare yourself for a shock. You won't see anything you'd expected. What you'll see won't even be recognizably human. It's a green, glass jar shut up with a cork stopper. In the jar you see a sluggish, glistening muddy-colored liquid. Neatly pasted on the outside of the jar is a white gum label with the words "Thirty-two-cents/Twenty-one-pence Worth of Chemicals" typed on it.

You gasp. What does this have to do with you, others or the universe? Where are your clues for setting up your operating instructions — the ones you need because your species comes live-born without them? What kind of clues can a glass jar give you about the business of living your life as a friendly, warm-blooded, group-dependent, large-brained primate stripped of the instinct-instructions all other animals come with at birth?

Well, one thing's obvious: if love was hard to get in Daddy God's world, it's on even shorter supply here. As a matter of fact, it doesn't exist. Neither does anger, sorrow, joy, jealousy or bitterness. This is a clean, lean and mean world, spare, and simple.

So, you're not born lovable or unlovable. In fact you're barely there — you could be traded in for a pack of chewing gum. Now look around. Other people — what do they look like? As it turns out, they look a lot like you: about as worthwhile as a pack of gum. And how are you to relate to them? Apparently you aren't — no one is relating to you. (Why am I suddenly thinking of snuff films,

33

those amazing twentieth-century inventions in which actual people are murdered on film for the purposes of entertainment?)

To me the message of the jar is this: *Mother's not running the universe, Daddy's not running it, no one's running the universe. So you'd better quick figure it all out yourself.* Ah. The purpose of life is to figure it all out. That's it. Nothing else matters. Others are important only as they serve as paths to enlightenment or knowledge — research subjects, say. Emotions of any kind get in the way and — through these glasses — look almost evil. Tenderness for humans for example might have halted the hand that first rose and fell to split the atom. Love for the species might have checked the minds that first broke open the path toward experimentation with genetic material in viruses, an unintended (?) byproduct of which was germ warfare and the threat of new, possibly uncontrollable strains of viruses deadly to the human species.

Figure 1.2. Three Broad Classes of Human Operating Instructions

I. GOD THE FATHER

How This Deity Sees And Treats Me: Loves me on condition — that I follow orders and give up positive emotion, freedom, sex, and pleasure. Harsh punishment for those who fail to follow orders.

How I See And Treat Others: I treat others the way Father treats me: love is conditional — on whether you give to, worship, and obey me. The earth is to be "subdued."

The Result: Social hierarchy, with those favored by Father at the top of the ladder; others enslaved to those immediately above them on the hierarchy ladder. War, torture, social violence, environmental degradation.

II. GOD SCIENCE

How This Deity Sees And Treats Me: I am 32c/21p worth of chemicals

– no more. On your own, bud. No help. It's all up to you. Impersonal.

How I See And Treat Others: Others are 32c/21p worth of chemicals. Our relationship: I study and probe them. Emotion is The Key Sin (first commandment of God Science is objectivity).

The Result: Neurosis, psychosis, anomie; pursuit of knowledge overshadows importance of continued existence of the species.

III. GOD THE MOTHER

How This Deity Sees And Treats Me: Loves me unconditionally, no strings attached.   I am born good and unutterably lovable. Impossible not to love me. Education versus punishment.

How I See And Treat Others: I treat you as Mother treats me: with unconditional, positive regard, no matter what you do or who you are. Same attitude toward animals and the earth.

The Result: Prosperous groups of healthy, happy, people. Earth in balance.

Mommy, Daddy and the Science Guy

Clearly big chasms yawn between Mother, Daddy and God Science in terms of how they see humans — where we came from, why we're here and so forth. And it's only logical that which of these three constructs we use to organize our world is going to make a difference in how we see ourselves and others. Our ancestors who rallied around the Great Guiding Mother Goddess basked in a world in which others saw them the way the Great Mother saw everyone: as unutterably lovable, valuable, and powerful. The majority today who use father gods to organize their operating instructions see themselves and others exactly the way Father sees them: as conditionally lovable. Only winners need apply for Daddy's love. The rest of you can go jump in a lake. People are lovable only when they make us look good, or when they say "How high?" when we say "Jump."

But love is in shorter supply yet in the world of God Science. To

God Science you don't even exist. You are 32c/21p worth of chemicals, remember? So in the God-Science world you see yourself and others the same way: as nothing important. You and they barely exist. You exist only as inanimate parts of the universe to be pulled apart, dissected, and observed. Or as a dissector yourself, i.e. a priest or priestess of God Science.

So we're looking at three vastly divergent possible worlds here. First, Mother's world, in which everyone treats you like the Emperor of Siam, and everyone on earth's doing just fine, because none of us would think of doing anything other than all pulling ourselves up together (we haven't witnessed this world for a while; for the past several millennia whenever it tries to rise it's sat upon by Daddy). Then there's Daddy's world in which unless you're on the top rung of Daddy's hierarchy ladder, most think of you as somehow not quite good enough (they don't wanna think that way, but they just can't seem to help themselves).

Finally, more and more of us around the globe are living in God Science's world, where what dominates is an explosion of technological advancement, along with a bunch of genies popped outa their bottles. For starters there's the nuclear-fission-fusion genie, the germ-warfare genie, the genetically-altered-seeds genie and the cloning genie. Knowledge gathered (in many cases lovingly) by anthropologists has been used by daddy war gods to crush the cultures studied. Science knowledge is used today to lock 90 percent of us into place on the lower rungs of Father's social ladder. Remember the 1960s science forecasters? "By the year 2000, robots will do the work, and no human will work more than three days a week." Uh-huh. Someone forgot to factor in Jehovah and his social ladder. Now like the rest of us, the robots are working for Father's top-rung class acts, and many in the US at least work not three but seven days a week at two and three different jobs.

In the end, both gods — Daddy-War and Science — are fatal reactions against the healthy Great Mother Goddess. As we'll see in a later chapter, the father gods are like many of us vis a vis our parents: we either adopt their traits wholesale, or we adopt the opposite. If Mom's temper's hot, ours is likely to be either hot or cold, not warm. If Dad's outstanding trait is his big, toothy grin, we'll have either a toothy grin or one with not a tooth in sight. The war gods too either stole outright the traits of the Great Guiding Goddess, or turned them 180 degrees backwards.

Although modern Western science might have been a reaction against the excesses of the war gods, hasn't it left us as bad off as the war gods did? With a basket full of toys we can't control? Mind you, I wouldn't want to live in a world without science. Could it be, however, that in the grand scheme of things, science is a two-year-old who needs a few limits set?

Deity Disarmament

By now some of you are saying, "Great jumping jelly fish, if we listened to this stuff we'd all turn into sixties flower children and the enemy'd be mowing us down with pruning shears." Although I understand your concerns, this is a paradox we humans have been dealing with for 6000 years, now — how to retain and even grow our humanity while many among us pour all their energy into shaping themselves for war. I think the solution is multilateral war-gods disarmament. We must identify our world war gods and then disarm them all at the same time. If any country disarms before others do, those still armed will simply crush the unarmed — as they've doggedly done in the past.

Actually, I should give credit where credit is due. Richard Dawkins came up with the idea of multilateral disarmament of war gods before I did — or at least a modified version thereof: "One of the stories told to the young Muslim suicide bombers," says Dawkins, "is that martyrdom is the quickest way to heaven — and not just heaven but a special part of heaven where they will receive their special reward of 72 virgin brides. It occurs to me that our best hope may be to provide a kind of 'spiritual arms control': send in specially trained theologians to deescalate the going rate in virgins" (Dawkins 1997:1).

But just dumping the metasymbol of the war god isn't enough. Even if we'd wave a magic wand and erase all memory of war gods from the minds of every human on earth, war-god culture wouldn't disappear. Well, it might disappear over a few millennia, but that's too long. We need war-god culture gone tomorrow. The way to dissolve the war-god way of life is not just to ditch the war gods, but to replace them with something. And that something should be a guiding metasymbol mirroring and modeling all we want to be: people who are loved unconditionally, people who are sexy and deep-down comfortable with that, and people who are gut-level courageous risk-takers, not sniveling slime-balls constantly bullying others to mask our own deep fears and cowardice. In sum, to rid ourselves of war gods, we need to replace them with something — and logic tells us a guiding mother goddess is just what the doctor ordered.

A Shot of Something Smooth

But it's not just logic that tells us Mother is the correct superordinate model to guide us — it's also biochemistry. Recent discoveries show mothers probably have a natural biochemistry that includes a chemical insuring they will behave toward their children the way we wish others would behave toward us: with unconditional regard and majestic anger and protective behavior when we're threatened. Fathers do not possess this biochemistry. If fathers learn "correct" human behavior, they learn it from people who come naturally equipped to exhibit it — mothers. But not all fathers learn correct behavior. 'Father' therefore is not the best role model.

To be perfectly fair and honest, moms aren't superheroes because they're better than dads or non-mom women either. No way, Jose. All dads would be 100-percent unconditional lovers of kids too if they had the same chemistry mom got as her birthright. Our births trigger a shot of a special hormone into our moms' bodies as they birth us. So powerful is this hormone that it uses the same track in the brain used when addicts shoot up with street drugs: "...the process of bonding to the newborn ... involves powerful activation of a system that ... can be artificially stimulated by drugs like cocaine and heroin" (Anderson and Middleton 2006: 1-2 of 4).

This hormone is called "oxytocin." During the last few months before your birth, you triggered in your mother a rise of the hormone estrogen. This estrogen built receptors in your mother's brain for the oxytocin to attach to. Then your sliding through the birth canal triggered the oxytocin, which made a beeline to those receptors in your mother's brain. So when mum took her first look at you, her newborn, her brain was literally flooded with love. What this boils down to is, your own mother became addicted to loving you. She can't help herself; oxytocin makes it a built-in part of who she is.

While oxytocin isn't new knowledge — we've known since 1906 that it stimulates uterine contractions and the flow of breast milk — only recently have we discovered that it acts as a neurotransmitter too, as a "chemical messenger that can guide behavior." And guide behavior it does: without it, ewes don't even recognize their own babies (Brownlee 1997: 1), and "virgin female rats, or even pregnant ones, will avoid or attack pups, but just before giving birth their behavior changes profoundly" (Anderson and Middleton 2006: 1). So dads who love their kids unconditionally should get triple credit, because to get to the same place moms are naturally, dads have to work like Hades. And although we don't know for sure, my guess is that a good part of the way good dads become good is by watching to see how moms do it.

Tend and Befriend

Actually it's not just mothers who seem to have a biochemistry making them the behavior model that would lead to the world we all want to live in. In stress situations at least, women in general seem to have biochemistry that makes their behavior a worthy model for all of us. On July 21, 2000, San Leandro California sausage-factory owner Stuart Alexander shot and killed three government meat inspectors. His buddy Michael Smith explained it this way: "Pressure, Pressure — everybody blows up under pressure" (Dess 2000: 22). But does everybody blow under pressure? Recent work suggests that while many men might, most women don't. The latest research suggests that women are hardwired to react differently to stress than men. The reason we didn't know this before is because until recently, scientists studied stress using male subjects only.

The scientists pioneering this work were Shelley Taylor and five of her colleagues at the University of California in Los Angeles. In 2000 these six published a paper in the journal *Psychological Review* called "Biobehavioral Responses to Stress in Females: Tend-and-Befriend, not Fight-or-Flight." This paper caused a stir. It's even easy to find it on the Internet; simply "Googling" the title with quotation marks around it will land you multiple copies.

Taylor was prompted to write the paper after listening to a lecture on the "human fight-or-flight" response to stress. As she sat through the lecture Taylor began to think "Whoa. This isn't right. It doesn't jive with what I know from years of dealing with women in therapy about the way they handle stress." So after the lecture Taylor dug around into the research on stress. What she discovered was telling: Until recently, all test subjects in almost all stress studies were either men or male rats. In other words, the fight-or-flight description of the human stress reaction had been "based entirely on research involving only male rats and human males" (Pitman 2003: 194).

This piqued Taylor's curiosity, and she began poking around in the more recent research — the studies including women. She and her colleagues looked at literally hundreds of studies done on both animals and humans. Needless to say, it's not easy getting people to sign up for studies testing reaction to "extreme stress," so this area has its fair share of animal studies. What Taylor discovered is, not only do women respond differently to stress than men do, their responses are radically different.

Instead of responding to disasters the way men do — by fighting or running — women respond with "tending and befriending" behavior. When under stress, women's tendency is not to strike out or go hide in the basement, but to move toward and "affiliate" with others. Numerous studies show that when things go wrong, men generally just want to be alone whereas women want to gather with other women. And while dads having a rough day at work come home and snarl or go hide in the basement, moms having a rough day come home and concentrate on the kids more ("Women's Response to Stress," 2002: 1; Dess 2000: 22). When under stress, women form defense groups by exercising positive, calming, endorphin-boosting human interaction ("Dear, your hair looks divine this evening" or "Sally, you have such a silver tongue; see if you can sweet talk that bank robber into putting down his gun.").

According to Taylor, women's befriending behavior under stress in contrast to men's fight or flight is "one of the most robust gender differences in adult human behavior" (Taylor 2000). Most striking of all is that in both men and women the stress response seems to be triggered by hormones — but by different hormones in each sex. Actually, during stressful situations, a whole avalanche of hormones comes raining down on both sexes, a "hormone cascade." But what rains down on men is mostly testosterone and vasopressin, while for women it's estrogen and the "mother's" hormone we talked about earlier, oxytocin. As we'll see in a minute, the fact that oxytocin is the hormone that bonds mom to baby is key to understanding women's 'tend and befriend' stress behavior.

Killing the Urge

Here's how oxytocin works: Like men, women's first reaction in the face of danger is to fight or run like Hades. But then oxytocin floods their bodies. The oxytocin "enhances relaxation, reduces fearfulness and decreases the stress responses..." (Azar 2000: p. 2 of 4). In other words, oxytocin kills women's urge to come to blows or to cut out in a hurry. Part of the way it does this is by stomping all over the hormone that produces fight or flight, namely, cortisol. Meanwhile, in men the opposite happens. In a sudden stress situation men don't get oxytocin, but something called "vasopressin." And vasopressin ramps up fight-or-flight behavior to an even higher state than it would be otherwise (McCarthy 2005: 3, 5).

Grandma Didn't Run

But why would women, when faced with threats, be flooded with a 'falling-in-love' hormone? For the answer, we need to hop into time-travel boots and trip back to the days of our early human ancestors.... Ah, here we are now on the old savannah. And there's our great, great (etc.) grandmother, only twenty-something now, lounging around camp with her girl friends and the babies. Where's grandpa? As usual, out with the guys hunting gazelle. Uh-oh, looks like we got here just in time to see the main event: moseying into camp is a mammoth lion, licking its colossal chops.

The women size things up in a hurry: "fight's out, flight's in." They run. But they all have babies hanging on them! As you might expect, the babies slow them down. In two swipes of his bushel-basket-sized paw the lion creams the bunch of them. He calls his pals, they all settle in for a feast.

Did I say all the women ran? Sorry; one didn't — Grandma. Grandma was the lucky inheritor of a mutated gene that gave her a rush of oxytocin just as she looked up into the green, glowing eyes of that drooling feline fiend. That oxytocin calmed her right down. This ramped up her courage and also let her think straight. As she watched the other women running and getting creamed, she said to herself, "I'm not going to run like those fools. I'm going to scamper up that tree over there and tend to baby — quiet her so she won't cry and let that feline fiend know where we are."

And that's what grandma did, and that's why she and her baby survived. That's why it was her genes and not those of the others that got passed on to the next generation. This is called "natural selection." Grandma's genes were 'selected for,' and all the other genes were stomped into the dust and consumed for lunch.

And since Grandma's descendents also got the oxytocin "tending" gene, they too were selected for. And they started doing the same thing to other women as Grandma did to baby in the tree: tending to them, fussing over them, saying things like, "You have the prettiest hair, where do you get it done?" and "You're so smart and strong; why don't we band together and beat that lion off with sticks?" So originally "befriending" was like "tending" only you did it with adults versus babies so the adults would help you tend baby. That way whenever a hungry anything moseyed into camp, he'd see you meant business and slink away, or you could fight him off as a group.

So the reason women under stress are flooded with 'falling-in-love' hormones is all because of evolution. Whichever women possessed this tend-and-befriend hormonal setup in early human evolution were the women most likely to survive deadly attacks. And of course when the men came home from hunting gazelle, the tend-and-befriend women were the only women left to act as our grandmothers. But what is men's fight-or-flight behavior adapted to? Perhaps to hunting. In hunting, males look after themselves only, not baby too. So the males most likely to pass on their genes were those who could fight and run the hardest — before the saber-toothed colossus landed on them with all four paws, and sabers rattling. (Pitman 2003: 194).

By the way, I don't mean to say women don't get aggressive — they do. It's just that in most women, aggression "occurs through a different pathway than the male testosterone-driven aggression..." (McCarthy 2005: 3 of 15). While aggression in men is

43

mostly run by hormones, in women it's softened some by culture and prior learning. Although "male aggression appears to be regulated by androgen hormones ... female aggression appears to be more cerebral" and "moderated by social circumstances, learning, culture and the situation..." (Azar 2000: p. 2 of 4).

But testosterone may play a key role here, too, and in both men and women. Trot into the women's and men's wards in any jail, and according to some studies you'll find higher-than-average testosterone levels in each ward. "Women with violent histories and female prisoners convicted of violent crimes were found to have higher testosterone levels in blood plasma and saliva respectively" (McCarthy 2005: 3 of 15, citing Ehlers et al 1988). It's obvious we need to work much harder than we have at training testosterone-heavy people to control their aggression. Let's begin by giving them a model of behavior to shoot for: the tend-and-befriend model of a guiding mother goddess.

Like all intellectual innovators, Taylor and her colleagues have their critics. Geary and Flinn (2002) for example point out that men befriend too. And indeed they do. But men's befriending comes from different places and for different reasons than women's. It looks, smells and tastes different. In short, while women befriend to protect babies, men befriend to protect themselves. Taylor and colleagues suggest that men's groups typically don't care as much about group bonding as about status hierarchies and power differentials (Taylor et al 2000: 419).

Time to Switch

In sum, women's tend-and-befriend behavior provides one more reason why we would benefit big-time by replacing God the Father with God the Mother — the ideal model not only for women but for men as well. We ask men to learn from women how to love children unconditionally; why not ask them to learn from women how to respond to stress? Men and women both purchased their stress-response hormonal packages in days long-gone — and for reasons no longer relevant. Just by luck, however, women's package still fits our modern needs, while men's is killing us.

Testosterone-heavy men and women need to learn from a larger-than-life model a better way of reacting to stress. We can no longer afford to have them leaking their prehistoric fight-or-flight behavior over us and the world. Hasn't the individual's ticket into the human group always been learning to modify his or her anti-group behavior? Now more than ever, fight or flight is anti-group behavior. And since women for six millennia have used God the Father as a role model, it's obviously no big deal to use cross-sex role models. By all rights, men should have no complaints over learning life's lessons from a guiding mother goddess.

Unfortunately no one's asking men to do this. Instead, the testosterone fight-or-flight response is being applauded and praised 24/7 by the war-god rule books, which now litter not only our homes and churches but even our public spaces (in the US at any rate, open the top drawer of your hotel bedside table and chances are you'll find a Gideon's Bible staring you in the face).

Shelley Taylor says we need a "new 'tending society' in which caretaking is cultivated on a broad cultural level as a means of eliminating psychological, social, and cultural ills" (Pitman 2003: 195). Although Taylor's right on the mark here, until we replace our daddy-god fight-or-flight behavior models (preferably with mother-goddess tend-and-befriend models), we'll never get to her tending society. The duds holding us down in the mud, now, aren't ordinary male gods, but the dregs of goddom: As Richard Dawkins puts it; Jehovah's a petty, jealous, vicious bully-boy. If you were itching to find a modern male on the order of Jealous Jehovah, the best place to look would be outside a bar Saturday night on the wrong side of town. Better yet, try the county jail. In short, trying to create a tending society with this kind of god at the helm would be like patching the holes in your truck tires without sweeping your drive free of tacks and nails first.

2

Kissing Cousins

A good next step would be to visit a group that uses a mother goddess as its guiding metasymbol. Unfortunately, over the past several millennia the war gods have pummeled all such groups into the dust. So none exist to look at. No pure ones anyway. The group that comes closest, however, may be the Moso of China mentioned earlier in this book.

The Great - Mother - Goddess-worshipping Moso of the Tibetan-China borderland were the inspiration for "Shangri-la," the mythical earthly paradise that was the setting for James Hilton's famous novel *Lost Horizon* (McElroy 2001). If you haven't heard of Moso Land, where women are gorgeous and men are hunky, it's probably because the Moso have managed to remain buried behind time in their beautiful, isolated mountain valley. Hidden high in the Himalayas in China's Yunnan and Sichuan provinces, the Moso live around what the rest of the world calls Lake Lugu but the Moso call "Mother Lake."

Fig. 2.1 Moso women dancing. The Moso were the inspiration for the mythical land of Shangri-la (Photograph by Christian Erni, IWGIA [International Work Group for Indigenous Affairs]).

The Moso of Mother Lake, or Land of Free Love

When the People's Liberation Army stumbled across the Moso in 1956 and "turned their world over," they (the PLA) were astounded at what they found. What astonished them most was this: in place of what was thought to be a universal institution — marriage — the Moso had an unheard of system of "free love." The Moso (or Mosuo as they're sometimes called) are "reputed to be the only people in the world who consider marriage an attack on the family." As the Moso writer Yang Erche Namu puts it "Women and men should not marry, for love is like the seasons — it comes and goes" (Namu and Mathieu 2003: 273-4, 7).

Due to a lack of roads reaching up to their mountain hideaway, even after Chairman Mao stumbled onto the Moso in the 1950s it took the rest of the world twenty more years to find them. Since then, men all over the world have been busy making beelines to Moso country — the "Country of Women" or "The Girl's Kingdom" as it's alternately called. These men are under the mistaken impression that Moso women hand out free sex; actually what they hand out is free *love* — they need to love you, in other words, before you get any loving.

In almost all ways, the Moso seem typical of the ancient guiding-goddess societies that existed before the war gods first burst onto the world scene some 6000 years ago. Today's 40,000 or so Moso are egalitarian, democratic, non-violent, generous, peaceful, playful, sensual risk-takers (mosuoproject.org). Moso men don't dominate Moso women, and vice-versa. "Men and women have ... limited authority over each other" (Namu & Mathieu 2003: 277) and families have not only a female but also a male "chief" (Hua 2001). "What is beyond argument" says anthropologist Christine Mathieu, one of the first Westerners to be granted access to study the Moso "... is that Moso society is not ruled by women as

Fig. 2.2. Moso man and woman boating on Mother Lake. Moso men don't dominate women, nor do Moso women dominate men (Photograph by Sara Gouveia).

is invariably publicized by the mass media.... Today, although there are no rules barring women from office," local government "is dominated almost exclusively by male cadres." This is partly because women are "constantly preoccupied with the housework and farmwork" and partly because for the past several centuries daddy-god conquerors have insisted that the Moso toe the line and let men run their larger governments. Nevertheless, women own half the family wealth — and manage all of it. They are the "owners" of the family bloodlines, and they possess remarkable sexual freedom known in few other places in the world (Namu & Mathieu 2003: 278-79).

Even though Moso families are headed by "chiefs," these select few aren't dictators — everyone in the family expects to help decide things. "Moso families are democratic units where all relatives expect to be included in decision making" says Yang Erche Namu. There's little crime. No Moso today "can recall either murder or beating or robbery, or a truly ugly fight between neighbors or jilted lovers" (Namu & Mathieu 2003: 277, 69).

The Moso are so generous they go beyond even Communist sharing standards. Says Yang Erche Namu, "The government ... sent special teams of soldiers and officials to our valleys to re-educate the people — because the Moso shared everything, including their lovers.... Moso men are sometimes gone for months at a time on trade caravans — sometimes a risky business but always full of excitement and adventure. The Moso gather constantly for parties, picnics, banqueting, dancing, flirting, teasing, joking, singing, wrestling and horse-riding contests (Namu & Mathieu 2003: 94, 96).

The Moso Guiding Mother Goddess

In addition to being the only society in the world minus marriage, the Moso are also one of the few still worshipping a guiding mother goddess. "[T]he Moso are alone among their neighbors to have a guardian mother goddess rather than a patron warrior god." This Goddess, Segge Gamu, guards and protects the Moso people, their animals and their fields. She's "intelligent, beautiful and powerful" (Mathieu 2003: 399; 1998: 225).

Fig. 2.3. Moso woman praying at Mother Lake. The Moso still worship a Guiding Mother Goddess (Photograph by Sara Gouveia).

The Moso also worship "ancient totemic deities" such as the mother tiger Lamu, the mother snake Zhemu and other benevolent mountain deities. These create harmony in the world "as they mediate between sky and earth...." Although the neighbors of the Moso also worship mountain deities, theirs show despotic, dictatorial overtones: "In contrast to the Naxi, the Moso regard almost all mountain deities as giant relatives, not as lords of the wilderness" (Mathieu 1998: 223-25).

In *Leaving Mother Lake*, Yang Erche Namu describes trekking on foot with her family around Lake Lugu and up the Goddess' mountain, Gamu, in order to honor their Mother. On top of the mountain everyone lit piles of sagebrush and bowed, prayed and sang to the Goddess. Before the People's Liberation Army came and forbade them their religion, this festival honoring the Goddess was not a day- but a week-long event. Across the plain at the foot of the mountain as far as the eye could see stretched blue, white, yellow and black tents, some painted with multicolored flowers. "And amid the spiraling smoke of smoldering sagebrush, amid drunken men, and women bright as flowers, hundreds of lamas in brilliant yellow would have performed the ceremonies for the Goddess. Their faces glowing … they would have chanted sutras in deep vibrating voices and blown their long brass trumpets into the heavens" (Namu & Mathieu 2003: 104).

At night big bonfires were lit and men and women danced in circles around the fire, the women singing about "how bad the men were" and the men singing teasing songs back to the women. The women would reply and so it would go, back and forth, everyone getting wittier and "more daring" as time flew by. After the dance, men and women drifted to the hot springs, where the women washed each others' backs and men lay in water drinking wine. When his glass was empty, and if a woman liked the gleam in his eye, a man might get it refilled by such a woman. As she poured, he would whisper about which tree and which gathering of stars he could be found under later that night. When no one was watching she would steal off to that place, and he would follow (Namu & Mathieu 2003: 103-104).

Fig. 2.4. Moso girl. A Moso household is made up of you, your mother, her siblings, your siblings, and all other children of the women in the family (Photograph by Dirk Borchers).

Here's how love and love-making work among the mother-goddess-loving Moso. First, don't worry about babies having no fathers. Babies are all taken care of outstandingly well by their families. It's just that their families have no biological dads. A Moso family is made up of you, your mother, her sisters and brothers, your sisters and brothers, and all the children of the women in the family. If you were a Moso kid, you'd have tons of people to care for and adore you, all living together under the roof of a large, two-story home surrounded by a courtyard. If you were a guy, your uncles would teach you guy things. Although you may have no idea who your biological dad is, neither you nor your biological dad give a fig.

When you become a teen, if you're a girl you get your own private bedroom on the second floor of your home, with your own private entrance. If you're a guy, you wait until cover of night, quietly steal out of your house, make your way to your lover's home, slip quietly into her courtyard, climb the stairs, and steal along the second-floor balcony to her door. At this point you use your wits to find a creative way to make your presence known. If your sweetie's not in the mood, you find somewhere else to sleep that night. If she is, she opens the door and lets you in. The next morning you get up before anyone else, sneak out of your lover's room, and hightail it back home before anyone sees you (the Moso are a bit modest about their "visits"; the less known about them the better).

Depending on the couple, love lasts anywhere from a night, to a month, to many years. Although most Moso claim hundreds of lifetime love partners, after a certain age everyone typically settles down with one partner. Although it's not considered kosher to have more than one partner at a time, it's not really against the rules either. Here's what one Moso man, Ai Le Shan Ma, 38, said about Moso "marriage": "Our marriage is better because it is for love only. I come over at night because I want to. If we didn't get on, if we fought all the time, we would split and find other partners.'" (McElroy 2001: 1 of 3).

Breaking up is not hard to do: guys, you simply stop knocking at the girl's door. Girls, stop opening the door. No one's allowed to get hurt or jealous over a break-up, let alone throw a fit. Those are the rules, Sam, and it seems most Moso follow them. "I had never heard of a woman fighting over a man" said Yang Erche Namu. Namu first heard of such weirdness after leaving her village to sally forth into the wider world of the daddy-war-god Han Chinese. After learning that such a thing actually existed (women fighting over a man), Namu "felt relieved that my mother and my sister and my little brothers lived in Zuosuo, where everyone took care of each other... and where people could love without fear of jealousy or punishment" (Namu and Mathieu 2003: 179).

Mothers Are the Model

Another exotic aspect of the Moso — to Westerners at least — is the deep power they give their mothers. Moso put mothers so high on a pedestal it's a bit boggling. Listen to this song, sung "enthusiastically" by Moso women:

> There are so many skillful people,
> But none can compare with my mother.
> There are so many knowledgeable people,
> But none can equal my mother.
> There are so many people skilled at song and dance,
> But none can compete with my mother... (Yuan and Mitchell 2000: 58).

Why doesn't the rest of the world write songs like this? Would mothers accept such songs? Or are we so deeply anti-mother now that even mothers themselves would be unable to handle such power-packed praise?

It's astounding that for so many millennia the Moso have managed to keep their guiding mother goddess and their beautiful way of life. They've done so only partly though, and only by staying secluded from the rest of the world. Nevertheless, they may provide a clue about the way all Tibetans used to live. Says British news reporter Damien McElroy, "The isolation of the Moso ... has enabled them to preserve a way of life once common in Tibet" (McElroy 2001: 1 of 3).

Although they've kept their guiding goddess alive, the Moso have not been entirely free of war gods even in their remote mountain villages. At the end of the fifteenth century, for example, Buddhism crept into their lives, and in the 1600s the Qing dynasty forced them to adopt strong-man rule, social stratification, and father-to-son inheritance. Although they've mostly returned to their pre-Qing ways, there's still a scummy residue of Qing hierarchy left, and "Buddhism once again dominates the Moso religious scene," including the Goddess Gamu. Today the Moso face a flood of tourism and Chinese government interference that has already reduced their Goddess religion to a pale shadow of what it was even half a century ago. And sadly, although hopes are high for them, most wonder whether the beautiful old Moso way of life will last much longer (Hua 2001: 470, 368; Mathieu 1998: 210).

I believe the history of the Moso is the history of goddess peoples generally. These vibrant, healthy, "Shangri-la" societies — the kind we all want to live in — are no match for the sky- and war-gods we've allowed to lay waste to most of our world. After being discovered in 1956, it took only five decades for the Moso to begin to wilt under the withering gaze of the war gods — after surviving for no doubt millennia. The dominant Han-Chinese society talks not to women, but to Moso men. Also, the STDs riding in on the coattails of tourists are leaving Moso women sterile. Finally, almost the entire Moso way of life — including their goddess religion — has been either discouraged or outlawed by the national government. In short, the old Moso way of life is crumpling like a hot-house flower in a hail storm. Unless something happens fast to end the hail storm, like all others, this guiding-goddess society too will drop underground — or fade away into oblivion.

The Mysterious Basques

Another modern society that's managed to hang on to a bit of its ancient guiding goddess are the mysterious Basques living high in the Pyrenees Mountains in the Spanish-French borderland. The Basques are mysterious because everything about them is out of sync with the rest of Europe — their customs, their traditions, their language — all are totally distinct from what's found around them. For example, most of the rest of Europe speaks "Indo-European" languages. This suggests that somewhere back in the BCs, the hypothetical ancient Indo-Europeans either pummeled Europe, or somehow sweet-talked her into giving up her old languages for those of the Indo-Europeans. (Although it seems obvious to me that some big-time pummeling went on, I'd be remiss if I didn't tell you scientists disagree on this issue.)

Somehow the Basques escaped the Indo-Europeans, and so got to keep not only their language but their customs as well. Here's how I envision it: those rascally Indo-Europeans shot everybody up all over town, and then stole their land. The last of the guiding-goddess peoples said "Okay we'll go live up in the Pyrenees Mountains, and you can have the rest of Europe. But step one foot into our mountains, and we'll eat you for breakfast." The result: the Basques are a scrappy lot known for fighting tooth and nail to keep others out of their hair.

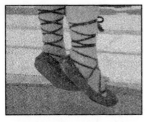

Fig. 2.5. Basque folk dancer on her toes. Much about the mysterious Basques is out of sync with the rest of Europe (Photograph by Alber Vazquez).

As a result, many Basques have kept many of their ancient ways, including a belief in a guiding mother goddess. Archaeologist and mythologist Marija Gimbutas, formerly of the University of California, says even today in remote areas of Basque country, the Goddess is still strong. "Even in the twentieth century, some mountainous regions escaped Christianity. There, belief in the goddess remains a living reality" (Gimbutas 2001: 173).

But how did the Basques escape the fate that befell the rest of Europe? Like I said, isolation was part of it. It can't be the whole story though, because all through history people were constantly passing through the Pyrenees to get from Spain to France and back again, and they had to pass smack through Basque country to do it. On the other hand, when passers-through have threatened their freedom, the Basques have never been afraid to fight back: "Successive invaders into the Pyrenees — Celts,

Romans, Arabs, Visigoths — all quickly learned some brisk lessons about Basque ferocity and bravery." The best explanation I've heard about how the Basques have kept their integrity goes back to their mysterious language. This language is incredibly difficult to learn. So the theory has it that this and the Basques' ferocity have made most would-be conquerors throw up their hands in disgust and move on to easier pickings (Hadingham 1992: 2; Coleman 2000: 3).

Actually there's new evidence hot off the press that the Basques are the first and oldest people in Europe. They, their language, and their customs are probably a tiny time-capsule of the first Europeans, who would have wandered into Europe between 15,000 and 7,500 years ago (Oppenheimer 2006). If all this is true, then chances are the Basque guiding goddess is very, very old.

Like the Moso Goddess, however, the Basque Goddess has been battered and bruised along the way. Through the millennia, no one conquered the Basques — not until the 1800s anyway, when the Spanish shoe-horned them into Spain — but between the third and fifth centuries AD they were overrun by father/war gods. And ever since, Daddy's tried his darndest to do a number on the Basque Mother Goddess. For example, when he discovered

Fig. 2.6. Basque folk dancers. Basque women used to officiate in Basque churches — until, that is, the Inquisition found out (Photograph by Alber Vazquez).

Basque women were actually allowed to officiate in his churches, Daddy was appalled. The result was, in the Basque town of Logrono in 1610, a major Inquisition witch burning (Shearer 2002; Hadingham 1992: 3).

Today most of the old holy days of the Basque Goddess have been run over by Daddy. Most have been forced to adopt Daddy's saint's names. For example, the famous running of the bulls in Pamplona is not a Spanish but a Basque ceremonial, Pamplona being a famous old town in the middle of Basque territory. There's no doubt in my mind that this bull ceremony harkens back to the Neolithic era or earlier, to the apparent sacred and widespread tie between the Neolithic Goddess and Her bulls. Yet for quite some time the official title of the Pamplona bull run has been "the festival of Saint Fermin."

But for Daddy, even Saint Vermin ... er, Fermin ... isn't enough of a hold on Pamplona. He's also made the town a stronghold of one of the nastier of his recent inventions, Opus Dei, the ultraconservative Catholic organization that plays a secretive, sinister role in Dan Brown's famous novel *The DaVinci Code*.

So who is the twenty-first-century Basque Goddess? Like the Basques themselves, She's swimming with mystery. My guess is that even today the Basques are careful to keep Her protected under thick layers of secrecy. The great Basque mythologist Jose Miguel de Barandiaran had this to say about Her supernatural aides the Laminak:

There are ... people who, in response to a question about the existence of such beings, remember this traditional Basque phrase ... : *Izena duan guztla omen da*, "Whatever has a name exists." Such a notion, and the Christianity which is opposed to it, has given place to an attitude of compromise which appears in many popular stories, and which is found stereotyped in the following phrase, alluding to mythical beings or spirits: *Direnik ez da sinistu bear: ez direla ez da esan bear*, "You don't have to believe that they exist; you don't have to say that they don't exist" (Everson 1989 translating from Barandiarán 1972: 140).

Shape Shifter

So my guess is, we know far from the full story on the Basque Guiding Goddess. We do know, however, that although She goes by many names, the most common is Mari. Also She's a shape shifter who can take on just about any shape She wants. When

Mari appears as a woman, She's stunningly beautiful (Buber's Basque Page online). Yet She can just as easily appear as a plant, animal, bird, cloud, rainbow or any other number of shapes.

Mari's as different from Daddy as a rainbow from a riot of plague-toting rats. While Daddy lives in the sky, Mari lives in the middle of the earth She created. Mari's inner-earth home is not, as Daddy's tried to con us into believing, an underground torture chamber (where he plunks those of us failing to follow his rules), but a beautiful land of abundance: of rivers running with milk and honey, and with gold and precious stones galore (Gimbutas 2001: 173, 175; Everson 1989: p. 14 of 30). And whereas Daddy rules by fiat and fear, often as not Mari leads by gentle prodding.

Mari's not too fond of Daddy, and the Basques tell a number of stories about how She deals with him. The following is supposed to be typical: Once a Christian shepherd wanted to build a hut next to a cave known to be a doorway into Mari's inner home, and, being a bit nervous about Mari's reaction to his plan, the shepherd decorated the cave entrance with a few Christian baubles. Well, how would you like your door decorated by your arch rival? Needless to say, Mari took offense. She sent a flock of vultures to roost on the dude's hut ceiling. The birds told the shepherd to take down the Christian crosses and other trimmings, and when the shepherd declined, the birds asked again. The shepherd begged off a third time, after which the birds repeated their request. This kept up and kept up, until the shepherd finally threw up his hands, trudged over to the cave door, and yanked down Daddy's stuff. Although the story doesn't say, my guess is the shepherd moved out of the neighborhood fairly soon after (Everson 1989: 16 of 30).

Like Jehovah, Mari is lawgiver and police officer all under the same hat. But half Daddy's laws are about him — no other god before me; no taking my name in vain, no dilly-dallying on my day Sunday; no carving any pics of other gods and worshiping them instead of me; and do what I say no matter what, just because I say so. Mari's laws, on the other hand, are all about us. Very simply, She's against lying, cheating, excessive pride, boasting, promise-breaking, lack of respect for people and property, and walking away when someone needs help. And whereas Jehovah punishes by popping you one, Mari's more likely to punish by turning the gold you stole into charcoal, or stripping you of whatever it was you lied about, cheated over, were too proud of, bragged about, and so forth (Everson 1989: 13 of 30).

Mari does, however, control the weather. And if it gets too bad, it's probably because someone's not living up to Mari's expectations of what the good person should or should not be doing.

Dashing, Daring and Democratic

As might be expected, the guiding-goddess Basques have a little more of a goddess style about them than do their European neighbors. For example the Basques have always been more egalitarian and democratic — and perhaps too a bit more dashing and daring. (It's what happens when you have a healthy mother backing you up.) Traditional Basque women for instance have always had their fair share of the power. As a matter of fact, in AD 7 the Greek geographer Strabo even said the Basques had "a sort of woman-rule." And for at least the past hundred years "scholars have widely discussed the high status of Basque women in law codes, as well as their positions as judges, inheritors, and arbitrators through pre-Roman, medieval, and modern times" (Hadingham 1992: 2, 3; Gimbutas 2001: 172).

While most of Europe from the days of the Romans on down to the modern era was run by war-god-like autocrats, the Basques stand out as a bastion of democracy. To a great degree the Basques were run less by people than by a set of ancient laws called *fors* in French Basqueland, and *fueros* on the Spanish side of Basque country. The *fors* and *fueros* were kept polished and shiny by a group "democratically" elected. These laws "governed every aspect of their lives ... and it was not uncommon for a fisherman

Fig. 2.7. Basque folk dance. The Basques never developed an elitist culture (Photograph by Alber Vazquez).

to preside over meetings in which Spanish noblemen were seated" (Shearer 2002). Evan Hadingham, author and science editor of the US television series "NOVA" says that Basque unity, which is supported by their distinctive language, "was cemented by unique social institutions startlingly different from those of feudal Europe. The Basques never developed an elitist culture, instead appointing a 'Lord of Biscay' by democratic election" as their political leader (Hadingham 1992: 2 & 3 of 10).

Risk Takers to Beat All Risk Takers

Finally, the Basques are risk takers par excellence. No one not a risk taker runs in their Pamplona bull run. Ever since 1926 when Ernest Hemingway wrote about it in *The Sun Also Rises*, the run has become flooded with outsiders wanting to test their mettle. Today up to 6000 "run with the bulls" annually in Basqueland.

Over the nine-day festival of Saint Vermin — er Fermin — a million and a half people flood Pamplona, population 200,000, turning the festival into something akin to "a Biblical visitation, a triathlon with music, for which the town provides medical emergency squads on 24-hour alert, thousands of volunteers to clean the streets of tons of garbage, extra police patrols and temporary toilets. Pamplonans who can't take it pack up and leave town" (Zwingle 2006). This flood of foreigners has dampened the Basque man's enthusiasm for taking part in the run. Although few do the run today, as little as a generation back it was a *rite de passage* for Basque men.

How risky is running with bulls through ancient, narrow cobblestone streets? Well since 1924 thirteen runners have died doing it, and many more have been bull-gored (Walker 2005).

"It's adrenaline over the top," said Eduardo Arregui.... "One or two months before San Fermin, I start thinking about the bulls, and I feel my heart pumping, and sweating. As the moment comes closer, it gets worse." And then? "When the rocket goes off," says Mikel Aranburu, a tax assessor who teaches the Basque flute, "the fear goes away and everything goes blank. And when the bulls pass by, you feel extreme relief. You feel exaltation, friendship, life. It's a very, very intense experience. You're hooked. It's like a drug, and you're almost begging for more" (Zwingle 2006: 5 of 7).

The last to die was a 22-year-old from Ernest Hemingway's hometown of Chicago, Illinois, one Matthew Tassio. Andrew Walker was there in 1995 when it happened. The run began at a corral near the Church of Santa Domingo "on the stroke of eight ... with the sound of an exploding rocket filling the air." As Walker stood watching near a corner of the church he saw that "... almost instantaneously, the crowd parted to reveal a huge black bull. Men were slipping on the dewy cobblestones, the look of fear in their eyes.... Within seconds, the horde was upon us, bodies crashed into the heavy wooden safety barrier in front of me with a dull thud...." And then, lying about 10 feet (3 meters) away on the ground, Walker saw Tazzio's body "eyes already glazing, a patch of blood spreading about it." A bull had hit the boy in the stomach, severing a main artery before tossing him 23 feet (7 meters) into the air (Walker 2005).

Fig. 2.8. Basque men: risk-takers to beat all risk-takers

(Photograph by Alber Vazquez).

Clearly, in this day and age at least, the Great Mother of the Basques does not suffer fools gladly. Her men are risk-takers to beat all risk takers. And taking risks sometimes means that some of them will end up with the short end of the stick.

The Hopis of the American Southwest

Another group that's hung on to their ancient guiding goddess longer than most, are the Hopis and their Pueblo cousins of the American Southwest. Like the Moso and the Basques, the Hopi too have helped preserve their Goddess — until the early 1900s at least — by plunking themselves down where war gods couldn't reach them. The Hopis stashed their villages some 600 feet (180 meters) above the desert floor on flat-topped land formations called mesas. Narrow trails hacked into the steep mesa sides — trails their enemies' horses couldn't mount — pumped up their isolation. Almost daily, however, the Hopi loped down these same trails to cultivate their crops on the desert floor.

Fig. 2.9. The Hopi village of Walpi, Arizona, lies seven hundred feet above the plain below it (From 1929 U.S. Government Document [Smithsonian Scientific Series: The North American Indians]).

In the early 1900s photographer Edward Curtis counted eight Hopi villages: "On East Mesa are Walpi and Sichomovi...; on Middle Mesa are Mishongnovi, Shipaulovi, and Shongopavi; on West Mesa are Oraibi, Hotavila, and Pakavi" (Hausman and Kapoun 1995: 43). Today atop the same three mesas, ten villages thrive, while two more sit below on the desert floor. When Reg

Saner visited Shipaulovi (now "Supawlavi") in 1997 he found life "little changed from ten centuries ago.... Here at Supawlavi," he said, "I'm standing so close to gone time as to be inside it. Prehistory alive in our midst and dancing. That's almost beyond astonishment. How many Americans realize?" (Saner 1997: 8 of 16).

But despite Her mesa hideaways, the Hopi Goddess has not escaped the hammering of war gods any more than the Moso and Basque Goddesses have. Dating back to AD 1100 and beyond, Hopi villages were probably badgered by war gods from the very first (Hopi Indian Tribal website). Four hundred years later the Spanish Conquistadores tortured the Hopi Great Mother for gold.

A little after that, Spanish missionaries began torturing Her in the name of Christ. In addition to torturing the Hopi, the Spanish pumped them into forced labor, "summoned" Hopi women for sexual favors, and tried to take down the Hopi Mother Goddess. Hopis caught practicing their age-old religion were either "whipped or executed" (Billard 1979: 174). Although usually peaceful and non-violent, the Hopi have never been shy about fighting for their rights. So after being manhandled by the Spanish for a few decades, they banded together with their Pueblo cousins and in 1680 royally routed the rogues.

Then in the mid 1800s, in stomped the Anglos with their missionaries and government

Fig. 2.10. Four young Hopi women climbing to their "cliff-perched homes." From 1900 to 1920, Hopi children were carted off against their parents' wishes to Anglo re-education schools (Photograph by Edward S. Curtis, ca. 1906. Courtesy of McCormick Library of Special Collections, Northwestern University Library).

policies. From about 1900 to 1920 the Mesa villages snapped and popped. For adults there was the US Religious Crimes Code, designed to root and stomp out Indian religion. For kids there was an even finer delight: the Indian boarding school. Against their parents' wishes, children were carted off to these re-education camps and cracked open like nuts (Dozier 1970: 88, 115). Pueblo English professor Paula Gunn Allen says "...millions of Indian people were educated in boarding schools ... wherein serious sexual and other kinds of physical abuse, neglect, terrorization, starvation, and humiliation were the order of the day..." (Gunn Allen 1992: xiii-xiv).

In 1934, with the US Indian Reorganization Act, things eased up a bit. By that time, however, the Hopi had crawled into a shell that even today they haven't completely broken out of. Even today they speak to few non-Indians other than the tourists who drive up the mesas to see the Hopi kachina ceremonies and ogle the handmade Hopi indigenous crafts. The Guiding Mother of the Hopis therefore is not easy to get to know. (Schlegel 2004: 30; Gunn-Allen 1992: 200; Dozier 1970: 5; Hultkrantz 1990: 213).

The Hopi Mother Goddess

In the near past, the Hopi Earth Mother was represented by several female deities — not only Spider Woman but Sand-Altar Woman, Corn Mother and others. Earth Mother birthed all living things. The entrance to Her womb was the *sipapuni*, the hole dipping down into the Hopi underground ceremonial chamber, the kiva. Another hole, this one in the floor of the kiva, was the doorway through which the human race crawled from inside earth to first greet earth's surface (Hultkrantz 1990: 213-14; Leeming and Page 1994: 28).

The story of Spider Woman exists in many versions, some with strong male elements, others without. University of Connecticut mythologist David Leeming says the male elements are recent additions, and that versions minus the male parts probably show what the Great Guiding Goddess of the Neolithic was like before She was bruised, battered and demoted by the Bronze-Age Hell's-angels gods (Leeming and Page 1994: 28). Here is the beginning of one version of the long story of Spider Woman:

> At a remote time, when there was no world and nothing else alive, Spider Woman thought out into space. She breathed, and sang, and thought, and spun a world into being out of the purple glow at the beginning. She spun a thread that stretched across the universe from east to west, and another from north to south. Spider Woman then set about creating the sun from turquoise, red rock, white shell, and yellow rock, carrying it to the highest point of the world and placing it in the sky. Seeing that half the time remained dark, Spider woman fashioned the moon from the same materials and placed it in the sky. After observing the sun and moon for a time, she noted that, in the course of the moon's travels, it left many nights without light. She put the crystalline eyes of the stars into the night sky so that even on moonless nights there would not be utter darkness…. (Leeming and Page 1994: 29).

To the Hopi, the Mother Goddess' power to create life was the source behind the source, the wellspring of all sacral magic. "The old ones were empowered by their certain knowledge that the power to make life is the source and model for all ritual magic and that no other power can gainsay it. Nor is that power really biological at base; it is the power of … Thought, of Mind, that gives rise to … social organizations, material culture, and trans-formations of all kinds — including hunting, war, healing, spirit communication, rain-making, and all the rest." Even among Pueblo Indians today, "motherness" pumps the brain full of "something other than the kind of sentimental respect for motherhood that is reflected in American's Mother's Day…. It is ritually powerful…. So central to ritual activities is it in Indian cultures that men are honored by the name mother..." (Gunn Allen 1992: 28, 29).

Pueblo English professor Paula Gunn Allen thinks the Hopi

Goddess has morphed recently into a male figure, "Maseo" or "Tawa" (Gunn Allen 1992: 41). Although possibly true today, it wasn't true in the recent past. Of course for insisting god was a mother, the parents of today's adult Hopis were humiliated, tortured and maybe even killed in government boarding schools. Who knows — perhaps the ticket to being released from these so-called schools was an agreement to abandon the Mother.

Fig. 2.11. Hopi Mother. To the Hopi, the concept of "motherness" is ritually powerful (Photograph by Edward Curtis, 1922. Courtesy of McCormick Library of Special Collections, Northwestern University Library).

But what kind of life did the Hopis enjoy while their Earth Mother was still steering their ship? Answer: the kind most of us can barely imagine. Like the Basques, the Hopi were democratic, independent risk-takers. Like the Moso, they were generally peaceful and non-violent. And compared to their nomadic neighbors the Apache and Navajo, they were swimming in riches.

Freedom-Loving Power Sharers

Hopi men and women shared both work and power. Women owned the houses, land and seed corn. And when most of your food comes from what you grow, owning seed is like owning The SuperDuper Food Mart Corporation. Each Hopi clan owned its own land and allotted each of its women a plot. Forking out the land was the job of the "Clan Mother" (Schlegel 2004: 21; Driver 1964: 258). On the other hand, Hopi men served as the village and religious heads. While men tilled and tended the fields, wove the cloth, and fashioned most of the clothing, women handled the housework, supplied the water, and manufactured the ceramic dishware. Residence was matrilocal, meaning newlyweds almost always moved into the bride's home.

Politically the Hopi were both free and democratic. Their 1680 defiance of the Spanish underscores another of their guiding-mother-goddess traits — their fierce love of freedom. The 1680 revolt has been called "... perhaps the most spectacular and successful act of defiance that Indians anywhere would ever accomplish in their relations with Europeans" (Maxwell 1978: 211). As the ancient Mother-Goddess societies no doubt did, the Hopi too ruled themselves by consensus; before becoming final, decisions must first be okayed by all members of the group. In 1929 Hopi towns were "entirely independent and self-governing" (Palmer 1929: 109-110). Today this is still true. Each Hopi village

... is a complete and independent government. The *kikmongwi* is the village leader.... [H]is power is limited because traditional Hopi decision making is based on community consensus .... A council of hereditary clan leaders assists the *kikmongwi*...." (Hopi Indian Tribal website).

Even vis a vis marriage the Hopi prized their freedom. Divorce and remarriage were common and simple. If your wife deposited your things outside the door of the house, your marriage was caput — period, end of sentence. Of course instead of seeing their adult caretaker group ripped in half as Western kids of divorced parents do, the kids of a Hopi divorce saw it drop only from, say, seven to six, or nine to eight. In other words still in your house after Dad two-stepped away were Mom's sisters, Mom's sister's hubbies, and Grandma and Grandpa.

The Hopi are one of nine peaceful societies highlighted in the book *Keeping the Peace* by University of Arizona anthropologist Douglas Fry and his colleague Graham Kemp (Kemp and Fry 2004). Although the Hopi engaged in warfare on a few occasions in the past, war to them was never a path to glory. Their attitude: war is a necessary evil. Inside Hopi villages today, violence is almost unheard of, and both police and policing systems are

Fig. 2.12. Court in Oraibi Village, Arizona, in the early 20th century. In Hopi villages, violence is almost unknown (From 1929 U.S. Government Document [Smithsonian Scientific Series: The North American Indians]).

absent. Public brawling — which is rare — is defined not as hitting, but as pushing and shouting. The anthropologist Alice Schlegel witnessed only one fight while she worked among the Hopi. She came upon it "just as it started, before onlookers had a chance to separate the contestants.... I saw no attempts to punch or kick. I was told that pushing was the major form of violent contest between men..." (Schlegel 2004: 24, 27).

The Hopi were also wealthy. They had what it took to manufacture awesome pottery, cloth, clothing, jewelry and other fine items. Since these bedazzled their nomad neighbors, who were always trying to filch the Hopi's finery and food stores, at times the Hopi were forced into defending themselves against looters. Nevertheless, among themselves they were almost totally nonviolent: children were not punished physically, thievery was almost unknown, and murder was totally out of the picture (Saner 1997: 9 of 16, Terrell 1998: 38, 39).

Fig. 2.13. Modern Hopi kachina doll symbolizing Butterfly Goddess. Yale art historian Vincent Scully calls the Hopi kachina ceremonies "the most profound art form in North America" (Photo by Mary Harrsch).

Creative and Playful

My favorite: the Hopi were creative and playful. They "manufactured toys, dolls, masks, and ... kachinas carved, painted and adorned with great artistry" (Terrell 1998: 39). Kachina figurines represented Hopi goddesses and gods. Even today the Pueblo kachina ceremonies, which Yale art historian Vincent Scully has called "the most profound art form in North America," are famous among tourists. (Page 2003: 114).

Profound or not, parts of the kachina ceremonies are downright jokey and fun. A few years ago novelist Jake Page witnessed one such ceremony:

> Within minutes the plaza has filled with spirits, maybe forty of them, bedecked in buckskin moccasins, pine boughs, white cotton kilts; bronze bodies all streaked with the same earthy colors; with multicolored, beaked faces, eyes flittering from slits. They chant like a low, distant wind while a drum thumps.... At which point all hell breaks loose. A band of the most appalling ragamuffins descends ... from the roof of a building.... [T]he rowdies ... do everything backwards, or

wrong... acting out the increasing corruption of mankind. They gossip, they fight, they covet things, they commit adultery. They are gluttonous.... The old Hopi ladies hug themselves with barely controlled mirth as each earthly sin unfolds (Page 2003: 113-114).

Pondering our Western religions Page adds: "I've never run across any yuks in the hymnals and prayer books I was brought up with, and the Bible is one of the most rigorously humorless books I've read.... Laughter is a gift, joy another form of prayer. For the Hopi a smile is sacred" (2003: 114-115).

Like all good mother-goddess peoples, the Hopis are also ace

Fig. 2.14. Hopi Snake Priest. During their snake dance, Hopi men carried live rattlesnakes around in their mouths (Photograph by Edward Curtis, ca. 1900. Courtesy of McCormick Library of Special Collections, Northwestern University Library).

risk-takers. In defending themselves they've been called "courageous warriors," and "brave and fierce fighters." And try dangling sometime on a rope 20 stories above the desert floor to steal an eaglet out of a cliff-side nest (you need it for a particular ceremony). Or try taking part in the Hopi snake ceremony — by carrying a live rattlesnake around in your mouth. Then tell me Hopis aren't risk-takers. Billard assures us that Hopi snake handlers "are remarkably free of fear...." They "do not believe the reptiles will bite a man with a pure heart..." (Dozier 1970: 4; Terrell 1998: 38; Billard 1979: 163).

Our Kissing Cousin the Bonobo

So mostly, our Mother has been forced underground for a while by war gods. In the next chapter we'll take a trip back in time and look at who She was before the war gods hit the ground running around 4000 BC. First, however, we need to sneak a peek at one of our long-lost recently-discovered primate cousins the bonobo. Bonobo societies look suspiciously like an animal version of guiding goddess societies — and we need to figure out why they get the good life while we and our other primate cousins have to suffer lives full of snooty snobbism, violent bully boys, and uptight stuffed shirts.

As it turns out, in the animal kingdom our two closest cousins are the chimp and the bonobo. We share 98 percent of our genes with each (this is about the same genetic distance as between dogs and foxes). The chimp and bonobo, however, are as different as Jekyll and Hyde. Whereas chimps are violent bully boys, bonobos are mostly even-tempered and tractable. While male chimps beat up female chimps as a matter of course and even kill their babies, it seems as if bonobo males would sooner eat dirt than do either. And compared to the bonobo, the chimp is a downright sex prude. Bonobos, in other words, rule. Says researcher Paul Raffaele, their "friendly family relations, peaceable males, powerful females, high IQs and energetic sex lives made the idea of sharing an evolutionary lineage with bonobos appealing" (Raffaele 2006: 10, 5 of 13).

"So," you say, "if bonobos are so awesome, why haven't I heard of them before?" Good question. First, because for a while after they were discovered in 1929 they were mistaken for chimps. Second, when it was discovered they were not chimps, our prudish grandparents were too embarrassed to talk about these — shall we say — "sexually-relaxed" cousins of ours. Turns out bonobos enjoy sexual activity exceedingly often. And not just males with females either. Bonobos don't even blink at same-sex sex.

But this isn't always sex for sex's sake. As a matter of fact, it's usually sex for the sake of chilling out. In other words, bonobos use brief sexual activity as a way to calm each other down. When the zoo keeper throws food out to a group, for example, there's frenzied excitement followed by a flurry of sex. With bonobos, sex is almost like saying grace before the meal. After "grace," everyone settles down and calmly shares the food. Chimps are another story entirely. Throw food out to chimps, and the alpha male zips over and hoards it for himself. Until Alphie's had his fill, everyone hangs back. Like the early war-god kings of Babylonia and Egypt, Alphie's attitude is "Me first. Let the masses eat cake."

Fig. 2.15. Among bonobos, one of our closest animal cousins, the sexes are equal (Photograph by Jean Kern).

Among bonobos the sexes are equal. All researchers agree: bonobo females do not allow males to push them around. Although in the wild, bonobo males seem to lead the group when it moves, if the alpha female isn't ready to rumba, she just plops into sitting position and refuses to budge. In this case the rest of the group follows her lead. "It's like the alpha male is the general and the alpha female is the queen" says Congolese bonobo researcher Mola Ihomi (Raffaele 2006: 10 & 11 of 13). In contrast, chimp males "reign supremely and often brutally" (de Waal 2006: 2b of 16).

Compared to the gruesome and vicious male chimp — who will fight to the death over females and territory — the bonobo male is a first-class gentleman. Male chimps are good at making fools of themselves: they "often engage in spectacular charging displays: ... throwing rocks, breaking branches and uprooting small trees.... They keep up these noisy performances for many minutes" (de Waal 2006: 4 of 16). Bonobo males on the other hand are metacool: not only peaceful and mild-mannered, but also "affectionate and attentive" around baby bonobos. Bonobo researcher Ihomi has "never seen a bonobo kill another bonobo."

It's not that bonobo males don't have temper tantrums; however, when they do, bonobo females either ignore them, or chase them off into the forest (Raffaele 2006: 10, 11, 4 of 13). The key to group peace: females bonding and banding together to counter male muscle and testosterone. In bonobo society, the female-female bond is the strongest social bond going (de Waal 2006: 15).

Hey Dudes, Chill, Will Ya?

When it comes to getting along with the neighbors across the way, once again bonobos outshine chimps. Rarely have researchers seen serious conflict between bonobo groups. The first time two bonobo communities were observed meeting, for example, there was squabbling, chasing, screaming and barking, but no physical fighting. Then females approached females and did some short sex. Then a few of the kids began playing together. Finally the males approached each other, and after that it was all smooth sailing. With chimps it's a different story entirely. "Those familiar with the brutal encounters between chimpanzee communities, described in gruesome detail by Jane Goodall, can only shake their heads in wonderment at bonobo intercommunity relations" says pre-eminent bonobo researcher Frans de Waal (de Waal and Lanting 1997: 88). While chimps in other words do the human equivalent of war, bonobos do not.

Like people in guiding-goddess societies, bonobos are creative and full of fun. "Bonobos have a playful, gentle manner that is often reminiscent of human beings at their best," says researcher Paul Raffaele (2006: 13 of 13). Frans de Waal agrees. "Bonobos are ... imaginative in play" he says. "I have watched captive bonobos engage in 'blind man's bluff.' A bonobo covers her eyes with a banana leaf or an arm or by sticking two fingers in her eyes. Thus handicapped, she stumbles around on a climbing frame, bumping into others or almost falling. She seems to be imposing a rule on herself: 'I cannot look until I lose my balance.' Other apes and monkeys also indulge in this game, but I have never seen it performed with such dedication and concentration as by bonobos" (de Waal 2006: 4 of 16).

Despite all their gentility and reserve, bonobos are no slouches when it comes to risk-taking. "My heart stops" says Paul Raffaele "as a youngster casually steps off a branch maybe 30 yards [27 meters] up and plunges toward the forest floor through branches and leaves. About 10 yards before crashing into the ground, he grabs a branch and swings onto it. I'm told by the trackers that this death-defying game is a favorite among young bonobos, and invariably concludes with a wide grin on the acrobat's face" (Raffaele 2006: 9 of 13).

As among the Moso, mothers are the core of bonobo society (de Waal 2006: 11; Raffaele 2006: 4 & 5 of 13). When a male chimp asks for help in a fight, it's other males who jump in to his defense. With bonobos, however, a male counts on his mom "for protection in aggressive encounters with other males." Franz de Waal asks the big bonus question: How do bonobos "manage to escape ... the worst scourge of humanity: our ... tendency to exterminate enemies on a large scale. Could it be that it is because bonobos do not fight for a fatherland but, if they fight at all, for a motherland?" (de Waal 2006: 10; de Waal and Lanting 1997: 89).

Part of what gives the bonobos their leg-up I think, is their ability to use sexual contact to flood their blood with the calming hormone, oxytocin. This quiets everyone down, and is probably at least partly responsible for making bonobo society close to idyllic. Sexual activity does indeed release oxytocin into the bloodstream (Moberg 2003: 67, 75, 118), as does touch. Frans de Waal notes that bonobos do sex whenever a potential conflict looms: When they get a new toy they need to share, group members have sex. After one male chases another away from a female, the two males have sex. De Waal has seen two females have sex after female A lunged at female B (because the latter hit the former's youngster).

De Waal tells about a female bonobo who used sex to calm a young height-frightened male who was blocking her way on a tree branch high above the central-African rain-forest floor:

> I once observed a young male, Kako, inadvertently blocking an older, female juvenile, Leslie, from moving along a branch. First, Leslie pushed him; Kako, who was not very confident in trees, tightened his grip, grinning nervously. Next Leslie gnawed on one of his hands, presumably to loosen his grasp. Kako uttered a sharp peep and stayed put. Then Leslie rubbed her vulva against his shoulder. This gesture calmed Kako, and he moved along the branch. It seemed that Leslie had been very close to using force but instead had reassured both herself and Kako with sexual contact (de Waal 2006: 8 of 16).

Like bonobos, I think we humans too are hardwired to trigger avalanches of oxytocin as a way of calming ourselves down. We don't, however, use sex to trigger the oxytocin. Humans everywhere are private about sex. To me, this human "universal" suggests we're hardwired for a distaste for the public sex bonobos use dozens of times a day to get their oxytocin flowing. We probably won't ever feel comfortable having brief sexual encounters at the corner of Broadway and Vine, or in Miltie's Meat Market, for example.

So if we don't use sex as our oxytocin trigger, what do we use? I think we use one of the primary traits setting us apart from all other animals: our wide-ranging and creative use of sound. Neither chimps nor bonobos sing, tell stories, recite poetry or play musical instruments. Neither they nor any other animal has the

Cadillac of language systems we have. Sure, they use grunts, peeps and squeals to communicate a few things, but they don't have *words*.

All humans learn literally thousands of words, which we use in infinite combinations and sound patterns to communicate ultra fine points about existence that bonobos will never be able to communicate. For example, "You're drooly handsome when you're not throwing a tantrum," or "Since I see you're about to kill my baby, let me invite you to imagine what the baby's father will do to you once he discovers what you've done...." And how about this song as a calming mechanism: "I'd Love to Run My Fingers through Your Handsome, Handsome Fur — But Let's Wait 'Til We Get Back to My Place" (sung to the tune of "Up a Lazy River").

But does sound trigger oxytocin? Dr. Kerstin Moberg thinks it does. Moberg, a Professor of Physiology in Sweden, is a recognized world authority on oxytocin. She says each of our senses probably influences our physiological reactions more than we used to think:

> Input from our organs of smell, taste, hearing, and sight most likely influences our physiological reactions to a much greater extent than commonly thought. When we think about it, this is not so far-fetched. We talk about being able to smell danger, or we experience a sound that makes us uneasy, or we see an 'alarming' sight. What if we can also be calmed and relaxed physiologically by input from our senses? A related question is whether such effects also work by causing the release of oxytocin. Several interesting research results imply that they do (Moberg 2003: 113).

Even though the relationship between sound and oxytocin production hasn't been studied formally, says Moberg, it's only common knowledge that certain sounds calm us down — quiet, peaceful music for example, or "a friendly tone" (Moberg 115).

Think about all the soothing, calm-inducing sounds we make that our primate cousins can't: not only singing and instrument music, but scads of categories of sound that come from complex language. Storytelling for example (talking on the phone to your sister about your duddy blind date); complimenting people ("Man, where'd ya get that sweet '56 Chevy?!"); and poetry ("To the dearest dear of them all, My best friend Dimples McGraw, You are true-blue, I'll always choose` you" etc.), to name just a few.

According to anthropologist Christine Mathieu, the peaceful goddess-following Moso use music 24/7. The Moso she says,

> … have songs for all moods and all events. They have songs to quiet infants, to heal the sick and to court lovers (duets), songs that celebrate the joy of love or cry its sorrows, songs that celebrate the beauty of the mountains and those which tell of the loneliness of shepherds…. Moso folk instruments are reed gourds (nio), tree leaves, flutes, and stalks of wheat which are blown and vibrated in the vein of the bamboo Jew's harp (k'a-kwuo-kwuo)…. Drums, conches, bells and cymbals are used only for religious ceremonies" (Mathieu 1998: 215).

Of course we humans also use plain old language to stop violence and other kinds of ugliness. We talk people out of jumping off bridges for example, or into handing over the gun they're using to shoot the sheriff. We pay trained talkers called therapists to use language to reduce our stress, and trained talkers called mediators to calm two partners so they can negotiate a well-thought-out divorce. We pay trained talkers called diplomatic negotiators to get international leaders to calm down and stop fighting, or to stop building weapons.

Could this be why language evolved in the first place — to give women a complex sound system that would flood everyone with oxytocin? Any female who could talk or sing males out of killing her babies would pass on more of her genes to the next generation than her sisters would. Some studies suggest that even today women may be born with more verbal ability than men (Hulbert 2005). And men — you can't deny it: you know that in the West, at any rate, women's "gabbiness" is frequent comedy fare for professional stand-up comedians.

But as we've seen earlier, it's not just their oxytocin-boosting verbal abilities that make women the calm-you-down sex. Women are also born hardwired to respond to stress with tend-and-befriend behavior. What's more, oxytocin may grind away longer in women than in men: "If oxytocin is given to female animals five days in a row, the lowered blood pressure lasts for three weeks. In male animals, the effect ... lasts only half as long." Finally, in some situations oxytocin packs a bigger punch in women than in men (Moberg 2003: 59, 74).

And if one woman is an oxytocin powerhouse, a group of them is an oxytocin bomb begging to go off. A group of women using language and tend-and-befriend behavior on each other is like a gigantic battery bulging with calmness energy. Each woman is boosting the oxytocin level of each other woman. The effect? The whole is far greater than the sum of its parts. And

Fig. 2.16. Minoan women conversing. From a 3500-year-old fresco in the Minoan palace-temple of Knossos on the Mediterranean island of Crete (Courtesy of the University of South Carolina Press).

now we're discovering that this group-generated calm can be transmitted to all the rest of us through touch, sound and maybe even smell. Beam us up, Scotty!

Blocking the Oxytocin Fix

So what happens when women are discouraged from gathering in groups, mingling with men, or even leaving their homes (the way they are in some war-god societies)? And what happens when men spend most of their time with men — as is the case in most industrialized nations today? Although it was worse before women entered the workforce in the latter half of the twentieth century, even today many to most workplace environments are top-heavy with men. And when women do waltz around at work, it's often in isolation, not in groups — one woman running the reception desk for example. The results are plain. We regress back to chimp stage, more primitive even than the bonobo. We not only go back to being animals again, but back to being low animals on the totem pole.

While bonobo males get to bask in a chilled-out society, our war gods may have stripped us of an important mechanism we evolved to stay healthy, happy and sane: organized groups of women producing soothing oxytocin and mingling in public with groups of men. Men then mop up the calm. Maybe this is why "houses" of prostitution are so popular: they're places where groups of women produce calmness-hormones for men to soak up. It's almost as good as — mmmmmm — m — sex!

In sum, who'd you rather be related to? The snooty, rigid, bully-boy, me-first chimps? Or the relaxed, sexy, egalitarian, generous, gorgeous bonobos? No-brainer, right? The thing is, the archaeological, historical, linguistic and mythological evidence show that our Neolithic and even some of our Bronze-Age ancestors were far more bonobo- than chimp-like. Although our current mother-goddess societies may have been temporarily driven underground, there's ample evidence that such societies existed openly in the past. Not only that, evidence shows when they *did* bask in the sunshine, life was golden — just as one might expect out of life lived with a Great Mother Goddess as the guiding light, a goddess who protects, validates and strengthens not only men but also the women who nourish and keep men healthy. This golden age is the focus of the next chapter.

3

Good Times

Just Any Ol' Goddess Won't Do

From the dawn of time, from the beginning of modern homo sapiens sapiens (and maybe even before that), the divine feminine has probably always been with us. As we saw in the previous chapter, great guiding goddesses still linger today among the Basque and Moso — and no doubt among others too shy to share the info with outsiders. Some modern societies worship goddesses openly. Along with their gods, for example, modern Hindus freely worship a range of goddesses, from Parvati and Sarasvati to Lakshmi and Kali (although some believe these are all aspects of one and the same deity). And from the ancient Sumerians and Babylonians to the Egyptians, Greeks, and Romans, most of the ancient world too worshipped goddesses.

The mere presence of goddesses in a society, however, doesn't guarantee peace, prosperity and pears and plums for breakfast. All you need to do is take a peek at Hindus to see that. Throughout their history, Hindus have been almost as bloody and violent as Muslims and Christians. And this is true double-over for the Sumerians, Babylonians, Egyptians and ancient Greeks and Romans.

This is so important I'll probably repeat it more than once: just any old goddess won't do. It has to be a special kind. For starters, it can't be one with a jealous war god hanging over her right shoulder. Also it has to be a goddess who, like bonobo females, either ignores god tantrums, gives these gods a hug, kiss and a kind word to calm them down, or if all else fails, chases the rascals off into the forest. And above all, it needs to be a guiding mother goddess who not only gives birth to everyone and everything in the universe (including any other gods and goddesses), but who also serves as a guide for our behavior.

Although they had them originally, neither the Hindus nor the ancients managed to hang on to their all-powerful guiding goddesses. These deities were all laid six feet under long ago by bogus war "gods" — who used every dirty trick in the book to put them there. A few of us hold hazy memories of our ancient guiding mother goddesses — the Greeks for example vaguely remember Gaia, and the Chinese their ancient Mother Goddess Nuwa (Leeming 2005: 295). But for most of us, the best the Guiding Mother Goddess has been able to do is disguise Herself in old nursery rhymes, folk tales and mythology (something we'll get to in a later chapter).

To get to the original Guiding Mother Goddesses, you need to go back to the days before the war gods roared into town on their Harleys, i.e. to the Neolithic and early Bronze Ages. Exactly when the Bad Daddies roared into town is different depending on where in the world you are. In Southeastern Europe and Mesopotamia, it was roughly 4000 BC. The Daddies roared into China around 2200 BC, into the Americas and India around 1000 BC, and not into Japan until about 300 BC.

Speaking of Time

But before we paddle on down this stream, a word about all the "Ages" archaeologists toss off the tips of their pens like gaudy baubles pitched off the sides of Mardi Gras floats — 'Palaeolithic,' 'Neolithic,' 'Eneolithic,' 'Copper Age,' 'Bronze Age,' 'Iron Age' and so on. As if this isn't bad enough, next they divide everything into sub Ages, and then into sub-sub Ages. Worse still, all these Ages are sly and shifty. Don't for example try to depend on them to be the same everywhere you go. For instance the Neolithic in New Zealand didn't happen 'til way after Norway's Neolithic, which happened well after the Neolithic in Nepal. Worst of all, however, since archaeologists dig up new stuff every year, or get new dating techniques, everything you thought you knew last year — is this year dumped in the dustbin.

Bearing all this sly slipperiness in mind, let's break the past down into four simple boxes: Palaeolithic, Neolithic, Bronze Age and Iron Age. At some point, almost every inhabited part of the planet has waltzed through these four main stages. But as I say, different people waltzed through at different times, and some even skipped a stage or two. For example less than fifty years ago and almost over night, the !Kung of southern Africa flew from the Paleolithic right over the tops of the Neolithic and Bronze Ages, and landed smack in the middle of the Iron Age.

If the Ages aren't tied to time, what are they tied to? Mainly to people's habits. For example the Paleolithic, coming as it does from the Greek words 'palaeo' (old) and 'lithic' (stone), is a stage when people didn't know a thing about steel, iron, copper or any other metal, and so had to make do with stone. If you chopped trees, you did it with stone axes. If you hunted hyenas, you did it with stone arrowheads or spearheads. If you scraped fat off skins, you did it with stone scrapers.

Not only did Paleolithic people use stone instead of metal, they didn't clutter up their calendars with planting, watering, weeding or stockbreeding either. They let nature do all that, so all they had to do for dinner was step out, hunt and gather. On the other hand, since the roots, shoots and berries they ate ripened at different times in different places, they had to hustle all over the place, setting up camp wherever the food decided to park itself. Fortunately the animals they ate also had their noses to the ground following the plants, so it wasn't too hard to throw a bit of meat into the pot each evening along with the veggies.

And then suddenly, at the end of the last Ice Age, the climate warmed up a notch or two. As a result, in certain places wild grain began growing like topsy. And if you were lucky enough to live in one of these places, you could just settle in, prop your feet up, and chow down without traipsing all over the place all year long like everyone else was doing. This was Big. This was the beginning of the Neolithic. The major new habit in the Neolithic was people settled down and began living in one, permanent spot.

But then the climate grew grouchy again, the grain disappeared, and people said "Whoa. Unless we think of something fast, we're going to have to hit the road again." So they invented farming—began planting wheat and barley seeds outside the front door. After that, for dinner all they had to do was step out and gather a bite or two from the backyard — and the same backyard all year long, no less. This happened first in Southwest Asia, or as I like to call it, the "Near East."

After the Neolithic comes the Bronze Age, when people traded in most of their stone tools for bronze ones. In the Near East the Bronze Age began roughly around 3000 BC, give or take a few hundred years depending, among other things, on which part of the Near East you happen to be standing in (Haviland 1997: 290). Finally came the Iron Age, which broke out first around 1000 BC, and in Europe (Fagan 2004: 474).

Old Snapshots of the Guiding Mother

It's in the Neolithic and Bronze Ages that we get our first clear picture of the Great Guiding Mother Goddess (although She puts in an appearance in the Palaeolithic, it's not as grand as Her Neolithic debut). Since for our purposes they're the Ages we're most interested in, figure 3.1 shows, for several places around the globe, when the Neolithic and Bronze Ages bloomed and blossomed.

Figure 3.1. Timeline: Neolithic and Bronze Ages in Selected World Locations (All dates approximate)

Place	Neolithic Began	Bronze Age Began
China	c. 10,000 BC	Before 3,000 BC
Japan	c. 10,000 BC	c. third century BC

Near East	c. 10,000 BC	c. 3,000 BC
SE Europe	c. 8,000 BC	Before 2,000 BC
Crete	c. 7,000 BC	c. 3,000 BC
India	Before 6,000 BC	c. 3,300 BC
Mesoamerica	c. 5,000 BC	After AD 1,000

Some of our earliest writers, the Indus Valley people and the ancient Minoans, both Bronze-Age civilizations, had still retained their Great Guiding Goddesses as late as the second and third millennia BC. Unfortunately no one's been smart enough yet to decipher their writing. The earliest writing we've cracked the code for belongs to the Sumerians of the ancient Near East. At the time Sumerian records were jotted down, the bully-boy war gods had already whomped everyone in town. After they elbowed their way in, these duds spun things their own way, making creation the joint handiwork of both a god and a goddess — sky and earth — 'An' and 'Ki,' respectively.

However, the Sumerian records also wistfully recall an earlier time when the Goddess alone had created the earth:

> the 'chthonic' theogony known from later manuscripts, which are said to reflect the earlier tradition in the city of Eridu, names the Goddess Nammu ... as the single prime element, the progenitress of all the deities, including An and Ki. She is 'a goddess without a spouse, the self-procreating womb, the primal matter, the inherently fertile and fertilizing waters' (Westenholz 1998: 68).

So although some ancient guiding-goddess societies had invented writing systems, and although the first deciphered written records speak about guiding goddesses of earlier times, we have no decipherable records written by a guiding-goddess society during the time they were following this goddess. Therefore what we know about the ancient Guiding Goddess comes from a few written accounts, from many art and archaeological remains, and from folklore and mythology. In the next section we'll look at how Neolithic and Bronze-Age artists depicted the Guiding Goddess.

Calling All Artists

If you're an artist, how do you paint a picture of a deity who's powerful but loving, pillowy soft but stronger than steel, a nurturing yet fierce protector, and a lover of flesh-and-blood bodies, freedom, adventure and playfulness? Oh. And She's also the birther of the universe and everything in it. Got that? Can you drop that down on canvas for us?

Tall order, huh?

Obviously even genius artists aren't capable of capturing such blow-you-away spirituality completely. Throughout the millennia, however, some artists have done a better job than others. Six to seven thousand years ago, an ancient artist in predynastic Egypt came close to perfection with a clay statue of what has been called a "bird goddess." Actually, more than one artist during this time period produced images of the Neolithic Egyptian bird goddess, all of them with bird-like faces and "winglike arms and hands." According to artist Buffie Johnson, "the vigorous stance of the figures expresses the energy and mystery of flight" (Johnson 1981: 27).

Although Her soft round curves whisper love and nurturance, there's no doubt this is a divine protectress with the strength of steel running through Her body. With this powerhouse holding watch, no one would dare harm a hair on your head. What's more I have no trouble believing She could birth the earth, the universe and everything in them. But this is also a Goddess who thrills with sensuality, freedom and adventure. This supernatural being, with Her half-woman, half-bird body, has been pegged as a possible forerunner of the Egyptian Goddess Nekhbet (Scarre 1993: 89).

Not long ago, in room 3a of a building they call Xeste 3, archaeologists dug up a fresco on the Mediterranean island of Santorini of another of my favorite goddesses. Here again an ancient artist has managed to pump an image full of soft tenderness coupled with iron strength. Dating from the mid-second millennium BC, this Minoan deity is electric with energy. Her eye swims with electromagnetic force, with the magnificence of the unknown, the mystery of the universe. But Her power doesn't seem to overtax Her; as She reaches to receive his gift, Her head is tilted gently toward Her monkey admirer, Her lips relaxed and slightly parted.

Fig. 3.2. Predynastic Egyptian Bird Goddess embodying mother love: soft nurturance coupled with the iron strength it can take to safeguard offspring. From Lower Egypt, ca. 5000 – 3100 BC (Courtesy of Werner Forman Archive).

Although this otherworldly beauty is our protector, She also simmers with sensuality. The monkey and griffin flanking Her on two sides make Her seem playful, and possibly now and again even prone to laughter. Far from being caged indoors She sits free as the wind on Her outdoor throne, wild crocuses sprouting around Her, Her feet free of shoes, Her breasts unencased in cloth.

Fig. 3.3. The ancient Minoan Guiding Goddess of Thera (located on the island of Santorini) This deity too has the softness to nurture, yet the power to protect us as well. From ca. 1500 BC (Courtesy of the University of South Carolina Press).

Divine Catwoman

For me, a marble statue

Fig 3.4. Close-up of Theran Goddess shown above. Notice the hypnotic, otherworldly look in her eye (From Ch. Doumas, The Wall Paintings of Thera, Idryma Theras-Petros M. Nomikos, Athens, 1992).

from Mesopotamia from c 3000 BC also packs a powerful punch. Despite the softness of Her woman's body, this goddess has the beefy hands and head of a wildcat. Who wouldn't feel safe encircled in Her arms? At the same time, this cat-and-woman combo sends a frisson of awestruck attention singing along your nerves. This is no natural creature; this being hovers somewhere beyond the world we know. This is colossal power, a convincing creator of the world and everything in it. And yet Her wildness feels like freedom and adventure, and there's a playfulness about Her that suggests a little fun and laughter tossed into the mix.

For contrast, in the Museo Nazionele in Naples, Italy, is a statue of the Goddess Cybele, sculpted only about two millennia ago, during war/sky-god times in the second or third century BC. Unlike the last three deities, this one seems anything

but powerful or interested in freedom, adventure, sensuality or playfulness. In Cybele the catwoman deity is fractured into one woman and two flanking wildcats. Even

Fig. 3.5. Santorini Island walkway today, fronting the island's watery center. Several millennia ago, a volcanic eruption blew away the core of the island, demolishing its Minoan population in the process (Photograph by the author).

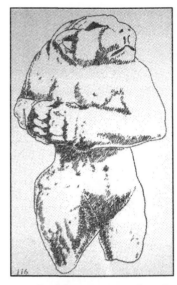

Fig. 3.6. Ancient Mesopotamian "catwoman" goddess. Age and provenance unknown; provsionally dated to ca. 3000 BC (Courtesy of the estate of Buffie Johnson. Reprinted by permission of the Charlotte Sheedy Literary Agency, Inc.).

though Cybele opens her right hand (heart?) to us, she hides Her soft nurturing body under clotted layers of cloth.

With this father-god Goddess, adventure, playfulness and laughter have flown the coop. This is a Goddess gone sad — beaten up inside, squandered. You can almost see the ropes tying Her to Her stone throne. She's parked not in the outdoor natural world but indoors. Although She's sweet, you'd have a hard time convincing me She could nurture or protect us — let alone create the universe.

Now compare Cybele to a mother goddess stretching back almost three millennia in time before Cybele was chipped out of stone by Her Roman creators. Hailing from the Neolithic site of Hacilar in modern Turkey, this Goddess lovingly holds a leopard cub. Unlike our Cybele from father-god times, this Hacilarian goddess is not only on top of things, She's deeply grounded, swimmingly self confident, completely at home in Her massively powerful body. It's a cinch

Fig. 3.7. Roman statue of the Goddess Cybele from 2nd-3rd century AD (Courtesy of the Archaeological Museum of Naples and Caserta).

Fig. 3.8. 8000-year-old Anatolian Mother Goddess caressing a leopard cub and sitting on an adult leopard. Although this goddess loves us like a mother loves her child, when warranted, she also restrains us (Courtesy of the estate of Buffie Johnson. Reprinted by permission of the Charlotte Sheedy Literary Agency, Inc.).

believing She's the all-encompassing Creator. This Neolithic Mother is a deep nurturer. She presses a baby cat to Her breast and strokes it. With its paw wrapped around Her shoulder, the baby clings to Her, and you can almost hear it mewling, feel its small heart thudding against Her chest. In stark contrast, Cybele has no physical contact with her cats. In fact, She barely seems to know they exist.

Although the Neolithic Mama is warm and fuzzy toward baby, She literally sits on baby's parent — complete master over this hunter and consumer of human flesh. In other words, even though She creates and adores us, She's also about keeping us — when necessary — under control. In contrast, Cybele neither nurtures nor controls her cats. As a matter of fact they seem almost to be controlling Her. Or maybe they're guarding Her. But guarding Her from what? Isn't She supposed to be all-powerful? Hm. Guess not.

For their beauty-queen posture, both Goddesses deserve pats on the back. Cybele, however, seems to have a ramrod up the back we just patted, and not one thing about Her inspires a sense of play, adventure or laughter. This is one uptight lassie. Our Neolithic Great Goddess on the other hand — well, what's more playful than a baby cat? And what's better for a chuckle than a kitten playing catch-mouse with a ball of yarn?

Great Mother of the Mountain

Like Cybele, the ancient Minoan "Goddess of the Mountain" from

Bronze-Age Crete also feels somewhat cut off from her animal creations — although you have to admit: that She can stand in wild nature unarmed and unharmed with two wildcats lapping at Her feet is a pretty fine promise of power. Unlike Cybele, one feels this mountain Goddess is in charge of her cats. You feel She could protect us from the cruel parts of Her world. Unlike Cybele too, the mountain Goddess stands not inside, but outdoors in the natural world. And like other pre-war-god goddesses, She's unselfconsciously in tune with Her body. After all, the female body's the prime symbol of creation, of the start of things, the cosmos, of all existence.

Unlike Neolithic goddesses, however, this Bronze-Age deity brings a whiff of power-over, a hint of possible power differentials that might have crept into Minoan society near its end (around 1450 BC). A male figure stands below his Goddess, hand pressed to forehead. In our day and age this feels like a "salute," like power-under acknowledging power-over. On the other hand, this could be all in our imaginations; most Minoan experts feel in Minoan times a hand on the forehead was recognition not of status differences but of divinity.

Fig. 3.9. Minoan Goddess of the Mountain, from ca. 1500 BC. This goddess seems to possess a combination of strength, nurturance and personal freedom. Did she demand that Minoans love each other unconditionally — as healthy mothers love their offspring? (Courtesy of the University of South Carolina Press).

One thing seems clear though: with Her flowing hair and full breasts, this Great Mother Goddess is a nurturer, a reminder that we're all Her children and therefore natural receivers of Her unconditional love. And as our major role model, She demands we love each other unconditionally too. Finally, compared to the Roman Cybele chained indoors to Her chair and guarded by lions, this Minoan Mother is freedom personified; She's in the wilds climbing mountains, breathing deeply, unafraid to travel to the ends of the earth, ready to drink in the pleasures of all Her creations.

Crazy about Goddess — All Over the Globe

Although what appears to be a Great Guiding Goddess pops up in all kinds of ancient art, by far the loudest surviving reminder of the way in which our Neolithic ancestors all over the globe adored the Goddess, are the thousands of clay and stone figurines they made of Her. Neolithic people all over the earth went crazy turning them out, sculpting and carving so many goddess figurines that at some excavations they have to be hauled off in carts (Ward 2006: 274).

These figurines vary from place to place and era to era. Some sit, some stand. Some are painted, some plain. Some figurines are naked while others labor under layers of clothing, jewelry and footwear. While some are worn and damaged, others are not. The 'disposal context' of goddess figurines — where archaeologists find them — changes too, with some discovered on altars, some inside house walls, some in graves and others in ancient grain bins or garbage dumps. And finally, while some goddess figurines look completely human, others are otherworldly or half human-half animal.

It seems that before around 4000 BC, the Guiding Goddess was widespread around the world, existing across the globe from Europe, Africa, and Asia to the Americas. University of California anthropologist Richard Lesure hit the nail on the head when he said that "small ceramic figurines representing predominantly human females are characteristic artifacts of many of the world's earliest settled villages." Of course in some areas — China and

India for example — they're still being crafted today. But the difference is this: along with goddesses, modern Chinese and East Indians also produce tons of gods, while our Neolithic ancestors didn't. As a matter of fact, Neolithic male statues are scarce as hen's teeth. That's why Lesure, for example, can talk about the "predominance of female imagery among Neolithic figurines," and "the widespread occurrence of predominantly female imagery" during the long Neolithic era (Lesure 2002: 587, 600).

Of course our Neolithic and Bronze-Age ancestors used things other than statuettes to keep in touch with their Great Guiding Goddesses. They painted Her on building walls and clay pots, pitchers and plates. They sculpted larger stone statues of Her (and probably wooden ones as well, which wouldn't of course have made it through eons of hungry munching bugs, damp dirt, creeping rot and so on). And in those lands where the Great Guiding Goddess swept on into the Bronze Age, She was etched onto rings, necklaces, other jewelry, and onto seal stones — identification gadgets the ancients kept to stamp and thereby identify their property.

To give you a taste of the ancient female-figurine situation, I'm going to take you on a tour of them in a few key world areas: the Near East, India, Japan and Southeast Europe. Are you ready? Okay, dear readers — let's rock and roll! Stop number one: the Near East — by which I mean today's Turkey, Syria, Lebanon, Israel, West Bank, Gaza Strip, Jordan, Iraq and Iran.

In the Near East, most ancient guiding-goddess settlements are today under water, and therefore, for the time being, beyond excavation (Fagan 2004: 345). Even so, Nilsson says that in the Neolithic, goddess figurines "appear over vast areas of ... the Near East" (Nilsson 1949: 290). And the renowned archaeologist Jacques Cauvin, who studied the Near Eastern Neolithic for twenty years, was crystal clear: a Great Mother Goddess reigned supreme in this area during the entire Neolithic: "Throughout the total duration of the Neolithic across the whole of the Near and

Middle East, a unique 'ideology' is found ..., organized around two key symbols: one, female, has already taken human form. Can she perhaps be derived from the first female statuettes known in the Upper Paleolithic of Europe and spread as far as Siberia?"

Cauvin is firm: this is not just any old goddess but a guiding goddess: "...[S]he was not a 'fertility symbol' but a genuine mythical personality conceived as a supreme being and universal mother, in other words a goddess who crowned a religious system which one could describe as 'female monotheism' in the sense that all the rest remained subordinated to her" (Cauvin 2002: 31).

The Guiding Goddess at Catalhoyuk

But enough already with the generalizations. What are these goddess figurines like in specific Near Eastern towns and villages? Let's zoom in on a big-time important guiding-goddess town, Catalhoyuk, "one of the largest and most populated Neolithic settlements ever unearthed...." We're standing now on the Konya Plain in south central Turkey, checking out a town that existed for some 1500 years — from about 7500 to 6000 BC. Although Catalhoyuk is now being dug up under the direction of British archaeologist Ian Hodder, it was first excavated in the early 1960s by one James Mellaart.

At its height, as many as 8000 people crammed themselves into the confines of this compact town covering 32 acres (13 hectares), and built like a beehive with each windowless house attached to the next, and with no house doors (as we know them anyway)(Fagan 2004: 245). According to Ian Hodder, the only way to get into your house was to drop through a hole in the roof and then creep down a ladder (Balter 2005: 3-4, 335). Hodder thinks people spent less time in their homes, however, than on top of them — on the roofs. If true, this would have zinged the Catalhoyukians into one big happy family of 8000, cruising around on top of a giant, raised-roof, social "square."

At Catalhoyuk you'll spot a few images of men, but not many. Images of women, however, are scattered everywhere. As University of California archaeologist Brian Fagan points out, most of the art at Catalhoyuk "depict(s) women or bulls, scenes of birth, dances and ancestors" (2004: 246). The reproductions of women at Catalhoyuk are not only common, they're majorly radical. One of the most amazing is a goddess settled into what looks like a stone throne edged by lions or leopards. This awesome clay goddess is about 4.5 inches high (11.5 centimeters). Her hands rest on the heads of Her felines, and from behind, the tails of these wildcats rise straight into the air and then drop down over Her shoulders.

This Goddess is not only nude — a sign of divinity — but massive. In days when everyone galloped around 24/7 planting, weeding, watering, hoeing, harvesting, grinding, hunting, killing, skinning, storing and sautéing food, everyone had the slim, svelte bodies today we all pray for. But Neolithics who for genetic reasons could store body fat were able to survive famines and the flu. So to the Catalhoyukians the ability to keep your fat must have been like magic — the sphere of the gods. Or in this case, goddesses. Between this goddess's legs down by her feet lies a roundish object the size and shape of a newborn's head. Of course we have no idea what it is, but the archaeologist Marija Gimbutas suggested the not-so-shocking possibility that it is indeed a newborn baby (Gimbutas 1989: 107).

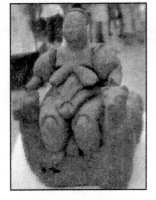

Fig. 3.10. Guiding Mother Goddess of Catalhoyuk, Anatolia, ca. 6000 BC. With this Goddess as their behavior model, Catalhoyukians were paragons of peace, prosperity and equality (Photograph by Pandora Yeung).

Jacques Cauvin said that at Catalhoyuk "the woman and the bull" are "predominant because of the number of their representations.... [T]his 'woman' is truly a goddess: in the ... monumental relief sculptures she dominates the north or west wall of the domestic sanctuaries ..., arms and legs spread, giving birth to bulls (or exceptionally rams)..." (Cauvin 2002: 29). And Ian Hodder, now head honcho at the dig and no lover of goddesses, nevertheless admits that at Catalhoyuk "It is difficult to argue against the importance of women in the symbolism. Especially in the later levels at the site the image of the enthroned or seated woman is powerful. There do not seem to be equivalent images of men" (Balter 2005: 322 quoting Hodder, message left on the Catalhoyuk website in 2001).

According to Cauvin, the world's first kings copied their thrones from the throne of this Catalhoyukian Goddess: "As universal Mother, the Goddess is well provided with explicitly 'royal' attributes, not least of which is her throne of Anatolian panthers.... [W]e can interpret it more readily as a throne when we think of the later thrones of the first oriental monarchies ... whose armrests will be sculpted in precisely the same form, with feline protomes" (Cauvin 2002: 71).

The animals chosen to hold court with this Great Mother — lions, panthers and vultures — help underscore Her power. Far removed from species Her people had tamed, these are wild guys that could rout, pound and cream human beings. In the Great Goddess, birth, death and wildness are compacted into one ball of wax; on Catalhoyukian building walls for example are breasts with bird beaks in place of nipples. And in 2006 a shocking goddess was unearthed: healthy and plump with pregnancy from the front, but from the rear a virtual skeleton — birth and death forced to deal with each other in close quarters — and as Cauvin puts it "as if suffering from a certain point of view paradoxically irrigates human life" (Cauvin 2002: 72). Or, maybe just a way of hitting home the truth of the birth-death cycle. Whatever. No two

ways about it though: death has to march on ahead of birth or —
if nothing else — we'd run out of room on the planet for birth to
march at all.

Elsewhere in the Near East

Trudging on down the timeline a tad to 5000 BC, we find the
Halafian people of Northern Mesopotamia churning out tons of
female figurines while blowing off social hierarchy, domination-
type government, war and violence (Maisels 2001: 136-146).
Halafian goddess figurines, says artist Merlin Stone, are found at
every Halafian site, and at Arpachiyah are found with symbols
coupled later in historical times with the
Goddess (Stone 1993: 17-18).

One day we'll know a lot more about
the fascinating Halafians, who lived in
today's modern Kurdistan (a "five-
corners" area covering thousands of
square miles/kilometers, and taking in
parts of Turkey, Syria, Armenia, Iraq
and Iran). For now, however, most
Halafian towns and buildings lie buried
still deep beneath the earth. Part of the
problem has been the political situation
in Kurdistan over the past 60 years.
In Iraqi Kurdistan for example,
Saddam Hussein intentionally crushed
archaeology — even destroying some
remains — because he thought knowing
who their ancestors were gave the
Kurds too much, shall we say, "energy"
(Axe 2006).

Fig. 3.11. Halafian clay
goddess from Tepe Gawra,
near Nineveh in Northwest
Iraq, and dating from ca.
3800 BC. The Halafians were
some of the earliest to
establish a commonwealth
form of government
(Courtesy of the University
of Pennsylvania Museum).

Everyone agrees: the Halafians
crafted fab pottery that was to die
for: "aesthetically superb" says

archaeologist Keith Maisels, and "superbly decorated" says renowned archaeologist V. Gordon Childe. There are those who think the Halafians were some of the earliest to use wheeled vehicles, and they probably also knew and used metal. Keith Maisels calls the Halafians an "oecumene," that is a commonwealth or group of people who ruled themselves, without any bully-boy rulers sitting on their heads (Maisels 2001: 137; Childe 1954: 81; Stone 1993: 17, 94).

Although we know only a pinch about their homes or other buildings, we do know that at the archaeological site of Arpachiya, Halafians erected round buildings with "well-engineered vaulted ceilings." These domed constructions measure 33 feet (10 meters) across (exactly two-thirds the width of an American high-school basketball court) and attach to rectangular corridors up to 63 feet long (19 meters) (three-fourths the length of that same court). Halafian towns, says Stone, boasted cobbled streets — fairly amazing for people who walked the Near East 2000 years before the ancient Egyptians saw the light of day (Stone 1993: 18).

Probably to help handle their complex economic system, the Halafians used lots of clay seals. They left behind "the earliest large groupings" of seals ever "found anywhere." What's more, many would consider their economic system classier than anything found even in today's modern industrialized nations. Maisels said this system worked more like "an egalitarian credit union" than a system of consumers and capitalists, or the systems bouncing around in days of yore in which "subordinates" forked over "dues" to "superiors."

One of the most dazzling traits of the Halafians is that at a very early stage in history they managed to jell together as a single people over a large geographic area. Maisels explains it this way: "It looks as if central places … served to knit-up the whole Halaf culture-area … through the exchange of fine pottery, obsidian (bowls and decorative links as well as blades) and

Fig. 3.12. Although most female figurines from Alishar Huyuk in Anatolia are made of clay, this one, with its elaborate headdress, clothing, and jewelry, is fashioned from lead (Courtesy of the Oriental Institute of the University of Chicago).

perhaps even animals, oils and fibers dyes, and medicines...." (Maisels 2001: 143, 146).

Moving on out of Halafian Land let's drop in on a few of the sizeable number of other Near-Eastern Neolithic sites where goddess figurines pop up. Let's go first to the Neolithic town of Yumuk Tepe in Turkey, where Goddess figurines surface all the way through to the Bronze Age, making a person think maybe "the worship of the Mother Goddess was a permanent tradition" in ancient Turkey. Next, at Alishar Huyuk, archaeologists have excavated "a number of" female figurines. Although most are clay, one wearing an elaborate headdress and bedecked in bracelets and a necklace with a rosette in the middle is made of lead (James 1960: 49).

Near the Jordan River in what is now the West Bank nestles one of the world's oldest towns — Jericho. In Jericho's Neolithic layers, archaeologists uncovered two small goddess figurines nattily dressed in long flowing robes cinched at the waist and with their hands supporting their breasts (James 1960: 47). And east of Jericho in southern Iraq, the first settlers at the town of Ur of the Chaldees fashioned female figurines with "well-modeled bodies" and babies in their arms. Pushing on east to Iran, in the early Iranian Neolithic, goddess figurines were "much in evidence." At the sites of Tepe Giyan and Susa for example, in western Iran, figurines are found with painted hair and eyes but with none of the usual fuss made over their maternal organs (breasts, bellies, navels and pubic regions).

India's Mysterious Indus Valley

The second major stop on our whirlwind tour of ancient guiding-goddess figurines is that mysterious and little understood ancient society, the mammoth Indus Valley Civilization, located in what is today Pakistan and western India. Blanketing a whopping quarter of a million square miles (c. 402,336 square kilometers) — double the size of ancient Egypt, which existed at the same time — these people had previously hung together for four millennia as a collection of small farming towns. Then around 2600 BC they morphed into a land of large cities, the largest home to up to 80,000 (Kenoyer 2005: 4 of 12). The ancient Indus-Valley people lived in two- to three-story houses and enjoyed super-sophisticated city-wide waste management systems as well as wide boulevards with dividers down the middle for two-way traffic.

Perhaps most impressive of all was their waste-management system. In the Indus-Civilization city of Harappa, for example, every house came equipped with bathing facilities, latrines, and sewage drains. Now this is startling, because it didn't happen again for another 4000 years — around 1950 AD to be precise, when the industrialized nations (in the West at any rate) abandoned most of their last lingering outdoor latrines and sprang for indoor plumbing for all.

Although the Indus people knew how to read and write, no one's been able to crack the code for their writing system. We can't therefore read what they wrote about their religion. We do know, however, that they turned out tons of what appear to be miniature Mother Goddess figurines, suggesting that their religion centered on one or more Mother Goddesses. Few doubt that the Indus Civilization goddesses are mothers. Their "maternal organs" as someone's so aptly named them, are prominent (Fagan 2004: 418; Wheeler 1966: 44; E.O. James 1960: 52), and occasionally they hold and nurse babies (McIntosh 2002: 114). Says University of California archaeologist Brian Fagan "The only clues we have to the origins of the Indian religion come

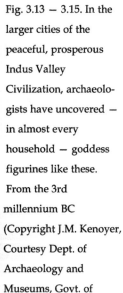

Fig. 3.13 — 3.15. In the larger cities of the peaceful, prosperous Indus Valley Civilization, archaeologists have uncovered — in almost every household — goddess figurines like these. From the 3rd millennium BC (Copyright J.M. Kenoyer, Courtesy Dept. of Archaeology and Museums, Govt. of Pakistan).

from minute seal impressions and small clay figurines from Harappan villages and cities that depict a female deity with conspicuous breasts and sexual organs."

Archaeologist Jane McIntosh agrees — the Indus Valley figurines are Mother Goddesses: "Individual aspects of the goddess, particularly as a mother, were well represented in Indus times, as earlier, by figurines" (2002: 198). And Heather Elgood, Course Director in Asian Art for the British Museum, drops us a nifty description of these deities: Most says Heather "are draped in a short loin-cloth, with fan-shaped headdress, and are highly ornamented with jewelry." They have "pronounced breasts, necklaces, large beaklike noses and circular eye holes" (Elgood 2004: 331). One final point about this Indus-Valley Mother

Goddess: She was no shrinking violet. In the cities of Harappa, Mohenjodaro and Chanhudaro says E.O. James, Her figurines "seem to have been preserved in a niche in the wall in *almost every house*" (emphasis the author's) (James 1960: 52).

The Goddess in Neolithic Japan

Leaving India, we're zipping northeast now over what's left of Asia, and on to Neolithic Japan. Once Japan climbed out of the Palaeolithic and into the Neolithic (the Japanese call their Neolithic the "Jomon Period"), it didn't budge for a record 13,000 years (Kobayashi 2004: iv; Pearson 2004: 2). The Japanese just danced merrily along in their peaceful Jomon towns and villages, churning out female clay figurines by the busload (or looking at it from their point of view, the wagonload).

During its Neolithic, Japan was a literal female-figurine factory. At one site alone, Shakado, archaeologists unearthed 1118 figurine fragments. And according to the National Museum of Japanese History "some fifteen thousand Jomon figurines are known to archaeology today." Furthermore it's been estimated that during the 2500 years most of these figurines came from (near the middle and end of the Jomon), as many as 200,000 were crafted (Pearson 2004: 5; Kobayashi 2004: 154).

These figurines, or "dogu," are different depending on where you are in Jomon Japan. Let's take a gander at them in one village, Kaminabe, on the bottom-most Japanese island of Kyushu. Even though Kaminabe in 800 BC was tiny as a tadpole (five houses for certain, 12 at most), during excavations there archaeologists unearthed a whopping 112 clay female-figurine fragments. The Kaminabe goddesses aren't fancy. Some have eyes and mouths but none have noses. Some have pierced ears. Measuring between 4 and 8 inches tall (10-20 centimeters) — think between a half-used pencil and a brand-new one — many have patterns on their heads representing hair or hats (we're not sure which). All, however, have the breasts common to most dogu, and all have the large stomachs characteristic of pregnant women and of many Jomon goddess figurines all across Japan (Minako 2004).

In the Early Jomon, goddess figurines were so small you could cradle them in one hand. Archaeologist Tatsuo Kobayashi of Kokugakuin University is a leading expert on the Jomon era. In Kobayashi's mind, the reason the creators of these early figurines crafted them with no arms, legs or even faces was to make them "mysterious" in the minds of beholders. Like most later Jomon figurines, these early examples possessed the breasts, narrow waists and broad hips common not to the human male, but to the female sex.

It wasn't until the Middle Jomon that people living on the Japanese islands begin giving their goddesses arms, legs and faces. Even then many figurines were still missing some to all their facial features. According to Kobayashi, halfway through the Middle Jomon, goddess figurines began featuring "facial expressions" (Kobayashi 2004: 146-9). Since neither their faces nor the expressions on them resemble what you'd find on an "ordinary" human, these dogu, too, were still steeped in mystery. Anyway, at this point the figurines begin picking up cute little nicknames from their modern researchers — heart-shaped (face), owl-shaped, mountain-shaped head, and goggle-eyed, for example.

Lots of goggle-eyed (or "snow-goggle") goddesses were made in the Late Jomon. These beauties look like they've slung on the eyewear many people crossing the Arctic snow used to

Fig. 3.16. Ancient Neolithic Japanese goddess figurine. To communicate the mystery of divinity, Neolithic Japanese artists created their goddesses without facial features — or with features as far from human as possible (Courtesy of PHG and Wikimedia Commons).

use as sun shades — wooden "lenses" with side-to-side slits in them. Unlike the hold-'em-in-your-palm early goddesses, many of the goggle-eyeds are "large enough to be held in two hands." What's more, although rare, the goggle-eyeds are classy works of art that obviously took talent to pull off. With delicate designs etched over every inch of them from head to toe, they're destined to strike awe in even the most jaded observer. They seem decked out in everything from earrings, bracelets and necklaces to groovy headgear, gowns and fine footwear. Most are also decorated with red pigment — interestingly a color choice favored by females in many parts of the world even today for fingernail, toenail and lip enhancement (Pearson 2004: 7).

Europe's Great Guiding Goddess

Let's shift into reverse gear now and whisk back to the Neolithic on the European continent. In Europe too we hit female-figurine pay dirt. During the Neolithic, these portable 3D works of art "appear over vast areas of Southeast Europe" (Nilsson 1949: 290) and come in a variety of shapes, sizes and postures. We're going to zero in first on the Neolithic Sesklo, who lived in what is today Greece from about 6400 to 5600 BC. (At this point some of you might be wondering how we know these figurines weren't just dolls, knick knacks, or playthings. We're coming to that soon, I promise.)

Since the Sesklo were fond of thinking of their Guiding Goddess as half woman-half bird, they gave many of their statuettes a woman's body but bird's head. When she dug up the old Sesklo town of Achilleion near Farsala in Southern Thessaly, archaeologist Marija Gimbutas stumbled onto several of these goddesses seated on what she calls thrones (1991: 253). Many of them appear pregnant, their hands propped on their stomachs. One, for example, tall and stately, is seated on what looks like a stone throne. While her right palm rests flat below Her belly-button, fingers stretched straight out, her left hand lies left of the navel.

Above Her knees, thighs and calves — all pressed tightly together — this goddess wears a short, tight skirt. On Her head is perhaps an 8000-year-old idea of a sacred crown. To me it looks like a large, soft, breast-shaped cloth hat filled with linen fiber or fleece, and fixed in place with a decorative headband. This Great Mother bears soft, full breasts the size and shape of Her crown, symbolizing the sustenance She offers the world and all its creatures. On Her slender neck rests a head bearing a bird's eyes, and in place of a nose and mouth, a bird's beak.

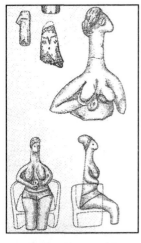

At the old Sesklo town at Achilleion, in a space blanketing about 1100 square feet (100 square meters; think of a three-car garage), Gimbutas uncovered almost 250 human figurines. Of these, says Gimbutas, two were male and the rest female. Half were pregnant. Gimbutas found 132 in temples and 99 near "a dais or oven" (1991: 251, 255, 22).

Also bearing the head of a bird is a Goddess found in another Sesklo town, Farsala in southern Thessaly. A little under three inches high (7 centimeters), this deity's posture is positively prize-winning — especially considering She's sitting with one leg tucked under the other. Magically, She's stored calorie-power in the form of a silky-smooth layer of fat. As we saw previously, in the eyes of our early ancestors, fat was without a doubt a Good Thing, built on

Fig. 3.17. Mother Goddess figurines from Old Europe's Sesklo culture. Archaeologists found them near altars in temples dating from 6000 — 5800 BC (Reprinted from Achelleion: A Neolithic Settlement in Thessaly, Northern Greece, Monumenta Archaeologica 14, by Marija Gimbutas, Shan Winn, and Daniel Shimabuku [Los Angeles, CA: The Cotsen Institute of Archaeology at UCLA, 1989]).

healthy calories and not the processed fake-food ones that in the industrialized world today piles bad fat onto many of us.

Her makers massaged this Great Mother into a high polish. Everything about Her is soft round curves: arms, legs, fingers, belly, neck, breasts. But this is no ordinary woman; this soft loving body sits under the head and beak of a bird, a head with otherworldly eyes taller than wide and missing their pupils and irises. Her neck is blown up twice human size — some call it phallic. A figurine that could be Her twin was found at Nicea near the Greek city of Larisa — same posture, same body fat, same high-polish shine.

To say female figurines are numerous in Neolithic Europe is like saying websites are plentiful on the World Wide Web. One culture alone, the Vinca, turned out "tens of thousands of figurines, almost all of them female." Coming a little later in time than the Sesklos, the Vinca existed for roughly a thousand years, from about 5200 to 4200 BC, in what is now Hungary, Bulgaria and Romania. There they erected hundreds of towns, and in just one of these, also named Vinca, so many figurines were dug up that they had to be "removed from the site by the cartload" (Ward 2006: 274).

While female figurines literally flood Neolithic Europe, male figurines are scarce as hen's teeth. At the site of Rakovets in the Republic of Moldova for example, a Cucuteni/Tripolye site from c 4500-3800 BC, excavators found 88 human figurines. Eighty-two of the 88 were clearly female, with the "chest, abdomen and breast area worked with great care." The final six were ambisexual, sporting phalluses along with breasts. At Golyamo Delchevo in Bulgaria, 32 percent of the figurines found were neither male nor female, a "small proportion" were male, and the rest were female. And the Neolithic Lengyel, who lived in what is today Hungary, Slovakia, Austria and the Czech Republic, churned out enormous numbers of clay figurines. Among the Lengyel there was a "mass occurrence of human, particularly

Fig. 3.18. Cucuteni-culture Mother Goddess figurines from Old Europe, excavated in Romania. Like many Neolithic Mother Goddesses, these too radiate soft nurturance coupled with iron strength. (Photograph Courtesy of Andreas Praefcke. From a collection in the Museum für Vor- und Frühgeschichte, Berlin).

female figures — 'Venuses,' indicating respect for the Great Goddess — Mother (Mother-Earth)" of us all (Popova 2005; Tringham & Conkey 1998: 27; Kovarnik et al. 2006).

But even though not as common as females, male figurines, as we'll see in the next section, do pop up occasionally in European guiding-goddess towns.

Men and the Goddess

The archaeologist Douglas Bailey tells a story about a Romanian man who was widening his garden when he stumbled across a stunning hoard of ancient clay figurines. After tearing it up totally, archaeologists decided the man's yard had once been part of a town belonging to the "A3 phase" of the Neolithic Cucuteni culture (second half of fifth millennium BC). The figurines came in two sets of six each. Set one were all male, with wide shoulders, legs straddled, phalluses prominent, and just a dab of body décor. Set two on the other hand, were female, with narrow shoulders, legs hugged together, and barrel-loads of body beautification. This delightful dozen are all six- to eight inches high (14.0 to 20.0 centimeters), and all are minus faces, hands and arms.

But here's the really strange thing: all twelve figurines have breasts. On all but one, these breasts are round little smushed pellets of clay stuck onto the chest. On the twelfth figure, however, the breasts are long, and etched into the chest. So Doug

Bailey (living in the war-god world he does), scratches his head and asks: "Why do the 'male' ones have the same size and shape of breasts as do the supposedly female ones?" (Bailey 2005: 90). To me the answer is simple: in guiding-goddess societies, breasts are symbols of nurturance. And since both males and females were reared to be nurturers in guiding-goddess lands, and both were rewarded for being nurturers, it's only fitting, symbolically speaking, to show men as well as women with breasts (symbolizing nurturing savvy).

But why do eleven of the twelve figurines have small versus large breasts? One possibility: the one large-breasted statuette might represent the Mother Goddess, while the smaller-breasted pieces could be other deities. It could be that in this culture, larger breasts symbolized motherhood, while smaller ones stood for people who'd not borne children. In other words, although we modern Westerners consider gender to be one of the most important ways to lump people into categories, maybe to the Cucuteni the most central division was not male/female, but mother/not-mother.

But maybe they're not deities at all you say. Why couldn't they be just people? The answer: because people don't come minus faces, hands and arms. All archaeologists would agree that these figurines were not meant to represent human beings but something beyond human, "natural" or "normal." Something in other words supernatural or supernormal.

A second clue we're dealing here with deities is the technical and aesthetic superiority of these pieces. Take it from someone who's not only worked with clay but is considered by some to be a pinch good at using it to represent people. It's not easy making clay figurines as beautifully proportioned as these. It would take radical time and talent both. I couldn't even begin to pull it off.

Remember — in guiding-goddess lands, oxytocin-high mothers were probably the role models — for men as well as for non-mother women. Boys learned not only to be studley macho men, but also to adore everyone around them the same way oxytocin-high mothers adore their babies. Men learned to nurture, in other words, by watching (and being reminded to watch) mothers under the spell of birthing hormones. Another reminder: don't think this made guiding-goddess men into "mama's boys." As we'll see a little later on, they were anything but.

Europe in the Bronze Age: The Fab Minoans

The final stop on our magic tour through Neolithic Goddessland is the Mediterranean island of Crete, famous for its shockingly sophisticated Bronze-Age Minoan civilization. In Athens we board a boat and in a few short hours land at the capital of Crete, Heraklion. Although the island boasts a bonanza of Neolithic goddess figurines, in the following (Bronze-Age) Minoan era, these are overshadowed by paintings of the Goddess on walls and ceramics, and by etchings of Her on seal stones, signet rings and jewelry in general. At the same time, the Minoans crafted few if any images of male gods (before around 1450 BC at least, when the war-god Mycenaeans took over).

Although the Minoans worshipped a few male gods, these were anything but war gods: "A male god appears surprisingly seldom" says Nilsson. And unlike their war-god neighbors in Egypt and the Near East, Minoan male gods were young and beardless. Unlike Egyptian male deities, they didn't seem to create people, plants or animals. And neither were they "gods of wisdom." Face it, says Minoan-religion expert Nanno Marinatos: among the Minoans "the indisputable predominance of goddesses" is just a fact of life (Nilsson 1949: 354; 292; Marinatos 1993: 166-67).

We've already checked out a few awesome images of the Minoan Goddess: the Goddess of the Mountain and the fresco of the Mistress of Animals (chapter 3). For years a third famous fresco image went by the name "La Parisienne," because She so reminded Her excavator Sir Arthur Evans of the cool French

Fig. 3.19. The ancient Minoan Guiding Goddess. This image is part of the remains of a wall painting called "The Campstool Fresco," uncovered in the Minoan palace-temple of Knossos (Courtesy of the University of South Carolina Press).

women he knew. That La Parisienne was a goddess is nowhere in doubt: She towers like a giant over the other figures in the "The Campstool Fresco", and around her neck she wears "the sacral knot" — something archaeologists agree signals the sacred, since it's found at sacred sites all over Minoan Crete.

Another place Minoans set down images of their Goddess is on signet rings — those devices the ancients would shove into wet clay in order to "leave their mark" (kind of like we do with pen-and-ink signatures). Although the faces of these rings are usually under an inch wide, ancient Minoan artists managed to drop a whopping amount of art onto some of them. On the face of one — the "Isopata" ring — an ancient artist managed to squeeze in five entire female figures — plus the lilies growing in the field four of them stand in.

According to Minoan archaeologist Nanno Marinatos, the four larger women in this image are priestesses (or adorants) waiting for the Goddess, who's still far away and high above the field, but sweeping in for a landing. Like all Minoan goddesses and priestesses, these are bare-breasted women wearing many-layered skirts that brush the ground. Above their waspish waists their breasts are large and full. Moving in like the wind, the

Goddess rushes to earth, Her skirt raised to her knees and billowing in what looks like an updraft in the wake of Her quick descent. As Nanno Marinatos puts it, "her hair is flying," a sign of "rapid movement" (Marinatos 1993: 163).

Fig. 3.20. Etched onto the inch-wide bevel of the 3500-year-old "Isopata" ring, are five Minoan goddesses and/or priestesses. To create such a tiny yet elaborate piece of art would have taken enormous skill — not to mention either spectacles or a magnifying glass (Courtesy of the University of South Carolina Press).

A second gold Minoan ring is also a little less than an inch across and also shows females — three this time. One woman tends a tree, a common Minoan religious symbol. The other two women — who look like they're doing a high-five — are probably performing a ritual or ritual gesture of some sort. Since she's larger and higher in the visual field, the female in the middle could be the Minoan Goddess (or one of them; the Minoans might have had more than one goddess). Could this Goddess be zapping the third woman with sacred energy? Healing power? Second sight? An idea for a stand-up comedy routine?

As for figurines, just because the Minoans slacked off a bit on manufacturing 3D goddesses doesn't mean they let goddess-figurine production die altogether. Possibly the most powerful Minoan objects ever uncovered are the two snake goddesses stumbled upon by Sir Arthur Evans in a stone-lined pit in the central sanctuary at the Minoan palace-temple of Knossos. These power-packed beauties are molded not from clay but from 'faience,' a substance made mostly of crushed quartz. Although they're each about a foot high, the one with her fists at face-level is a bit shorter than the other. J.A. Sakellarakis, former director of

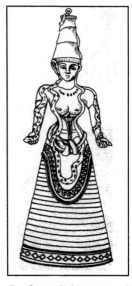

Fig. 3.21. Minoan snake goddess. About a foot high and made of crushed quartz, this reptilian-encrusted deity is roughly 3500 years old (Courtesy of the University of South Carolina Press).

the Heraklion Archaeological Museum on Crete — which is where these statues spend their days now — thinks the taller figure might be the Minoan Mother Goddess and the shorter Her daughter (Sakellarakis 2000: 36).

The Mother Goddess is literally crawling with snakes: up and down her arms, over her chest, her legs and her hat. Snakes slither over her ears, even. In front of her womb snakes tangle and twine — a suggestion maybe of her twin abilities to give the gift of life and to take it back when the time is ripe (Baring and Cashford 1991: 111). In her right hand, as if seduced, rests a snake's head; in her left lies its tail. One thing is clear: in control here are not the snakes, but our fearless protector Mother.

For more reasons than one, snakes are explosive religious symbols. If the idea of snakes slithering up and down your trunk makes your skin crawl, you're not alone. Many of us feel a

stomach-churning fear at the mere mention of snakes. Even monkeys and apes are afraid of them, making some say our cowardly-lion response to these reptiles might be biologically-based

Fig. 3.22. Minoan snake goddess No. 2. Could the snakes have represented reincarnation? (Courtesy of the University of South Carolina Press).

(Marinatos 1993: 158). But the panic they produce in us isn't the only reason snakes are powerful. Freudians insist snakes are phallic symbols. Also, snakes hibernate and shed their skin, which made some think these critters had cracked the code to eternal life:

> It was a general belief in the ancient world that snakes don't die of old age ... but periodically shed their skins and emerge ... reborn into another life. Greeks called the snake's cast skin *geras*, 'old age.' The Chinese envisioned resurrection of the dead as a man splitting his old skin and coming out ... as a youth again.... Melanesians say 'to slough one's skin' means eternal life (Walker 1983: 903).

Although some argue these two figurines aren't goddesses at all but only priestesses, I have to agree with Baring and Cashford: It would take a deity to handle all those snakes all at the same time (1991: 111).

But Are They Really Goddesses?

So all across the globe our Neolithic ancestors snapped out female figurines by the megaton. But are these goddesses — or something else? Unfortunately, since no one's translated the written languages of the guiding-goddess-Neolithic- or Bronze-Age societies, we can't lope over to the local library and read what these societies had to say about the why's and wherefore's of their figurines. Through the 1800s and most of the 1900s, however, our best minds taught that our early ancestors worshipped mostly goddesses. With archaeologists unearthing all those otherworldly female figurines and no male figurines to speak of, what other conclusion were they to draw? Not only that, when written records do begin, they say that similar historical figurines are, indeed, goddesses.

So before the 1980s, books like Robert Briffault's *The Mothers* and Eric Neumann's *The Great Mother* were all the rage. These authors said that for most of early human existence we probably all worshipped a Great Mother Goddess; however (they continue), that was because back then we were all dumb as mud. When we got smart (in their minds not until around 4000 BC), we began worshipping male gods. In other words, with time we evolved into proper worshippers of such deities as Indra and Odin the war gods, and later, Jealous Jehovah and Yahweh the "control freak" — as Oxford University professor Richard Dawkins calls him (Dawkins 2006: 31).

Go Directly to Jail, Do Not Pass Go

Then in the 1980s a cluster of books tangoed into town that turned everything on its head: Our evolution from goddesses to gods, said these authors, was not a step forward, but a giant leap back. Merlin Stone, University of California archaeologist Marija Gimbutas, Riane Eisler and others pointed out that when the new male gods roared into town, peace, equality and human health morphed into non-stop war, bigotry and general societal sickness. When this cluster of books hit the stands, a hailstorm of controversy fell over the literate world. As long as thinkers stuck to the party line ("before 4000 BC Mother was everywhere but not worth the paper She was printed on") all was peachy keen. The second someone suggested goddess was equal to god, however, all hell broke loose. The result: since the 1990s, a backlash of unprecedented proportions has raged against the Neolithic and Bronze-Age Great Mother Goddess.

Backlash

Backlashers lightly pepper the ranks of theologians, feminists, anthropologists, and archaeologists as well. Among them sit assistant professor of religion Cynthia Eller, theologian Rosemary Radford Reuther, anthropologist Richard G. Lesure, feminist archaeologist Lynn Meskell, and the writer-combo team of Lucy

Goodison and Christine Morris (Lucy and Christine are also feminist archaeologists).

Here's an example of some of the backlash folderol emanating from this group: "The Victorian scholars' notion of the all-powerful, all-sexual and potentially all-destructive Mother Goddess ... mirrors the obsessive sexual love, fear and hate of the small Freudian boy in his mother's lap" (Goodison and Morris 1998: 20). And get a load out of this: After the female figurines "are no longer limited to ... objects of male desire or 'the Mother Goddess,'" then we can imagine other things their makers meant them to be. And then there's this about why we should pitch the ancient Goddess out on Her ear altogether: "I have reservations about" the prehistoric Goddess, says theologian Rosemary Radford Reuther. "If women, and women alone personify the forces of nature ... either they need to be dominated ... in order to control these forces ... or they are the primary gender that will somehow 'save' us from the destructive effects of millennia of male domination of nature" (Tringham and Conkey 1998: 37; Reuther 2005: 39-40).

Whoa Rosemary, say I! If goddess replaced gods, men would feel an itch to dominate women? Rose, have you glanced out your ivory-tower window lately? Personally I can't fathom how men could feel a greater itch to dominate than they do today — under your war gods. In Nigeria during the 2002 Miss World Pageant, for the crime of wearing bikinis in public, Muslim men felt an itch to set women on fire and burn them to death; over 200 people died as a result (Harris 2004: 46). In Deorala, India, in 1987 men felt an itch to publicly burn to death a teenaged Hindu widow in the ancient practice of suttee (in which widows are immolated simply for the crime of becoming widows) (Sarkar 1997). And in the glorious Christian US, men every year feel the itch to beat to death 1300 women — their intimate partners — with 1.5 million women "raped or physically assaulted or both," and with "one in three of these ... injured to the extent that significant medical intervention is required" (Jafee et al. 2005: 713). What's worse, Rose, ample evidence shows this delight in domination began exactly when your gods stomped the goddesses, and began telling men to beat women into the dust as well.

Rose also moans and groans that if gods were swapped for goddesses, she might be handed the crackly task of cleaning up the mess her war gods have made of the planet. But Rose! Why not let women try to put the world house in order? Some might have more energy for it than you do. Besides, women have been handling the housecleaning for millennia now. We've gotten good at it. My biggest concern is that since the world's women have been punched and crushed by war gods for six millennia now, we aren't the powerhouses we could be. So although we *can* make life sweet and exciting again for men and women alike, to do so we need to begin immediately rearing our daughters under new rules — rules that restore their innate, Goddess-given powers.

Tricky-Dickies

I'm warning you: these anti-goddess people are tricky. Since they know they couldn't get away with it, they never say our Neolithic grandparents *didn't* worship goddesses. So they do the next best thing: throw page after page at us of confusing, stuffy, tangled, academic language that boils down to this: before 4000 BC the world *might* not have worshipped goddesses. Which of course is something you can say about anything archaeologists dig up. A piece of obsidian with all the features of an arrowhead and buried near a bear skeleton might have been an arrowhead — or it might not. We'll never know. In archaeology all we can ever do is go with our best bets.

These backlasher naysayers get not only silly; they get downright shrill about goddess figurines. Listen to Lynn Meskell for example, a feminist archaeologist, as she moans that "evocative images from antiquity ... are ... open to ... political manipulation.... Claiming ... social utopia and a single 'Mother Goddess' at Catalhoyuk may be seen as ... dangerous ..." (Meskell 1998: 55). "Evocative"? "Dangerous"? Those innocent little three-inch, 5000-year-old clay statuettes? Howza! Let's all dive under the couch!

Other backlashers say just because a figurine is breast-bedecked doesn't mean it's female. For gosh sake, men have breasts too! (Lesure 2002: 602). Tatsuo Kobayashi, a leading archaeologist of the Japanese Jomon period, proceeds as follows: Golly gee! Men have breasts! Who cares if all the Jomon clay figurines have breasts — that doesn't make them women! Kobayashi goes on to say that if the breast-bedecked figurines can't be his sex, they can't be any sex at all: "it is considered here that these clay figurines are neither male nor female ... but rather they are images that surpass the realms of gender..." (Kobayashi 2004: 155).

Still others say, "Gee if that clay statuette over there doesn't have breasts of a certain heft, don't try to sell me on its being a woman — could be a man, darling" (See Meskell 1998) (never mind the poor statuette is also minus a penis). Well I say if breast-bedecked figurines sans penises are men, our ancestors were trying to tell us something. My bet is it's this: Whether you're man or woman, the important thing is feeding and nurturing others. Breasts are a jim-dandy symbol of feeding and nurturing, and maybe Neolithic men who had them were put up on pedestals. On television today, 90 percent of women are blond — even though blonds make up a miniscule portion of the population. Maybe a similar thing was happening back in the Neolithic. Maybe it was the ideal, not the real, man who was pictured in these little pieces of art. Have to tell you, though: my bets are still on most of the figurines with breasts being women, not men.

Silly, shrill idea number three: Neolithic figurines were mostly female because Neolithic women were so much trouble no one could concentrate on anything but them: "Could it be that [almost all human] figurines were female because the status and powers of women in social relationships were the source of ongoing struggle?" Silly, shrill statement number four: Even though the Neolithic Mesoamericans made figurines "with two heads or two faces" we should still give heavy weight to the notion that these figurines weren't goddesses, but just ordinary women (Lesure 2002: 598).

Idea number five is just shrill (not to mention shabby): prehistorian David Anthony compares world-renowned University of California archaeologist, author, and excavator Marija Gimbutas to the Nazis. Nazis tried to use archaeological evidence to "prove" blond, blue-eyed humans were better than the rest of us. Anthony says Gimbutas is just as bad, because she tried to "prove" Neolithic Europeans worshipped a guiding goddess (Anthony 1995).

I know, I know. Makes no sense. Like all scientists, Gimbutas painted a theory to account for the tons of evidence she uncovered and studied during her long, successful career as an archaeologist. It's what all scientists do. Then other scientists calmly weigh in on what they think is weak or strong about your theory. What most good scientists don't do, however, is call other scientists nasty names.

You do have to wonder: Just what exactly are these backlashing naysayers saying? That before writing was invented no one ever worshipped goddesses? That would be a tad wacky, since once writing *was* invented, the female-figurine-producing people wrote this: "We worship goddesses." So, what — as soon as they invented writing, people shot overnight from no goddesses, to goddesses galore? (Sound of author scratching her head.)

Like Rosemary Radford Reuther, post-modernist feminists worry that goddess figurines will hurt women, that they will cause scientists "...to essentialize women, falling into the androcentric assumption that 'women's bodily functions ...

117

define entirely women's capacities as social actors'" (Lesure 2002: 595, quoting McNay). To me this is a puzzler. Men's bodily functions don't "define entirely" men's social roles — so why should women's bodily functions define theirs? If trained away from our war-god fear and loathing of women, their bodies, and bodily functions (birth, labor, breastfeeding, monthly controlled bleeding, and sexuality), this kind of thinking would never pop into anyone's head. And even if it would — when did we start calling it kosher to lie when we don't like the truth?

Frankly my dears, in case you haven't noticed, scientists aren't always perfect. Especially when it comes to explosive, ride-'em-cowboy issues (like goddesses potentially regaining a seat on the planet), scientists can easily run amok. Scientists themselves have been known to spill the beans about this fact. Listen to Yale University scientists Bloom and Weisberg: "[S]ome skepticism toward scientific authority is clearly rational. Scientists have personal biases due to ego or ambition.... There are also political and moral biases, *particularly in social science research dealing with contentious issues...*" (Bloom and Weisberg, 2007; emphasis the author's).

A great case in point is archaeologist Doug Bailey's noodly notion that some of the Neolithic figurines from Thessaly he studied modeled sadomasochism and "the potential mix of pain and pleasure that comes both from bondage ..., from such physical abuse ..., and furthermore, from the distanced spectation of the abuse of others (which the act of looking at the figurine of a bound woman evokes).... There is a dynamic tension between pain and pleasure in the bound bodies, especially the female..." (Bailey 2005: 165).

Doug, I think you need to get out more. You're "reading" the figurines with your twenty-first-century daddy-war-god lenses lined up square on your nose, and firmly fogging your view of the Neolithic. It's the war gods who teach there are kicks in seeing women suffer, and that pain is pleasure and pleasure pain — no healthy Mama teaches this kind of hogwash to Her children.

Out-to-Lunch Ideas?

Although goddess naysayers love painting long lists of things the female figurines could be (other than goddesses), most of their ideas seem out-to-lunch (See Lesure 2002: 596-98, 604; Meskell 1998: 52; Eller 2000: 139). Based on fieldwork done by anthropologists, many suggest the figurines are "objects that heal people," "objects that protect the dead" (Eller), and/or "magical items" (Meskell). All of which suggests the little statues are supernatural females. And how much different is this from calling them goddesses? Just because a modern informant tells an anthropologist something is a "magical item" rather than a goddess, doesn't necessarily mean the anthropologist is being given a clear picture of the situation. For many, religion is a private matter, the knowledge of which is not always shared with outsiders (Gunn Allen 1992).

Other naysayers overlook that many Neolithic female figurines are otherworldly — for example part human-part animal. That these could be "portrait[s] of an individual," an "allegory of womanhood" or representations of "ancestors" (Lesure) seem farfetched ideas, to say the least. Likewise with ideas that otherworldly figurines represent "concubines, slaves, subdued enemies, puberty models, training items, wish figures ... communication devices, ... contracts, territory markers" or "individual tokens" (Meskell).

Finally, many of these "explanations" fail to account for the fact that the figurines are female: "Ancestors"? You mean the Neolithics had only female ancestors? "Props in initiation ceremonies"? (Lesure). You mean only women had initiation ceremonies? "Subdued enemies"? (Meskell) You mean no one had anything but female enemies?

Cauvin Pooh-Poohs the Toy Notion

The great, recently deceased French archaeologist Jacques Cauvin pooh-poohed notions that Neolithic goddess figurines were toys. These figurines are some of the earliest clay objects our ancestors made, and child's play doesn't precede adult life — it imitates it. Cauvin also got a chuckle over the idea that because some figurines were designed simply, they were merely foo-foo items. After all, whether it's made of gold, wood, or chrome-plated fiberglass, a Christian cross is a Christian cross. And Cauvin nixes notions like Ian Hodder's that goddesses found in grain bins aren't goddesses: "[N]or, as is equally often said, is the variety of archaeological context" in which goddess figurines are uncovered "whether funerary or domestic, an argument against their significance" or identification as goddesses (Cauvin 2002: 105-06).

But here's the best evidence that many if not most of these prehistoric figurines were Mother Goddesses: as soon as the page turns and people began keeping written records, these records *say* the figurines are Mother Goddesses. As the archaeologist Arthur Evans pointed out, it "can hardly be ... coincidence that all these provinces of ancient culture — the Aegean, the Anatolian, the Syrian, Cypriote, Mesopotamian, and Elamite — where the habit prevailed of forming" the Mother Goddess figurines "were the later scenes of ... Great Goddesses who often combined ... motherhood and virginity" (Nilsson 1949: 291, footnote 9, quoting Arthur Evans PM, I, p. 52).

But in the End Most See the Light

In the end, however, even the harshest critics admit that many if not most of the Neolithic and Bronze-Age figurines probably represent goddesses. Lynn Meskell's True Confession: "This is not to say that a theory of female deities or entities is implausible, but rather that it may be something specific to Catalhoyuk, or Anatolia, at that time and not what the twentieth-century Western viewers have constructed was the 'Mother Goddess'" (Meskell

1998: 51). And here's Ms. Cynthia Eller 'fessing up: "Certainly we are aware of numerous cross-cultural instances of goddess worship accompanied by widespread use of ... figurines, so this is one of the most likely explanations of the Neolithic figurine assemblages." Eller goes on to say that "Especially persuasive is the fact that goddess figurines — and larger-scale goddess images as well — exist in later cultures in the same geographic area" as the prehistoric figurines, and are labeled "goddess" in the written records of the time (Eller 2000: 139).

Others are even clearer than Eller and Meskell that many if not most Neolithic female statuettes were probably goddesses. It's likely some were specialty goddesses concentrating on, say, weather control or fertility. Others might have been half-goddesses (remember the Basque Laminak from an earlier chapter?). Undoubtedly many, however, represented powerful Great Guiding Goddesses, birthers of the universe and everything in it.

4

Before Snoots, Snobs and Bully Boys

Did the Guiding Goddess Guarantee Utopia?

The evidence clearly points to many Neolithic peoples worshipping goddesses more than they worshipped gods. But did these people also live in utopia? No. No human group has ever lived in utopia, and I doubt any ever will. But compared to what came after them, yes. Compared to most of their Bronze-Age descendants and to us their twenty-first-century descendants, our Neolithic ancestors did indeed live in utopia. The evidence is strong that the Neolithic was a time of little if any warfare, little if any interpersonal violence, little if any social ranking, and no tyrannical dictator governments. And in the very next era, the Bronze Age, when the male war-sky gods make their first unmistakable appearances, all of the above nasties suddenly pop up in spades in several places over the planet. And ever since, up to the present day, they have continued to plague us.

As I said, I doubt if we can totally understand how golden life was in those days. I think the only way we can do it is through some of our most talented artists, our visionaries. I think I've come closest while watching certain old films, including one of my favourites, by the Swedish filmmaker Ingmar Bergman: *The Seventh Seal*.

Ingmar Bergman's *The Seventh Seal*

Antonius Block, a drop-dead gorgeous knight in shining armor who's just returned home from fighting the Infidel in the Holy Land, is sick of war, fighting, and munching cold-meat sandwiches on the fly between battles. He just wants to prop up his feet and smoke a cigar or two back home in Scandinavia. But Lady Luck isn't tagging along on Block's coattails: The plague's hit Scandinavia, and everyone — surprise, surprise — is a bit crotchety.

But wait — it gets worse. Death sashays into the picture next and starts following Block home. Out on a spooky stretch of grey beach, Death challenges Block: "Hey dude. Game 'o chess, dude. You win, you walk. I win — well you know what *my* gig is." So what could Block do? In those days, no one argued with Death. So as Block continues home, Death pops up every day or so with his chess board tucked under his arm, and they play a bit of chess.

Meanwhile, the countryside is awash with war-god people. Long trains of monks snake through town squares beating themselves with chains until the blood bubbles up on their backs. Broken-down, witchcraft-accused young women ride inside high-walled carts on their way to burning at the stake. Bar crowds sit around dousing themselves with beer and obsessing about death. Block's squire saves a woman from rape by a priest — and then rapes her himself (half-heartedly).

Just about when you're ready to stick your head in an oven, in waltz four people who shake you back to life again. The contrast between them and the war-lord people almost rips the breath right out of your lungs. They're a troupe of traveling medieval poet-actors: Mia, her husband Jof, their son Mikael, and their entertainer colleague Jonas Skat. The first time we meet Mia, Jof and Skat, they're sleeping with the tops of their heads touching in a close triangle inside the SUV-sized horse-drawn traveling wagon they call home. First to wake is Jof, who slaps at a fly, somersaults out of the back of the wagon, juggles a bit, talks to their horse ("It's a pity you can't teach me to eat grass...."), and then sees a vision of the Goddess (disguised as the Virgin Mary) gliding across the meadow. Breathless with excitement, Jof runs to tell Mia. "She smiled at me!" he exclaims in wonder.

Jof and Mia aren't perfect — only very human. While the god people are burning and raping their women, beating themselves to bloody pulps, and talking non-stop about death, Jof sits in the sun, lets Mia clean a minor head wound, and says "Ouch. It hurts." He tells Mia he'd "been in a fight" (when mostly what had happened was a crotchety bar crowd of war-god men had beaten him up a bit). But Mia knows her husband. She says she knows he was probably singing and dancing again, which typically made the god-people hot under the collar. "I roared like a lion!" Jof protests. And what did people do when you roared? Asks Mia. "They laughed..." admits Jof.

Jof and Mia know Death is nearby, and they're respectful of him. As Jof sits in the sun next to their wagon playing his lyre, perched on a post nearby is a human skull — the war-god priests have paid Skat to wear it when he performs for the god crowds. Unlike Block the knight, however, whose senses are so filled with Death that he's suffocating with him, Mia and Jof never let Death break their stride. They go on living life to the fullest — drinking it in, laughing in the sun. Death can't prevent them from being creative, impish and wide-eyed with wonder about the world around them.

In the end, Jof and Mia watch Death and Block trudge away, two black silhouettes moving high on a rocky bluff against a sullen sky. Death is leading Block by the hand. Then Mia and Jof turn and walk away beside the sea, symbol of the Goddess' loving womb.

Our Ancestors: Playful and Creative

Like Mia and Jof, our Great-Goddess ancestors were as playful, sensual and creative as they come. Take for example our ancestors who lived in southeastern Europe from about 7000 to 2500 BC. Marija Gimbutas, only one archaeologist who's dug up their remains, positively croons about their creativity: their "anthropomorphic, zoomorphic and ornithomorphic vases" she says, are "exquisite," and the "symbolic signs and decorative motifs" they lovingly applied to their dishes and other ceramics are "rich" — especially in comparison with the pottery of the

Fig. 4.1. Conversation among Minoan women. Unlike both modern and ancient war-god peoples, Minoans did not dictate that women cover their bodies above the waist (Courtesy of the University of South Carolina Press).

war-god peoples who followed them in time. Gimbutas calls these later war-god peoples 'Kurgans.' The "stabbing and impressing technique" the Kurgans used to decorate their pottery "is quite primitive" sniffs Gimbutas "and seems to focus on only one symbol, the sun" (Gimbutas 1982: 26, 30).

And take the people of the Bronze-Age Indus Valley Civilization, who carved female and animal figurines that "display great liveliness and imagination" and who produced a variety of crafts from A to Z, including "polychrome pottery, superb jewelry ... finely woven cotton textiles and woodwork..." and so forth (McIntosh 2002: 48; 9). Or the ancient Minoans, who have to rank among the top ten of all times when it comes to cool. If you've never seen any Minoan art, get a book and drink in an eyeful. Minoan art is wild but sophisticated, and the sexy Minoans trucked it around everywhere.

The Minoans even slathered their walls with flowered landscapes of wild deer, flotillas of ships sailing the high seas, dancing women, laughing men, blue monkeys, airborne birds, and flying dolphins. One of my favorite pieces of Minoan art is a lentoid-shaped flask covered over every inch of one side with an octopus, its tentacles spread in undulating loops that smother the jar from top to bottom, left to right. This sea creature looks exactly like a modern cartoon, whose only purpose in life is to put a smile on your face. The Minoans also decorated their walls with octopi — purple no less: "In Cretan homes, walls and ceilings were lavish with flowing lines and bright curves, plants and flowers, birds and forest animals, and sea creatures — purple octopi!" (Sjoo & Mor 1991: 217).

The ancient Minoans "... appear to have been gentle, joyous, sensuous and peace-loving" say artist Monica Sjoo and poet Barbara Mor (Sjoo and Mor 1991: 213). On the Minoan Harvesters Vase, men are shown laughing, singing and maybe even joking. This is amazing, because there's absolutely nothing else like it from this early in time — and not for a long while after. Other Minoan art shows acrobats completing somersaults in mid air, and bull

Fig. 4.2. 4500 years ago, a playful Minoan artist painted a cartoon octopus on this flattened, ovoid flask (Drawing by the author).

leapers leaping lengthwise over the backs of bulls. In contrast to their neighbors the ancient Egyptians, whose paintings of human bodies are stiff as boards, Minoan artists made the human body look natural, graceful and flexible. And in contrast to the Mycenaeans who followed them, the Minoans never felt the need to erect massive "Cyclopean" walls around their cities.

One of the most drop-dead gorgeous pieces of Minoan art, though, is the Bulls Head Rhyton (a rhyton is a kind of drinking vessel). Carved out of shiny black stone, this bull is a masterpiece. Its eyes are made of rock crystal and its muzzle of mother-of-pearl. Its horns are covered with gold. Like the Minoans themselves, this animal is full of itself — in a good way — and so

Fig. 4.3. Minoan bull leapers on a wall fresco at Knossos. While their war-god Egyptian contemporaries made the human body rigid and unbending, Minoan artists made bodies look natural and fluid (Drawing by the author).

Fig. 4.4. In addition to bull leaping, Minoans were fond of boxing (Photograph by the author).

life-like that at any second you expect it to begin moving.

This bull is full of magic too — you can feel it. And mystery: in the top of its head is a hole, which is okay, except that there's a hole in his mouth too. So if an ancient Minoan poured beer or wine or whatever through the top of this bull's head, the liquid would have come straightaway out his mouth. And why would anyone want to do that? What exactly did the Minoans use this bull for? We don't know. It's just one more mystery.

George Lucas and Ron Howard's *Willow*

Another film that gives us a taste of the old paradise our goddess ancestors basked in is George Lucas and Ron Howard's *Willow*. Although I love Mia and Jof for their sensuality and innocence, they seem a touch cut off from the world. They have power in their small group of four, yes, but in the wider world, forget it — they're virtually powerless. In *Willow* things are different. One thing that's great about *Willow* is that women have political and spiritual power right alongside the men. According to Lucas and Howard, in other words, women with power don't drain an ounce away from men's power. People, it is possible to share the sandbox!

What I see in *Willow* is what's at the core of a book still popular in the Goddess Community: Riane Eisler's *The Chalice and the Blade*. Eisler says what we're shackled with now is a 'dominator model' of how we all should relate to one another. It's like there's this big, tall ladder, and we're all sitting on one particular rung of this ladder. Whatever rung you're on, you're expected to dominate the people on the rung below — and get dominated by the people on the rung above you. So Eisler pops the question: Why do we have to live like this? The answer, of course is, we don't. Eisler says we need to trade in this dumpy old dominator model for a spanking new 'partnership model,' in which we're all equal. Ditch the ladder and bring in a circle for all of us to stand in, hand in hand.

And that's what we have in *Willow*. Everyone shares the power: women, men, young, old, little person or otherwise, everyone's in the game on equal footing. Men not only lose nothing by sharing the power with women, little people, baby girls and old women, they actually seem to gain by it. *Willow* men seem larger than life, stronger, more courageous than the norm. The world savior is male (the little person Willow), as is the film's second hero, Madmartigan, who calls himself 'the greatest swordsman that ever lived,' and who single-handedly in the film's final battle takes on an entire human army and a two-headed dragon, crushing them both.

So 'mama's boys' is not a label easily pinned on the men in *Willow*. And yet the political power and a good part of the spiritual power in this film rest in the hands of women. From the very start of the film, women hold center stage: a baby girl is born, and the ruler of the land, the Queen Bavmorda, orders the baby killed, since according to prophecy the child is destined to destroy her one day and filch her throne. In a smashing turn-around of the Moses myth, the baby's midwife places her in a basket of rushes and sends her floating down the river, where she's found by Willow. The Goddess appears to Willow (in the form of the fairy queen Cherlindrea), and clues him in on who he's rescued: she's Elora Danan, destined one day to overthrow Bavmorda and bring peace and harmony to the land. And she's chosen Willow to save her from the evil Queen.

From one narrow escape to the next, Willow slashes his way through the film, panting hard to deliver Elora Danan into safe hands. He doesn't fight his battle alone, however, but in partnership with three others. Madmartigan and Sorsha, daughter of the evil Bavmorda, fight with him on the material plane with swords, and on the spiritual plane he fights with the help of Raziel, a mighty and wise old sorceress. And although it's Willow who throws the winning punch in the end — the one that finishes off the evil queen — it's Raziel who teaches him the magic he needs to know in order to do it. And it's Raziel who teaches him that his powers won't work until he has faith in himself. In the end, Willow hands Elora Danan over to Madmartigan and Sorsha, who together will raise her till she comes of age and can rule the land on her own.

Although Sorsha handles a sword as well as any man, she can't take Madmartigan down in a fight. On the other hand, Madmartigan can't govern as well as Sorsha can. As a pair, however, they'll be awesome protection for Elora Danan until she's old enough to govern the land herself. Lucas and Howard are very clear on this: Elora Danan is saved only through two male-female teams dancing together as co-equals: on the spiritual plane it's Willow and Raziel, and on the physical plane Sorsha and Madmartigan.

No Snoots in the Near East

In a lot of ways our Neolithic guiding-goddess ancestors were like the people in Willow. For one, neither showed many signs of being bitten by the bug of social ranking, that is of considering some people 'better' than others. In his overview of human prehistory, anthropologist William A. Haviland, Professor Emeritus at the University of Vermont, says Neolithic people generally did not rank each other on the basis of good, bad, better and best. Like a good mother with her brood of babies, they saw everyone around them as equally valuable and lovable: "Archaeologists have been able to draw some inferences concerning the social structure of Neolithic society," says Haviland. And what they've found is that Neolithic society was "probably egalitarian" (Haviland 1997: 280; 274).

But what about the guiding-goddess people we just visited — the ones who churned out the goddess figurines? Were they or were they not snooty snobs? Climb into your traveling clothes, and let's go see. First stop: The Near East, land of modern Turkey, Syria, Lebanon, Israel, Jordan, Iraq and Iran.

Sure enough, during their Early Neolithic (10,000 — 6000 BC), the Near East was generally egalitarian, with little or no snooty snobbism. Even in the Later Neolithic (6000 — 5000 BC) most of the Near East was "still egalitarian." It wasn't until the first Near Eastern cities were born at the end of the Neolithic that trouble began brewing: rigid social classes popped up, separated one from the other by yawning chasms as wide as the Atlantic. At that time "the communal control of land by kin groups gave way to ... private estates owned by noble families. The eventual result was a stratified form of social organization rigidly divided along class lines" (Fagan 2004: 339).

For ancient Sumer (in what's now Iraq) we have written evidence that when the Goddess reigned, no one was poor: in 2300 BC, well after the father gods had roared into town in Sumer, reforms called 'amargi' were snapped into place. Interestingly, the

Sumerian word amargi has two meanings: 'freedom' and 'return to the Mother.' Even more interesting was what the amargi reforms did: they ripped fruit and other food away from the father-god priests and turned them over to the poor. Shades of Robin Hood! The Sumerian tablets "repeatedly mentioned that these reforms harked back to the way things were done in earlier periods" (Stone 1993:41).

And remember Catalhoyuk, the 8000-year-old town in ancient Turkey where houses had no recognizable doors or windows, and people seemed to spend their days cruising around on everybody's rooftops? In this happy little town, too, the evidence comes down on the side of women and men being equal.

First, excavators don't see any differences in how Catalhoyukian men and women were buried — both got stuffed in the same way into the same type burial urns with the same amount and kind of "grave goods" to lug with them into the afterlife. Second, men and women were spending the same amount of time indoors (lots of times excavators find fire soot on the insides of their rib bones), so "whether you were a man or a woman did not determine the life you could lead." And third, the fact that women's teeth were just as worn as men's means both sexes ate the same stuff. No grabbing the better food for men, in other words, and leaving the scraps for the women. Although more meat was being gobbled up in some Catalhoyukian buildings than in others, this could be just because people in the "meat-poor" buildings spent part of the year away from town — on trading expeditions for example (Balter 2005: 289-91), or Mediterranean carnival cruises.

No Snoots in the Indus Valley

So goody for the Near East; it stacks up on the low end of the snooty-snobbery scale. But how do our other areas measure up — say the Indus Valley, currently home to that pinnacle of all snooty snobbery, the Indian caste system? Well, scratching her head in puzzlement, archaeologist Jane McIntosh says ancient Indus people show "few overt signs" of having an "elite" class. She says she's clueless as to why no one got buried in big fancy graves with lots of stuff piled in it to prove they were 'important': "It seems particularly surprising ..." says Jane in a quiet voice, "that to date there have been no burials or cemeteries discovered that stand out by the lavishness of their funerary structures or the wealth of their grave goods..." (McIntosh 2002: 126, 118).

In big-city Harappa, almost every house boasted sewage drains, bathing areas, and even indoor latrines — virtually unheard of that early in the ancient world: "even during the Roman Empire, some 2000 years later," says archaeologist Jonathan Kenoyer, "these kinds of facilities were limited to upper-class neighbourhoods." In the other big ancient Indus city too, Mohenjodaro, everyone seems to have gotten an equal share of the pie: "In its prime, the whole city bespeaks middle-class prosperity..." (Kenoyer 2005: 5 of 12; Wheeler 1966: 21).

But wait. Stickler for detail that she is, Jane McIntosh points to a weeny wrinkle in all this perfection: "a small number" of graves contained more jewelry than others. "In some cases, the deceased wore more elaborate and abundant jewelry — long bead necklaces, sometimes including gold beads, worn around the neck or used to tie up the hair — and some of the women were buried with a copper mirror" (McIntosh 2002: 126; 118).

Now although archaeologists agree if you find some graves with more and better stuff, what you're looking at is snooty snobbery, remember: we're talking here about only "a small number" of jewelry-loaded, mirror-bedecked graves. Isn't it entirely possible that these were burials of priestesses of the Goddess? In the Near East, archaeologists have dug up seals showing women on thrones holding what some think are mirrors. Instead of the Indus grave mirrors showing snooty snobbery, isn't it just as likely that mirrors were considered magic sacred objects — so hot only a priestess could risk handling them?

McIntosh also speaks a bit about some Indus houses being larger than others (2002: 100; 127). Although she insists this shows snooty snobbery, I say, Hold on a minute, Jane. A smaller house may simply be a sign of a 20-something couple with no kids yet. Or — who knows — maybe the Indus people had a marriage system like the Moso, where most lived in their mother's house all their lives. The more kids Mom had, the bigger a house she'd need. On the other hand, some Moso women leave Mom's household to start their own. In *Leaving Mother Lake*, the Moso woman Yang Erche Namu left her mother's house and built her own — which, since she had no children and hadn't established herself yet, was much smaller than most Moso homes.

It's in daddy/war-god societies that we have to find a hundred ways to sundown to show which rung of the social ladder we're perched on. We collect fancy degrees, big boats, hefty houses. But in a guiding-goddess system, we're all equal children of the same mother. In Mother's eyes, no one's more important than anyone else, and big houses are big usually because more people live in them.

All in all, it seems pretty clear to me that the evidence for snooty snobbery (aka "social ranking") in the Indus Valley Civilization is pretty slim. When future archaeologists dig up twenty-first-century North America, Europe or Australia, will they find what they found in the ancient Indus Valley, i.e. 99 percent of houses equipped with the same modern conveniences, and all of the same high quality?

No Snoots in Old Europe

Okay let's shuffle on over to Neolithic Europe now. Any snooty snobbery there? "Early European farming societies" says archaeologist Brian Fagan "were basically egalitarian," with graves generally showing few status differences between individuals. In southeastern Europe at least, the sexes seemed equal: "...cemetery evidence throughout the fifth and most of the fourth millennia BC does not suggest any imbalance between the sexes or a subservience of one sex to the other." Even a bit later, among the Bronze-Age Minoans, we've generally stumbled over few rich burials that would act as flashing red lights signaling snootiness: "Survival of gold and silver vessels in neopalatial Crete is no doubt affected by the fact that we lack the rich burials in which they might be expected" (Fagan 2004: 264; Gimbutas 1991: xi; Fitton 2002: 157).

No Snoots in Jomon Japan

All agree the Jomon in the early Jomon period weren't snooty. After that there's disagreement, with some saying the later Jomon were snoots, and others insisting not. Here are some of the signs people have thought might signal late-Jomon snootiness:

a. Some late Jomon have different (but not necessarily better) stuff in their houses.
b. The late Jomon traded "ornaments," i.e. "non-functional items" with each other, and some say this is "evidence for non-egalitarian society" (Pearson 2004: 4 of 9).
c. Some late Jomon have better stuff in their graves — or at least stuff with a higher "degree of refinement."
d. And in "17 percent-25 percent of all cases in Hokkaido and the Kanto in the Final Jomon" era, there are extra goodies in the graves of Jomon teenagers.

Pretty slim-jim evidence, is what I say. I'm not even going to bother with item a. Beyond me too is the reasoning behind item b. So what if the Jomon had time to make and trade stuff they didn't need in order to survive? How is that evidence of a social ladder of any kind?

And to me item c. spells trouble. What does the author mean by "refined"? Something that took longer to make? Is more elaborate? Is more pleasing to look at — and would be for anybody? How much of "refined" is in the eye of the beholder?

Item d. is fascinating. Usually archaeologists agree that whoever has more grave goods is higher on a social scale of some sort. So what are we talking here? The nightmare of every parent — rule by teens? Or could it be that snooty-snob Jomon adults did conspicuous consumption by "buying" stuff for their teens instead of buying it for themselves? Kind of like, "since my kid has more than yours, our family's better"? On the other hand, suppose the late Jomon in Hokkaido and the Kanto thought teens with certain physical characteristics needed extra things to stay safe in the afterlife. If so, this would be a non-snooty-snob explanation for why some teens had more grave goods than others. Tricky stuff, archaeology.

When asked if the later Jomon did social ranking, our old friend Tatsuo Kobayashi also says "maybe." Not surprisingly, some of Tatsuo's main evidence is the amount of stuff certain Jomon carted off to the grave with them. The example he gives is three Jomon women buried with lots of jewelry. These three were loaded down with earrings, bracelets and "serpentinite pendants.... Burials such as these" says Tatsuo "with rich assemblages of grave goods indicate a degree of social differentiation within Jomon communities.... Typically," Kobayashi goes on, "less than one-tenth of burials from Jomon community cemeteries have earrings, and it seems that only certain people within these communities were allowed to wear them..." (Kobayashi 2004: 134-5).

Thing is, my friends, as Tatsuo himself later points out, all this body paraphernalia could be a sign not of social ranking but of "spiritual power":

[I]t is not until towards the end of the Early Jomon that clay figurines really begin to come into their own. Interestingly, at about the same time, body ornaments ... start to become popular.... [W]e need to be wary of assuming ... that these objects were really just ... to enhance the beauty of the person wearing them. Given what we know about the use of similar objects in other societies, we should probably expect that *those wearing such objects would derive spiritual power* or social status from them (emphasis the author's) (Kobayashi 2004: 144).

In other words, Kobayashi's three jewelry-bedecked women might very well have been not snooty snobs, but priestesses of the Goddess.

Goddess Daredevils

Never let it be said that Guiding-Goddess people were wet-noodle wimps. In the courage department, my guess is they outshone us two to one. Like the people in Willow, Guiding-Goddess men and women were gutsy risk-takers and valiant adventurers. For example, Indus Valley mariners "roamed the known world" (McIntosh 2002: 7) and the ancient Minoans traveled and traded "to every port of the archaic world and even — boldly — to regions far beyond" (Campbell 1964: 62).

Archaeologists have dug up scores of images of Minoans

Fig. 4.5. Minoan bull leaper in mid leap. Although modern matadors say it can't be done, bull-leaping is a frequent focus of Minoan art (Photograph by the author).

Fig. 4.6. Bull leaper snagged on the horns of the bull. Bull leaping was not for the faint of heart (Photograph by the author).

somersaulting — from front to rear — over the backs of bulls. Although modern matadors say this can't be done, I don't believe it for a second. Just because we can't do something, what makes us think our ancestors couldn't? I suspect our Goddess-centered ancestors packed a lot more pluck than we do. Mother-Goddess societies would drape people with a kind of self-sense we god peoples can't even imagine. We're birthed and 'loved' by deities who'd just as soon see us stoned to death as look at us. How could we ever have healthy senses of self?

Rich as Rockefeller

Although from movies like *Willow* and *The Seventh Seal* it's possible to get a whiff of what guiding-goddess life might have been like, neither film tells the entire story. The truth is, things were even better than these movies suggest. If the characters on our fantasy screen waltz ahead of us in the vim-and-vigor category, guiding-goddess people waltz even beyond them. When it comes to being solid-gold examples of humanity, the people of *Willow* beat us hands down. They do not, however, begin to measure up to our ancient guiding-goddess ancestors.

Our modern world seems unable to plunk "happy" and "creative" into the same sentence with the word "rich." Even our best filmmakers don't seem able to do this. Mia, Jof, Willow and Madmartigan were happy and creative — but poor when it came to worldly goods and material things. What's more, our artists often paint rich people as the bad guys.

But the ancient goddess people weren't dumb. They knew rich people can't relax if they're an island surrounded by a sea of poor. Twenty-four/seven, these surrounded rich worry about their alarm systems. Or about the people they hire to worry about their alarm systems. To avoid this situation, our smart ancestors simply made everyone rich. Ancient Southeastern Europeans not only enjoyed "...accumulations of wealth — gold, copper, marble ... and exquisite ceramics," nothing suggests anyone had more of

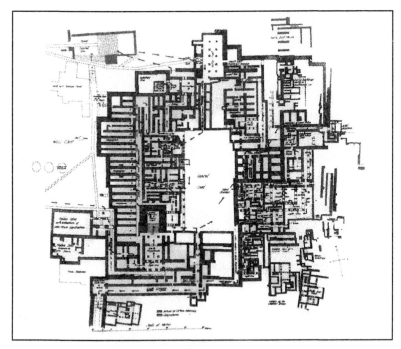

Fig. 4.7. Plan of the multistoried Minoan palace-temple of Knossos. Shot through with light wells, all 1000+ rooms of this mammoth 1450-BC building were fed with natural light and fresh air (Courtesy of the University of South Carolina Press).

this stuff than anyone else: the "distribution of wealth in graves speaks for an economic egalitarianism." These Europeans held no truck with "contrasting classes of rulers and laborers"; what they basked in instead was one big, "rich middle class" (Gimbutas 1982: 23, 324).

Fig. 4.8. In larger Minoan buildings, storage rooms were often heavily lined with these giant storage jars, or "pithoi," which could reach two meters in height (6-1/2 feet), and which bore olive oil, wine and grain (and who knows what else) (Photograph by the author).

Fig. 4.9. Author's fifth finger fits inside the decorative bowl-shaped buttons on the pithoi shown in the previous photo. These buttons were made 3500 years ago, probably by the forefinger of an ancient Minoan (Photograph by the author).

Also rich — with their mammoth multi-storied buildings, road systems, bridges, water fountains, fabulous gold and silver jewelry and indoor plumbing — were some of the final ancient guiding-goddess people we're aware of, the ancient Minoans. "The amount of bronze ... to have been in use" by the later Minoans, says J. Lesley Fitton, curator at the British Museum and a specialist in the Greek Bronze Age, "certainly shows the wealth of neopalatial Crete, particularly since the survival of such artifacts is greatly compromised by the fact that metals could be melted and re-used" (Fitton 2002: 156).

Only the Best — For Everyone

In the Indus Valley, says archaeologist Jane McIntosh, not only did everyone have all they needed, everyone had the best of all they needed:

No one seems to have wanted for any essential objects, and the same high-quality goods were present in households in villages and in cities.... All houses ... provided a comfortable existence with good facilities.... Despite the differences in size, the housing in the major Indus settlements was generally of a high standard, suggesting that even the 'least important' [sic][emphasis the author's] individuals led a comfortable existence (McIntosh 2002: 126-7, 100).

And while in the war-god societies you can take a gander at graveyard bones and tell who was eating lousy food and who wasn't, in the Indus Valley Civilization the bones all look alike. Why? Because every Indus person was dining on the same high-quality food: "[W]hereas in most stratified societies the elite show signs of being better nourished ..., no such differences can be seen in the ... Indus people ... — on the contrary ..., everyone had access to an adequate and balanced food supply" (McIntosh 2002: 126).

Astoundingly, even in the so-called "modern" era, India falls far short of the level of overall health, wealth and equalitarianism it enjoyed 4000 years ago under the Great Guiding Goddess. As a matter of fact, most of the rest of the world falls short, too. Archaeologist McIntosh hits the nail squarely on the head when she says the Indus people lived "a lifestyle that would be the envy of most today" (McIntosh 2002: 7).

Fig. 4.10. Modern Pakistani boys explore the ruins of Mohenjodaro. In this ancient goddess-centered city, the ancestors of these boys enjoyed an economic egalitarianism unknown in Pakistan today — or in most of the rest of the modern world (Copyright Images of Asia).

No Dictators, Despots or Bully boys

But darlings, I'm not done. Our ancestors weren't just brave, peaceful, fun-loving and rich. In his general survey of world prehistory, anthropologist William Haviland says they were politically savvy as well. They didn't allow themselves to be run over by despots. Instead, their organizational needs "were probably met by kinship groups and common-interest associations" (Haviland 1997: 274). If you could go back and visit the Minoans, Neolithics, or Indus-Valley people, you'd see among them not one evil Queen Bavmorda. You wouldn't even see a good Queen Alora Danan. Nuh-uh. Our Goddess ancestors would not have stood for it. The evidence is good that they governed themselves, thank you very much, and to heck with bully-boy (or bully-girl) rule.

And getting down to specific brass tacks, in some Near-Eastern areas at least, it looks as if the leaders weren't single, solitary individuals, but *groups* of people: "Several documents and myths suggest that Neolithic and early historic goddess-worshipping communities were governed by assemblies.... One Mesopotamian tablet said that 'Under the guidance of Inanna at Agade, its old women and its old men gave wise counsel.'... (B)efore the arrival of the Hittites, the Hattians," who were Goddess-centered people, had "originally been loosely organized in a number of independent townships, each governed by a body of elders" (Stone 1993: 130-31).

When it comes to the leaders of the glorious Indus Valley Civilization, the big problem is — no one can find them. Jane McIntosh pins on these phantom people the label "elusive." Unlike the rulers in their neighboring god societies, Indus leaders had no fancy-schmantzy burials: "It seems particularly surprising," murmurs Jane, "... that ... there have been no burials ... that stand out by the ... wealth of their grave goods and which could ... represent the rulers of Indus society." (Could be Jane's surprised because all her life — like most of the rest of us — she's called snooty-snob societies her home, and it's hard to imagine anything else.) What's more, says Jane, we'll probably *never* trip over any fancy graves for Indus leaders: "One could argue that, given the small numbers of cemeteries that have been found, the royal graves lie yet undiscovered. This is certainly a possibility, although it becomes increasingly unlikely as the volume of evidence of the civilization grows" (McIntosh 2002: 126, 118).

Not only did the Indus leaders have no fancy graves, they had no fancy, upscale homes either: "The Indus Civilization has no evidence of royal palaces" says Jane. What's more, they didn't do

"Look at me! Look at me!" the way the ancient Egyptian pharaohs and Assyrian bully-boy despots did: The Indus leaders showed "a complete lack of priestly pomp or lavish public display. There is nothing of the ardent militarism of the Assyrian kings or of the slavish glorification of the pharaohs.... These were no bombastic rulers boasting of their achievements on grandiose palace walls" (McIntosh 2002: 210).

Finally, McIntosh throws up her hands in despair and wails "Why are the Indus rulers so difficult to find?"!? Then she pauses, gets a grip, and says, "The answer must lie in the nature of their authority and the way of life and ideology associated with it." I agree, Jane. If you live in a Mother-Goddess world, where anyone's as good as anyone else, you don't try to stand out like a sore thumb. You blend. You downplay whatever makes you different. Bragging and strutting are totally uncool.

I suggest that the Bronze-Age Indus leaders, like leaders in the Neolithic, were outstanding people asked by their community to play leader for a while. What for gosh sakes makes us so certain the Classical Greeks of the first few centuries BC invented democracy? Until whites mashed them into the ground, most North American Indians ruled themselves. As a matter of fact, some scholars even make a good case for the US lifting its democracy not from the Greeks, but from democratic societies the American colonists danced with for 150 years before they concocted the Constitution: the tribes of the Iroquois Federation (see Jack Weatherford's *Indian Givers* and Paula Gunn Allen's *The Sacred Hoop*). So I ask: what makes it so hard to believe our Neolithic and Bronze-Age ancestors also enjoyed rule by the people?

For Japan too, we're minus evidence that despots, dictators, or bully boys forced themselves down the throats of the people. Same for Neolithic Southeastern Europe. Archaeologist Marija Gimbutas says "There is no evidence in all of Old Europe of a patriarchal chieftainate.... There are no male royal tombs and no residences in megarons on hill forts." But this, however, doesn't mean Old Europe was just a piddling place, too basic to need complex government. It wasn't "simply composed of small-scale segmentary societies...." For example, one of its people, the Late Cucuteni (4000-3500 BC), "reached an urban stage with towns of up to 10,000 inhabitants." And these sizeable towns sat "at the center of a district surrounded by medium and smaller size villages" (Pearson 2004: 4, Gimbutas 1991: 324, xi).

Moving on to the Minoans, if the experts agree on nothing else it's this: there's no evidence Minoans put up with dictator-type leaders running their lives. Like the Indus-Valley people, the Minoans plunked no clear pictures of rulers into their art. Meanwhile, the art of their father-god neighbors of the same time period — the Egyptians, Babylonians, Amorites and others — bristles with pompous pictures of pharaohs, dictators and miscellaneous tyrants. Even J. Lesley Fitton, one of the most scrupulous Minoan experts anywhere, admits that "we really do not know who, in Minoan society, held the reins of power" (Fitton 2002: 135). In sum, it seems more likely the Minoans were led by popular councils than by monarchs or hereditary rulers.

Guiding Goddessites: Ancient Techno Wizards

So far, the Guiding Goddessites sound way too good to be true: brave, playful, peaceful, prosperous and possibly democratic to boot. It's almost too rich for the blood. But believe it or not, I'm still not done. Mia, Jof, Willow, Raziel and Madmartigan all five are — I hate to say it — technological dunces. Even when you compare them to their neighbors, these five are technologically challenged. Since they're wandering gypsies, Mia, Jof and Madmartigan are minus the 'niceties' their non-wandering neighbors have: water wheels or wheat grinders, for example, or farm plows.

And technologically speaking, Willow's village lags behind other towns of the times. At least Madmartigan owns a spiffy suit of metal armor, and in some *Willow* battles he brandishes some pretty fancy metal weaponry. Willow's village, on the other hand, seems to have none of this stuff. Here again, our best visionaries have trouble plopping certain cultural characteristics onto the same page together — this time it's creativity, sensuality and playfulness onto the same page with technological know-how.

But tech-savvy our Goddess grandparents definitely were. It's been said that in 1700 BC, the Minoans were as technologically advanced as Europeans were in — get this — AD 1700. To me, this is an astounding statement. What it means is, after being beaten to a pulp by father gods, Europe took 3400 years to bounce back onto its feet again — technologically speaking at least. Like the rest of the industrialized world, in most other departments Europe still has far to go to get to where it was in guiding-goddess days.

At any rate, the ancient Minoans built bridges, fountains, architectural gardens, a system of paved roads, and as noted before, complex architecture that would have taken a heck of a lot of math and science to plan and construct. On tiny gold and silver rings they etched complicated scenes packed with goddesses, gods, boats, animals, plants and people — scenes so small scientists say they could not have been done without magnifying glasses or eye glasses — or both. Ten centuries before their great, great grandbabies the ancient Classical Greeks waltzed into view, Minoans were erecting super-sized buildings up to five stories high and covering a ground area the length and breadth of the modern American football field. With at least 1000 rooms and maybe more — we dunno if it rose three stories or four, or more — the "Palace" of Knossos near the modern city of Heraklion, Crete, was a stunning example. By using light wells shot from the top story to the bottom, the architects of this massive building were able to feed all its 1000-plus rooms twenty-four/seven with fresh air and natural light.

Of course "palaces" are where kings and queens hang out, and as we saw a few pages ago, there's no evidence Minoans

Fig. 4.11. Modern ruins of the palace-temple of Knossos, viewed from the northwest (Photograph by the author).

Fig. 4.12. Ancient Minoan steps inside the 1000-room palace-temple of Knossos, Crete. Who trod these steps 3500 years ago? And for what reasons? (Photograph by the author).

had either. Personally I think Knossos was more like a modern shopping mall than anything else. In it were not only retail shops and government offices, but anything else you'd want in the world outside your home: barber shops, beauty shops, theaters, concert halls, factories, lawyers' offices, college classes, science labs, saloons, schools, sacred spaces, and probably a nice sit-down restaurant or two.

Among all the world's earliest "civilizations," the Minoan and Indus alone show no signs of either war or braggart, bully-boy politics. One other thing these two guiding-goddess societies shared in common was indoor plumbing. Ten centuries before the Classical ancient Greeks, the Minoans boasted an "elaborate plumbing system that ran throughout the ... enormous" Knossos palace/shopping mall. This system "centered around a massive underground sewer that was of stone and cement, and ran downward to the nearest river. Attached to the sewer were four large, vertical shafts. Kitchen refuse, wastewater, household trash, and bathroom waste could be dropped directly into the shafts from any floor ... or flushed into drains...." There was even "at least one 'modern' bathroom, complete with tub and toilet" (Kugler 2002: 2).

Moving on now to the Indus Valley, homes there were two- to three-story affairs with court-yards, outside stairs and indoor bathrooms that boasted both bathing facilities and latrines. Some ancient Indus people even had showers: "a small stair along one side of the bathroom allowed another person to ascend and pour a steady stream of water over the bather. The bathroom floor, constructed of stone or sawn baked bricks, allowed the water to flow off into the efficient drainage system that served the city." And in "almost every house" was a latrine. Although most latrines consisted of clay

Fig. 4.13. Knossos, outside and from the northwest. Shown here is what was once probably part of the advanced plumbing/drainage system of this giant building (Photograph by the author).

Fig. 4.14. The ruins of what was probably a sit-down, indoor latrine in the 3500-year-old ancient goddess-centered Indus Valley Civilization city of Mohenjodaro. Almost all homes in Mohenjodaro had latrines — something never again to happen in the urban world until the middle of the 20th century (Copyright Images of Asia).

jars set into the floor, some Indus toilets had seats, and others were even connected to the city drainage system (McIntosh 2002: 100, 101).

The crowning glory of the Indus Civilization was their wicked good municipal waste-water system. Running under their streets and through their towns and cities, the plumbing pipes of the Indus people were punctuated with periodic covered inspection centers — so workers could drop down into the pipes and fix things when necessary (McIntosh 2002: 100). And if you think the fancy-schmantzy father-god "civilizations" of the same time period — Egyptians, Sumerians, Babylonians, and others — had anything like the Minoan and Indus grand plumbing systems, take another think. As a matter of fact, it wasn't for another 2000 years that things got this good again: The Indus Valley "management and use of the domestic and urban water supply were way ahead of those of any other civilization of their time. Not for another 2000-odd years were hydraulic engineers of this caliber to reemerge, with the Romans in the Old World and Chavin in the New." Unfortunately, the father-god Romans were snooty snobs. So unlike the case in the equalitarian guiding-goddess Indus Valley, in ancient Rome only the rich were treated to indoor bathrooms and latrines.

5

Before War

As Far as the Eye Can See: No War!

Of all the praises that can be sung about our Great-Goddess ancestors, probably the most stunning of all is their ability to live for hundreds — and in some cases thousands — of years without plunging into the hell that is human warfare. As we'll see later, as soon as father gods roared into town and mowed the Mother down, we had war 24/7 — for breakfast, lunch and dinner. But while the Mother Goddess watched over us, we had no war. In other words, there seems to be a link between on the one hand, guiding goddesses and peace, and on the other, father gods and war.

Imagine: a world without war. Otherwise well-educated people will tell you we're born biologically primed to wage war. That it's in our genes. Frankly my dears, these people don't have a clue. Before about 4000 BC, give or take a few years in either direction, and depending on where you are on the globe, there was no war. At least not what's called "institutionalized" war, where war is built into our social systems, so it's almost impossible to dig it out and pitch it on its ear, and where wars happen every few decades or so, regular as the beat of your heart.

Biologically Built for War?

I'm sure you've heard the fantasy tale — doubtless more than once as a matter of fact — that humans are biologically built to war, and that war's been with us from the beginning of time. For whatever reason, during the twentieth-century big batches of academics convinced themselves humans are born violent. Although some today still believe this hogwash, others are pointing to the obvious: given what we know now about our peaceful first cousins the bonobos and the numbers of nonwarring societies in the world, there's just no way human beings can be born violent. Pure and simple: if you're not taught war, you're not going to do it.

Come on: be logical, for Goddess' sake! If war is stuck in our genes, there wouldn't be any peaceful societies anywhere on the globe — no way Jose. But scads of peaceful peoples do exist, and scads more writers have written about them. For a list, go visit *www.peacefulsocieties.org*. Although my favorite peaceful societies are the Semai of the Malay Peninsula and the Paliyans of Southern India, there are dozens of others, which you'll see if you visit the website (or if you read *Keeping the Peace* by Kemp and Fry; Fry's *Beyond War*; Ashley Montagu's *Learning Non-Aggression*; Signe Howell and Roy Willis' *Societies at Peace*; Bruce Bonta's *Peaceful Peoples*; Leslie Sponsel and Thomas Gregor's *Anthropology of Peace and Nonviolence*, or one of dozens of other resource books. For more, tap those keys on over to *www.peaceful-societies.org*).

But it's not just peaceful societies that show war's not in our genes. Evidence is coming in from all directions: "archaeology, hunter-gatherer studies, comparative ethnography, the study of social organization, cross-cultural research findings on war and justice seeking, research on animal aggression, evolutionary theory, and ... cultural belief systems ... about war and peace." As University of Arizona anthropologist Doug Fry puts it, all this evidence is fitting together to make a whole greater than the sum of its parts. Humans are "really not so nasty after all," says Fry. We're more flexible than we think, and we have tons of ways other than war to manage conflict (Fry 2007: 211-12).

Despite all this evidence, however, some doodle-bugs just won't give up. "Scholars who study war are at war with each other" says anthropologist Keith Otterbein (2004: 11). Keith has dubbed the two armies in this war the "Hawks" and the "Doves." "But," I can hear you protesting, "if tons of peaceful societies exist, how could Hawks say (without blushing at least) that we're born to war?" The answer is, some doodle-bugs are just darn good at doodling. But look at it from their point of view: if we begin to suspect war is not something ordained on Day One, think of all the poor dears who'd suffer: the military industrial complex would be only a small start of a long list. Think of all the spies who'd be shoved out on the dole. West-Point instructors, military songwriters, The CIA — who'd need them anymore? C'mon! Have a heart!

Anyhow, in 2004 Doug Fry took pity on these potential losers, and published a little treatise called "Seven Ways to Make Peaceful Societies Disappear" (Fry 2004: 187-194). From the start of his essay, Fry warns that "peaceful" doesn't necessarily mean perfect. In all societies, people bicker and bark at each other. Not all societies, though, let this bickering boil over into violence. Also, we're not talking black and white, here. Societies fall onto a continuum that starts with "very peaceful," and slowly oozes on over to "very violent." Plus, even though among themselves some societies are peaceful ("low levels of physical aggression and nonviolent core values"), they still might do war every once in a while. Or maybe in the past they did war, but not now.

Pay particular attention here, because I'm going to pass on to you Fry's list of ways to eliminate peaceful peoples. You'll want to pass this list on to all your military-industrial-complex buddies, so they can use it in their spin about how we've always had war — and always will:

1. Hold up the peaceful society, "stridently emphasize violence, and simply ignore all evidence to the contrary." Dudes who are aces at this are Mikie Ghiglieri (*The Dark Side of Man* 1999) and the duo Richie Wrangham and Dale Peterson (*Demonic Males* 1996). Mikie ignores peaceful societies altogether, and like a dog worrying a bone keeps up a steady chant about how violent we all are. Unlike Mikie, Richie and Dale dare to dip a bit into the

peaceful-society lit. But they "mention and then dismiss the nonviolent Semai" — probably the most peaceful people on the planet — "in one short paragraph."

2. Another way to make peaceful societies disappear is to "set an impossible standard" — like demanding "a peaceful society ... be absolutely ... free of all ... aggression across time." Then, "find a few real or apparent exceptions to the impossible standard" among the world's peaceful societies. Last, pitch these societies "as clearly NOT peaceful." A dude getting gold stars for successful use of this little trick, is the ethologist Eibl-Eibesfeldt. Mr. E-E successfully confuses his readers by saying that since the Ju/'hoansi of the Kalahari Desert have their cranky moments, they are definitely not peaceful.

3. A third trick is to "count any type of conflict as if it were aggression." Oscar nominees for outstanding use of this technique, are Laura Betzig and Santus Wichimai ("A Not So Perfect Peace" 1991). These two say that since the Ifaluk of Micronesia have social inequality and "conflicts of interest" among groups, they are not peaceful (Shhhh! Don't tell anyone, but when four different trained observers spent a combined total of six months with the Ifaluk, they saw not one instance of violence, and only twice saw kids smacked for bad behavior).

4. Another nifty little item in Fry's bag of tricks is this: "cite an inflated homicide rate to exaggerate violence." For example, when no one's looking, drop a society's population down from 15,000 to 300, which will balloon their murder rate to 50 times what it really is. This was actually done to the Semai of Southeast Asia, and Master Lawrence Keeley (*War before Civilization* 1996) and others plunk the 50-times-too-high murder rate into their books to "prove" that the Semai are not peaceful paragons, but vile little vermin. Fortunately for the poor military-industrial

complex, once errors like this get into print, they never really go away.

5. Trick number five for making peaceful people disappear into thin air: "Regarding warfare in particular, make clever use of terminology to exaggerate the number of societies that engage in war." To be awarded for brilliant usage of this fine technique are Mr. Quincy Wright (*A Study of War* 1942) and — again — the cunning Master Lawrence Keeley. In *A Study of War*, Mr. Wright 'forgets' to include a category to plunk nonwarring societies into — he just lumbers around pretending that if attacked, all societies will fight back. As a matter of fact, they don't: "the ethnographic record shows many instances of nonwarring and other societies fleeing or moving away from aggressive neighbors rather than automatically fighting back."

If someone in your society sneezes, Master Lawrence Keeley lumps your whole society into the warring-society category faster than you can say "slick as a whistle." At this little trick, Keeley's an ace. A few of the big barrel of things that will cause Keeley to pitch you into the war category: Did a murder happen once in your society — say back in 1699? Whoops! Into the war category you go! Did two guys die when a landslide plunked a bucket of rocks on their heads? Whoa! For you it's the war category! Back in Great, Great Gramma's day, did a bunch die in a typhoid epidemic? All those bodies buried at the same time make Keeley think of — you guessed it: war!

6. Doug's final tip: Make it a habit to "create a bogus peaceful society, then destroy your creation." For boning up on this most creative of techniques — and getting the Samoans of Polynesia to help him carry it off — kudos go to Mr. Derek Freeman, author of *Margaret Mead and Samoa*. After insisting Margaret labeled the Samoans a peaceful people, Mr. Derek then sheds buckets of sweat proving they weren't. Just think: Mr. Derek could have spent all that time on his deck with his feet propped up sipping

fine wine. But no, he spent his hours in public service for all those potential welfare recipients in the military-industrial-complex. Anyhow, in technique six, the final crowning-glory step is to "extrapolate from the single case to a broader conclusion, that peaceful societies in general do not exist."

The plain fact is, we've dug up no evidence that the Neolithic and Bronze-Age guiding-goddess societies did war. As archaeologist Jonathan Haas puts it, "'endemic warfare was much more the exception than the rule until the first appearance of state-level societies between 4000 and 2000 B.C.E. in the centers of world "civilization."'" (quoted in Otterbein 2004: 34). Bill Haviland chimes right in behind Jonathan: in his survey of human prehistory, Bill mentions war only when he talks about the first state-level societies. And in her "The Natural History of Peace," Leslie Sponsel follows suit: "nonviolence and peace were likely the norm throughout most of human prehistory" (quoted in Otterbein 2004: 34).

Anthropologist and war-analyst Mr. Keith Otterbein says we don't have evidence that war or killing occurred in the early Neolithic at all, anywhere, anytime. There's "a lack of data" he says "to support the notion that homicide and warfare occurred in the early Neolithic..." (2004: 17). Otterbein's take on things is this: any scholar who thinks "the natural propensity of humankind is to live in peace and harmony can find in ... the early agriculturalists support for his or her position...."

But let's get down to the nitty gritty. Get out your fine-toothed combs, now, and let's go over each of the guiding-goddess areas we checked out before — Near East, Southeast Europe, Indus Valley, Japan — and hunt for signs of war. How about beginning in the Near East? Spin the wheel Willie.... For the Neolithic Near East, where will the needle stop? On "War" or "No War"?.... (Sound of wheel spinning...)

And it comes up ... No War!

Before War in the Near East

Keith Otterbein says war was unknown in the Near East until the Uruk period, which toddled along after the Neolithic around 4600 BC in what's known as the "inchoate early-state" era. Going on, Otterbein gives a whopper of an example of the monumental peacefulness of the Neolithic Near East: Located in what is today Syria, "… the settlement of Abu Hureyra, occupied from 9500 to 5000 B.C.E., is a wonderful example — nearly five thousand years of continuous occupation *and no warfare*" (emphasis the author's). This conclusion was based on "an examination of all aspects of the culture as well as numerous human skeletal remains," says Otterbein. Over its lifetime Abu Hureyra blossomed from a few hundred to roughly six thousand people. After almost 5000 years, it seemed to be nothing more than "increasing aridity" that finally forced the Abu Hureyrans to pack up and abandon their old home area (Otterbein 2004: 144, 222, 71, 92).

Let's move on now to another Neolithic Near-Eastern town — one we've visited before, the famed Catalhoyuk in what is today the country of Turkey. Michael Balter, the official site biographer, says everyone's still scratching their heads over why the Catalhoyukians scrunched themselves together into their tight, interwoven thicket of homes. Mostly stuck together like a bunch of honey pockets in a beehive, Catalhoyukian homes are separated now and again by the rare, narrow street. To get into this ancient town, you apparently had to climb a ladder onto someone's roof — archaeologists haven't found one single gate in the wall that circles the place.

Of course some of Keith Otterbein's War Hawks would no doubt whine that the Catalhoyukians huddled together for protection against other raging, war-like Neolithic lunatics. But for this there's no evidence: "there were few artifacts at Catalhoyuk that could have been much use as weapons; nor did the skeletons show any evidence of injuries from warfare." Digging at Catalhoyuk in the 1960s, the original excavator,

James Mellaart, "thought that some of the axes and daggers he found there were used in warfare...." However, "physical anthropologists who have studied the bones at this and many other early sites seldom see the kind of traumatic injuries that would be expected if warfare had been a regular occurrence." And as Otterbein points out, whatever the walls around the town were for, they *weren't* for defense against other humans — armed with a few ladders, anyone could have slunk over at night, swarmed into the town, and taken it in a trice (Balter 2005: 155-56, 283; Otterbein 2004: 242 n 26).

Before War in the Indus Valley

To make a long story short, while the Great Guiding Goddess steered the ship in the Neolithic Near East, war didn't happen there. But how about the Indus Valley? Indus Valley people had moved out of the Neolithic and into the early Bronze Age. Did the Great Guiding Goddess keep them too free from war?

The answer here also is — Tah Dah! Drum roll please: "Yes indeed She did." In total and mind-blowing contradiction to "what we would expect from experience elsewhere," says Jane McIntosh, "the clues from the Indus Civilization seem to be showing us a state without violence or conflict." Jane is dumbfounded: "Can this really be so, in defiance of all our experience of the world elsewhere? Who were these peace-loving people? Where did they come from? How did they come together to create a state?" (McIntosh 2002: 12).

Societies doing war leave behind a trail of telltale clues that give away their dirty little secret. They can't stand it, for example, until they paint and etch scenes of their battles, hand-to-hand combat, and armies facing each other with weapons bristling and war flags flying. In their cemeteries they leave men buried with shields, helmets, swords and battle axes. We find telltale signs on skeletons, such as parry fractures of the right forearm, and blades imbedded in bone. In their fields we find dead giveaway clues such as catapults, war chariots and siege engines.

Thing is, we don't find any of these dirty little clues in the ancient Indus Valley. No war art, no war weapons, no parry fractures, no siege engines. Oh sure, some of the towns and cities were surrounded by walls, but there's no sign that these took abuse from attackers (McIntosh 2002: 179-80; Kenoyer 1998).

What makes the peacefulness of the Indusites even more astonishing is that in their era, warlessness was totally unheard of: "When we look at the other civilizations we can see how unusual and unexpected this is. The texts of contemporary Sumer and Egypt are full of references to warfare and this is underscored by numerous depictions of soldiers, battles and war captives. The same was true of China, Mycenaean Greece and many other areas." While the ancient Egyptians and Mesopotamians hired artists by the hundred-pack to paint pictures of their rulers conquering enemies, the guiding-goddess Indus people dabbled in none of this kind of art (McIntosh 2002; Kenoyer 2005: 6 of 12).

Not only did the Indusites keep no armies (Kenoyer 2005: 4 of 12), the evidence suggests they didn't even have city police forces (McIntosh 2002). So what in the world kept them toeing the line? Here, ever ready with her thoughts on the matter, is archaeologist Jane McIntosh: Instead of a police force or army "there seems to have been some social mechanism," says Jane, "probably backed by religious beliefs, that ensured cooperation between the people...." Jane thinks this 'mechanism' might have been the caste system — you know: that daddy of all snooty-snobbism, found in India today, even as we speak? But as we've seen, umpteen signs show that the Indusites lived as equals — and that doesn't quite jive with the notion of caste divisions.

Scratching her head, McIntosh tosses out a second possibility: the threat of religious punishment. The problem with this, Jane, is that most of the world today sits shivering under the threat of father-god punishments (mostly 'hell'), but I don't see any father-god countries toodling along without police forces.

So Jane suggests a third reason the Indus people could live in cities without police: the "jajmani" system. Under the modern Indian jajmani system at least, "everyone within a community ... has obligations to provide the fruits of their ... labors to meet the needs of others, the potter making pots for all the village, for example, or the priest providing ritual services (such as marriage and funeral rites) for all, supported by food grown by the community's farmers.... Payment for these services are made in kind and are fixed by tradition" (McIntosh 2002: 180-81).

Although jajmani could be part of the answer, I don't think it's the total explanation of Indus self-control. Imagine it: cities almost double the size of Portland, Maine — the largest city in the state — toodling along year after year with not one police officer to hand out parking tickets, hound graffiti artists, or round up rowdies collecting outside Popeye's Ice House Bar and Grill on a Saturday night. I think what allowed the Indus to live in cities of up to 100,000 (McIntosh 2002: 104) without police was a sociocultural system based on the concept of a Guiding Mother Goddess. As common children of a Mother who sees you all as gorgeous and unutterably lovable, you see each other that way too. And if you've learned to respect and adore every last person you bump into, who's going to punch out anyone's lights? What's more, when you have all you need (not to mention the same-quality stuff everyone else has), why steal?

Before War in Japan and Europe

Okay. So much for India. Let's truck on over to Japan and find out about things over there. When they followed a guiding goddess were the Japanese also peaceful and nonviolent? The Japanese press has painted a picture of the Japanese Neolithic era, the Jomon, as a time of utopia (Pearson 2004: 7). But was it really?

Of course not.

As noted earlier, given our nature it's impossible for humans to crank out utopia. Even so, there's no telltale evidence that the

Jomon people, for almost 13,000 years, did warfare. And although during Jomon times there's "some evidence for disputes or aggression" there are "many fewer cases" than in the following Yayoi period — and nothing like what followed later when father-god people purloined the islands (Reimer 2004: 29; 31; Pearson 2004: 7, 9).

And Southeast Europe? After excavating in the area for decades, Marija Gimbutas was clear: while the Guiding Goddess steered the ship there, war failed to rear its ugly head in Southeast Europe: "The absence of weapons of war and hill forts over two millennia, from c 6500 — 4500 BC, argues for an absence of territorial aggression" (Gimbutas 1991: 331). In this area too, it's not until father gods roar into town that war struts onto stage.

In his overview of world prehistory, University of California archaeologist Brian Fagan says that at the end of their Neolithic (c. 2800-2400 BC), a cultural revolution erupted among central and Eastern Europeans. During the European Neolithic, the group was King. Suddenly, however, at the end of the Neolithic, the group took a back seat to the individual, i.e. to "individual power and prestige." And, says Mr. Fagan, although the sexes had been equal during the Neolithic, at the end of it, women suddenly become dirt under everyone's feet, with "prestige" reserved for men only. Old men got thrown under the bus too, with respect for elders giving way to respect for "men in their prime." And on top of everything else, suddenly there are weapons galore, with towns and cities moving from few if any weapons, to serious production of daggers, swords and battle axes. Finally and most alarmingly, Mr. Fagan says this: "everything points to the emergence of individuals who thought of themselves as warriors" (Fagan 2004: 260-61).

Folks, here come the daddy war Lords.

At the same time things switched from egalitarian peace, to war and snooty snobbism, Europeans also stopped making female figurines. When archaeologists Tringham and Conkey talk about

"...periods and places when clay figurine imagery is *not* made" one of the first places they tap on the shoulder is — you guessed it, southeast Europe at the end of the Neolithic, "the Late Eneolithic-Early Bronze Age of south-east Europe..." (Tringham & Conkey 1998: 36).

Moving on south now, what about the Minoans? Like the Indus Valleyites, the Minoans were people who had waltzed out of the Neolithic and on into the Bronze Age. In a nutshell, no one even bothers to suggest Minoans did war before they built their "palaces." For the palace/shopping-mall period, though, it's another matter. There's a bit of a fight on, over that.

In the recent past, archaeologists considered the Minoans totally peaceful throughout their centuries-long history. The Minoans lived where anybody could have picked them off in a fight — mostly on flattish land and in cities unprotected by walls. What's more, like the Indus Valleyites, they had no armies, never painted pictures of war, didn't have war weapons, and showed no battle scars on their bones.

But an important thing to remember about archaeology is this: one of the best ways to make a name for yourself is to kick dirt in the faces of the archaeologists who came before you (preferably the dead ones, who can't kick back). So these days, some are actually saying silly things like "Well yeah, we don't really see any Minoan weapons or walls or war art, but Hey! Look! Here are a few towns that were up on hills! Unquestionably that means war!" Krzysztof Nowicki, for example, "... presents a list of difficult-to-access settlements he calls 'defensible sites.' These sites, claims Nowicki, suggest Minoan warfare. Yet Nowicki's sites are vastly outnumbered by indefensible sites — a fact he neither denies nor adequately explains" (Studebaker 2004: 30).

To see how peaceable the Minoans were, just prop them up next to any of their neighbors — the Egyptians, Near Easterners, Mycenaeans and others — and than gawk at the contrast. It's literally black and white. Huddled like caged birds behind massive city walls, the Egyptians, Near Easterners and Mycenaeans also built their cities on the highest ground around, so attackers would have to sweat bullets to get to them. As regular as clockwork, their art shows war scenes in blood-dripping detail. "The contemporaneous Mycenaeans, for example, circled their cities with fifteen-foot-thick, fifty-foot high stone defense walls, and Mycenaean art clearly and frequently shows armed conflict" (Studebaker 2004: 28). And the skeletal remains of these war-god peoples are marked clearly with signs of war — mass graves with blades embedded in bones, parry fractures of the forearm, and other signs of armed group conflict.

Turning to the Minoans, the contrast literally smacks you in the face: you get a piddling number of Minoan towns and cities sitting on defensible sites. You get no fifteen-foot thick defense walls. In the art where there should be warriors, you get laughing men, dancing women, happy dolphins, flowers, and flying fish. You get no signs of war on skeletons. No blades imbedded in bones. No parry fractures. Sure there are so-called Minoan 'weapons,' but these were probably hunting weapons or work tools, not weapons of war. According to archaeologist Keith Branigan, "95 percent of so-called Minoan weapons possessed hafting that would have prevented their use as weapons. Furthermore some of these 'weapons' show virtually no wear and are made of metals too soft to even support their use as tools" (Studebaker 2004: 30).

Remember though — none of this means the Minoans were mama's boys. "Since war appears to have been relatively scarce in Minoan Crete" says Minoan expert Nanno Marinatos, "it should come as no surprise that contests, often of a violent character, took place" (Marinatos 1993: 212). Minoan art is stuffed, for example, with scenes of men and even small boys engaged in the sport of boxing. And then there's the remarkable Minoan game of bull leaping — so difficult and dangerous modern matadors say it can't be done. Finally, a full millennia and a half before the

Romans built ships making it even passably safe to do so, Minoan sailors were boldly sailing the high seas in search of trade and adventure.

The Myth That Underpopulation Means Peace

Maybe now's the time to tackle the myth that there was no war in the Neolithic because populations were small. I guess the idea is that Neolithics snuggled up in little groups of ten to fifteen, with the next nearest neighbor nowhere in sight. Or maybe the idea is that whenever you get more than a few of us humans together in one place, stuff gets scarce and everyone begins to fuss and fight over it — land, ladies and the last bottle of Lindemans Reserve Chardonnay, for example.

The fact is, however, there's no good relationship between underpopulation and peace, or overpopulation and war. According to University of Michigan anthropologist Raymond Kelly,

> population density ... does not provide a means of accounting for observed differences in the frequency of warfare among foraging societies.... This finding is consistent with Keeley's conclusion "that absolutely no correlation exists between the frequency of warfare and the density of human population" within cross-cultural samples that encompass all types of societies (Kelly 2003: 71; Kelly quoting Keeley 1996: 118).

Actually, instead of preventing war, underpopulation sometimes leads to it. For example when the Koreans were becoming a state (c 200 BC — AD 300), they began to do war because they needed a workforce, i.e. slaves. So in this case "underpopulation rather than overpopulation predicted warfare" (Otterbein 2004: 110).

What's more, not all Neolithic peoples were underpopulated. Take the peaceful, Goddess-centered, Neolithic Old Europeans for example. Their countryside areas seemed as densely peopled as any I know (outside modern large cities, that is). Old Europe took in the territory of modern Greece, Bulgaria, Romania, Hungary, Slovakia, Moldova, Croatia and Serbia and parts of the Ukraine, Poland, the Czech Republic, Austria, Bosnia-Herzegovina, Macedonia and Montenegro. Out of this vast territory, the archaeologist Marija Gimbutas pinpoints a relatively tiny area in the Uman region of Western Ukraine — one only 70 miles across and 50 tall (113 by 80 kilometers). Nevertheless, back in the Neolithic a remarkably dense carpet of Cucuteni people covered this pint-sized area.

Back in Neolithic Cucuteni times, this little spot was literally peppered with towns and settlements. The largest, Tallyanky, was 2.2 miles across and 1 mile deep (3.5 by 1.5 kilometers) with possibly up to 10,000 inhabitants. In Gimbutas' diagram, five large black circles symbolize settlements from 1 to 1-1/2 miles large (250-400 hectares). The next-to-the-largest circles represent five more settlements that are 62 to 185 acres large (25-75 hectares). Beyond that, however, the diagram bristles with almost 250 population centers under 62 acres each. And all this in an area only 70 x 50 miles large. One of the smallest Cucuteni towns, Petreni, measured 62 acres (25 hectares) — picture ten football fields lying side-to-side and end-to-end. Petreni inhabitants arranged their 498 houses (each about 26 feet by 16 feet, or 8 by 5 meters), in ten concentric rings (Gimbutas 1991: 104-107).

In short, in spite of its hefty population, Old Europe did not do war. Among the early-Bronze-Age Minoans, the same stood true: sizeable populations but no war. Recent population estimates indicate that in its heyday the Minoan town of Knossos was home to from 12,000 to 18,000 people (Muhly 2006). And in addition to Knossos, Minoans had four other large population centers: Mallia, Chania, Zakros and Phaistos. What's more, on the roughly 155-mile by 37-mile island of Crete (250 x 60 kilometers), archaeologists have excavated scores of smaller Minoan settlements. And it's not as if the Minoans were locked up on their island with no opportunity to plunder and lay waste to surrounding lands. As we saw previously, they traded on a regular basis all over the Mediterranean and up and down the Atlantic coast. Nevertheless, we have no evidence they made war on any of those they visited.

In the Goddess-centered Indus Valley Civilization, we find the same story: large towns and cities but no war. Blanketing a whopping quarter of a million square miles (402,336 square kilometers) in what is today India and Pakistan, the Indus Valley Civilization included over 1000 cities and settlements. Some of these were definitely hefty in size. Harappa for example was 60,000 people large. Looking at the UK, that's roughly the size of Maidenhead, Stafford or Royal Tunbridge Wells — nothing to sneeze at. In the US it's the size of Portland, Maine, the largest city in the state. Mohenjodaro, size-wise the runner-up to Harappa, contained a not-so-shabby population of roughly 30,000. The next three largest Indus cities were between 200 and 250 acres each (80 and 100 hectares) (McIntosh 2002: 103, 104; *City Population*; Maisels 2001: 187).

Each of the five Indus cities above seemed to be a hub for its own 38,000-square-mile population area (100,000 sq. kilometers) (McIntosh 2002: 105). Many small countries aren't 38,000 square miles large (take Portugal, Austria or Hungary for example), making these Indus cities somewhat akin to capitals plunked down in the middle of their own small countries. Nevertheless, the Indusites failed to carry on wars, conquests or attempts at subjugating each other. The five Indus city-states did not struggle to smother one another — which is exactly what was going on in the same era down the road in Egypt and Mesopotamia. And like the Minoans, the Indus Valleyites too were great long-distance traders, traveling as far as Mesopotamia to ply their wares. Like the Minoans, if they'd wanted to raid and plunder, they had plenty of chances to do so.

End of the Female Figurines

In many places around the world it's when large cities shoot up that female figurines quietly fade away. In his global look at ancient figurines, Lesure says that at the end of the Neolithic, female statuettes "often disappeared" (Lesure 2002: 587). And with their disappearance comes the world we've known since, one in which we're all ranked as good, bad, better and best. This is a world of mammoth cities and cobbled-together nations run by centralized, fire-eating political dragon-machines. And it's a world of war. Since the Goddess left us, our lives have been one big, voluminous valley of violence, conquest and empire-building — all courtesy of the daddy war gods.

6

Bad Times

... the coming of the Lord,
He is trampling out the vintage where the grapes of wrath are
stored;
He hath loosed the ... lightning of His terrible swift sword;
His truth is marching on.
Glory! Glory! Hallelujah! Glory! Glory! Hallelujah!
Glory! Glory! Hallelujah! His truth is marching on....

Who Popped Us in the Chops Ma?

Unlike our guiding-goddess ancestors of the Neolithic and early
Bronze Age, most of us today are clearly not living lives free of
snooty snobbism, violence, and war without end. So what
happened? What went wrong? I think in part it was this: What I
call a war-god dystopian package fell out of the sky onto the
world's comparatively utopian societies. Of course this is a gross
oversimplification. The package didn't fall at the same time in all
places around the globe (far from it), and the pieces of the
package didn't always fall all at once. And I'm not saying this
particular package and it alone is the cause of all the dystopia
dominating the historical era and the world today.

As much as some today try to deny it, large-scale general
patterns of change can be seen in the history of the human race.
One example is the shift, in various places around the globe, from
pre-state sociocultural organization, on the one hand, to the
dysfunctional "state" organization on the other. This was a
relatively sudden switch into dystopia, i.e. into institutionalized
warfare, political domination, divergent social classes ending in a
slave class at the bottom of the hierarchy — and dominating war
gods. The state first appeared around 4000 BC in the Near East

and Egypt, then a bit later in China, and lastly down the west coast of the New World. The shift from pre-state to state in several places around the world is not a post-modernist "narrative story"; it's a fact. (What caused this shift is the subject of scientific investigation and debate.)

Coined not that long ago, the word *dystopia* means "a place where everything is very bad" (*Encarta World English Dictionary* 1998-2004). Although where the first dystopian state packages came from we don't know, there are a few theories floating around — which we'll get to later. For now, let's check out the situation from the diagram shown in figure 6.1:

Figure 6.1: The Black Box

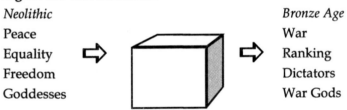

Neolithic		Bronze Age
Peace		War
Equality		Ranking
Freedom		Dictators
Goddesses		War Gods

As the diagram suggests, at the end of the Neolithic, people in many world areas were sailing along in the lap of peace, equality, and freedom, and with mother goddesses at their backs guiding them like a good wind. Next thing you knew, it was as if those societies suddenly ducked into a black box. Inside that box something bad happened. And although we don't know exactly what it was, we do know that when the goddess societies we've been following stumble out of the box in the Bronze Age, they're almost unrecognizable. They've morphed into brutish, snooty-snob, war-lovers, flattened out under the thumbs of war gods and repulsive bully-boy rulers.

When exactly our guiding-goddess ancestors ducked in and out of the black box differs from region to region. In southeastern Europe, people popped into the box around 4300 BC and stumbled out around 3500 BC. In the Near East, the Mesopotamians went in c 4000 BC, and came out again around the same time. The Indus Valley peoples lasted quite a bit longer, not entering until c 1500 BC, and popping out again about a thousand years later. On the Mediterranean island of Crete, the Minoans dropped into the black box c 1450 BC, and out again almost immediately — as the "Mycenaean-Minoans." The last holdouts were the Japanese Jomon, who didn't duck into the box until around 300 BC; like the Mesopotamians and Minoans, they too exited almost immediately — as the "Yayoi" (see figure 6.2).

Figure 6.2. The Switch from Guiding Goddess to War Gods

Area	Entered the Box	Exited the Box
Southeast Europe	4300 BC	3500 BC
Mesopotamia	4000 BC	4000 BC
Indus Valley	1500 BC	500 BC
Minoans	1450 BC	1450 BC
Japan	300 BC	300 BC

Now, the black box isn't totally black. It's as if we're shining a flashlight/torch with very weak batteries into it, one that throws thin, dim light onto a few murky clues about what might have happened when the goddess societies entered. As we'll see, the story differs in each of our five world areas, and yet the overall pattern is the same: a war-god-dystopian package gets its foot in the door, and the guiding-goddess utopia is weakened if not out-and-out erased (for a time at least).

So plunk yourselves into your traveling shoes again because we're heading across the world once more to check things out in person. This time though, we're about to enter some rotten sink holes. So please — hold your noses and hang on tight.

Europe in the Big Black Box

Since Europe seems to have been earliest to drop into the box, let's head on over there and tackle it first. From the thin stream of light shining dimly in the box, one of the first things we see is that between around 4000 and 3500 BC, the goddess peoples for some reason seem to be moving out of their gorgeous valley-bottom homes up onto higher-elevation, but lower-value real estate. Also, they seem to be throwing palisades up around their towns — as if trying to protect themselves from something or someone. The archaeologist Marija Gimbutas says that at this time the following European female-figurine-producing cultures begin to "disintegrate": Varna, Karanovo, Vinca, Petresti, Lengyel, Tisza, Butmir and Danilo-Hvar (Gimbutas 1991: 43, 436; see also Christensen p. 136; 153).

The next thing we see in the black box, is that between 3500 and 2500 BC all our lovely Goddess figurines disappear. Archaeologists Tringham and Conkey wonder, "What is the historical context of periods and places when clay figurine imagery is not made, such as ... the Late Eneolithic-Early Bronze Age of south-east Europe (3500-2500 BC)....?" And the great British archaeologist V. Gordon Childe says that in Europe, "as warfare becomes the norm ... female figurines, so ubiquitous in the earlier levels, are now 'no more in evidence'...." Archaeologist Bailey too, of the University of Cardiff, UK, says that in the Balkans (basically modern Greece) at the end of the Neolithic, the goddess figurines disappear from view (Tringham and Conkey 1998: 36; Childe 1958; Bailey 2005: 3).

Finally, by about 2800-2400 BC the stream of light in the black box is outlining a fairly clear picture of a new type of people stepping onto stage — in Eastern Europe at least. Unfortunately these new kids on the block are showing signs of snooty snobbism, with young men getting all the grave goodies and "personal achievement and prestige associated with males" (Fagan 2004: 260-61). In contrast, the Goddessites had typically laid themselves to rest in "communal" graves, in which everyone was buried together — and more or less equally.

To archaeologists, group burial is almost always a sign that people are considering the group a little more important than any one individual person. But with these new kids on the block, the young men with all the grave goodies appear too "good" to be buried with everyone else. Instead they're buried in "individual graves," making some archaeologists think they thought themselves a bit better than everyone else (Fagan 2004: 260). (Whether anyone else thought so is another story altogether.)

Chillingly, archaeologists call these people "the Battle-Ax culture," since their men are buried with them — battle axes that is. In their arsenals these Axers kept not just battle axes but "many weapons, such as daggers and swords...." According to University of California archaeologist Brian Fagan, everything points to the fact that Axers "thought of themselves as warriors" (Fagan 2004: 466, 261).

On the subject of Battle-Axer religion the black box is fairly mum. Some, however, think the Battle Axers were also "Indo-Europeans," and we do know a bit about Indo-European religion. What we know about Indo-Europeans is based not on archaeological artifacts they left in the ground, but on the fact that most Europeans and East Indians speak languages that are cousins to each other. European and several East Indian languages are so similar that it's almost certain they're descendants of the same grandpapa proto-language. And of course where there's a language, there's usually a people.

Anyhow, by looking at how similar or different two Indo-European languages are, linguists can tell how long ago the languages split from each other. And most say the European branch did actually split from the Asian branch at about the time the Battle Axers waltzed into Europe. In other words, the Battle Axers could very well be the fabled Indo-Europeans. We are, however, treading on thin ice here, since there's a whopper of a war going on over the Indo-Europeans (see for one Leeming 2005: 200, and for another Kristiansen 2005). After all, we're talking about what appear to be ancestors of quite a few of us around the globe, so we're all a little touchy about who these people were, where they came from, and how bad they were (for a recent skirmish in the war see Kristiansen's "What Language Did Neolithic Pots Speak?").

Nevertheless, Miriam Robbins Dexter of the University of California at Los Angeles says there's a boatload of evidence — genetic, archaeological and linguistic all three — that beginning around 4500-2800 BC the snooty-snob, war-like Indo-Europeans "expanded" into Guiding-Goddess territory in Southeastern Europe (Dexter 2005). Archaeologist Kristian Kristiansen (2005) agrees. Meanwhile, University of Connecticut mythologist David Leeming cuts to the chase: Whoever the people were who came charging into Eurasia around this time, they were definitely warlike snooty snobs, and they definitely brought in new deities who knocked the old ones for a loop:

> What can be said for certain is that there were several stages of conquest … from the north into … cultures of the Bronze Age in Europe, Anatolia, Iran, and India; that the conquerors … brought a body of myths … reflect[ing] the patriarchal, hierarchical, and warlike social and political structures of the conquerors; and that the new gods, goddesses, and heroes undermined but did not completely eliminate the ones found in the lands they invaded (Leeming 2005: 200).

But getting back to the Battle Axers: if they actually were Indo-Europeans, we could say a few things about their religion. All we'd have to do is pick out the cards the early historical Indo-European peoples held in common — religion-wise, that is. For example, from early historical records we know the religions of the Indo-European ancient Greeks, Germans, Scandinavians, East Indians and others. If we pick out the religious stuff they all shared in common, we'd have Axer religion — or at least something akin to it.

When we do this, the first thing we notice is the Indo-Europeans have no Great Guiding Goddess. As a matter of fact, they barely made room for goddesses at all. And the ones they did let hang around outside the kitchen door, didn't do anything fancy or important. For example, none of them created anything — they just hung out with the male gods. Indo-European "female goddesses, like the Dawn and Sun Maiden" says Marija Gimbutas, "were not creatrixes but … simply brides or wives of male deities" (Gimbutas 1991: 399 col. 3).

What Indo-European religion did have, however, was a ton of tough-guy gods — thunder gods and war gods for example. One of the toughest was the "God of the Shining Sky," also known as "Dieus," a dude who gets his main points across not through words, but through his weapons (Gimbutas 1991; Jackson 2002). Dieus is "known in various Indo-European groups from early historic records" as "the Indic Mitra, Baltic Dievas, Roman Dius Fiduis, Janus, and Mars, Celtic Lug (called 'Sun faced'), German *Tiwas, … Anglo Saxon Tiw, German Ziu, Icelandic Tyr, northwestern Slavic Jarovit-Sventovit, and others…. His powers are transmitted by his weapon, the dagger …" (Gimbutas 1991). In ancient Greece, Dieus became Zeus.

Frankly folks, I hate to say it, but this dude Dieus was a dirtbag. Turns out he was into incest. In the oldest myths we have of him, "he once approached his own daughter, Usas, in the appearance of a bull," and "more or less successfully tried to rape her," after which he "was punished for the act by the other gods" (Jackson 2002: 73). Since every culture known to humans has stamped incest a taboo, we need to suspect that the god Dieus had something seriously wrong with him. Unless of course we suddenly decide to reverse all of human history and catapult incest into the "mentally healthy" category.

Second only to the mentally deranged Dieus was the Thunder God, "Perk-uh-nos" aka "Striker." Perk-uh-nos (I like to call him

"Perky Nose") was a "hunter and warrior," and the god "best preserved in all Indo-European mythologies...." Perky Nose had a cute habit: he "smiled (*smei-) down lightnings [sic] on[to] earth" (Gimbutas 1991: 399; Jackson 2002: 75-76). Lightning — the stuff that sets fire to things, including forests, home to many of the earth's living creatures. So what — out of Perky's happiness comes fiery destruction? What kind of god are we dealing with here? Does the word "sadistic" come to your mind like it does to mine?

To the early Indo-Europeans, weapons were gods. Literally. No I mean it — they thought certain weapons *were* gods. Some Indo-Europeans actually made sacrifices to particular spears or swords. "'Weapons ... were worshipped as representations of the god himself. The sacredness of the weapon is well evidenced in all Indo-European religions. From Herodotus we know the Scythians made sacrifices to their sacred dagger, Akenakes'" (Eisler 1987: 49, quoting Gimbutas). I wouldn't be at all surprised if before climbing into bed at night, Indo-Europeans didn't get down on their knees in front of their weapons. Can't you just hear them? "Now I lay me down to sleep, I pray my Sword my soul to keep..."?

Some of the earliest images we have of Indo-European gods are securely or tentatively dated to around 3000 BC. In *The Civilization of the Goddess*, Marija Gimbutas shows four of these: ancient humanoid-type stone slabs decorated with weapons (Gimbutas 1991: 396, 398). Two come from

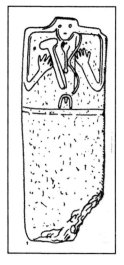

Fig. 6.3. One of the earliest known portrayals of a war god. Decorated with nothing but weapons and a belt, this stone-slab deity hails from the Ukraine, north of the Black Sea. Ca. 3000 BC 144 cm high (4.72 ft.) (Courtesy of the Journal of Indo-European Studies).

Fig. 6.4. To ancient Indo-Europeans, weapons were gods, and gods were often weapons. Some early Indo-Europeans actually made sacrifices to particular "holy" spears, axes or other weapons. This stone god too comes from north of the Black Sea. Ca. 3000 BC c. 1.5 m high (4.92 ft.) (Courtesy of the Journal of Indo-European Studies).

the Ukraine, north of the Black Sea — considered by most part of the original homeland of the proto-Indo-Europeans. The second pair — remarkably similar to the first — comes from northern Italy and Transylvania (Romania). Three of these gods are decorated with nothing but belts and weapons. In addition, the fourth seems to be wearing a scarf or tie of some sort. The stone-slab god from Italy is almost ten feet tall (3 meters). His 14 arms are represented by 14 halberds. For those of you minus a good weapons education, a halberd is a pike fitted with an axe-blade at one end. This darling deity also wears a dagger at his throat, four daggers on his chest, and five daggers above and below his belt.

Whomped Again in the Near East

Dropping down south and east from Europe, now, let's wing our way over to the Near East and scope out the situation there. Like the war-god package that pounded Europe, the one that routed the Near East (beginning roughly around 4000 BC) was also stuffed full of snooty snobbism, domination, war and violence. In the Near East, the bearers of this delightful package were called "Urukians," after one of their major cities, Uruk, located on the lower Euphrates River. The Urukians were ancestors to the famous Sumerians, inventors of the world's first "civilization." You know, the Cradle of Civilization you studied in elementary school, the one cradled between the Tigris and Euphrates rivers in what's now Iraq? (As we'll see later, what our school teachers called civilization was anything but civilized.)

Figure 6.5 Timeline: Ancient Mesopotamia (data from Maisels 2001: 125)

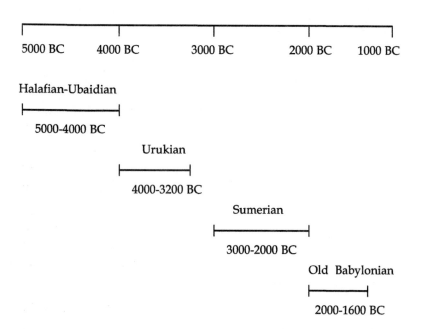

For now, however, one way to look at the switch from goddess to god in the Near East is to watch it quickstepping into one ancient city, Ur. Also located on the lower Euphrates, Ur was excavated from 1922-1934 by a joint expedition of the British Museum and the University of Pennsylvania, an excavation headed up by one Sir Leonard Woolley. At Ur, Sir Leonard found the last traces of guiding goddessites in a layer of earth cradling the remains of a people called "Ubaidians."

The Ubaidians lived not just at Ur, but all over ancient Mesopotamia. While they churned out a fair number of female figurines, they made almost none of the male sex. For example, out of 76 Ubaidian human figurines unearthed by archaeologists before 1968, 18 are sexless, 3 are male, and a whopping 55 are female. (Ucko 1968: 366). And at Ur, says Sir Leonard, Ubaidian anthropomorphic figurines are "always female" and are "goddesses who must not be represented otherwise" (Woolley 1965: 31, 34).

According to anthropologist Keith Otterbein, the Ubaidians were peaceful, non-warlike people who lived around 4700-3700 BC and had little snooty-snobbism or dominating stuff clanking around inside their towns. He does, however, see snootiness and a wee bit of pushiness happening at the end — stuff totally absent from the earlier goddess populations in Mesopotamia (for example, the Halafians we visited earlier). As far as Sir Leonard Woolley's concerned, the Ubaidians he uncovered at Ur were a "fairly sophisticated community," their pottery "superior to any ... until the Arab Conquest." (Otterbein 2004: 144; Woolley 1965: 23.)

Resting on top of the Ubaidians, Woolley uncovered a massive layer of flood silt — in some places a whopping eleven feet (3.3 meters) deep. And on top of the flood layer was another layer of Ubaidian stuff, but only a very "thin" one — which of course means the Ubaidians didn't do very well climbing back up onto their feet after the mammoth flood hit them. And then, on top of the pitifully thin final remains of the post-flood Ubaidians, is a dirt layer laced with Ubaidian and some entirely new stuff: a kind of inferior pottery and other paraphernalia that signals the coming of — ta da! — the grungy, war-god Urukians.

Chillingly, in the next layer the Ubaidians have vanished, and all that's left are the "invaders," who "settled down there alongside" the Ubaidians "and ended by acquiring such a supremacy over them that the old arts and techniques were superseded by those which" the Yukky Urukians "brought with them." According to Woolley these invaders "very soon made themselves the masters of the country."

No doubt about it, the Urukians were big, fat bully boys. Anthropologist and expert on the ancient Near East Charles Keith Maisels lays it out point blank: the "Uruk period of the fourth millennium" BC was the start of "social control" and domination. And according to anthropologist Keith Otterbein, with the coming of the Urukians "coercion based on priestly authority" first reared its ugly head (Woolley 1965: 37-38, 32; Maisels 2001: 146).

There's even evidence that Urukian "assistants of officials" used mace heads to bully people into doing their bidding. Maceheads were manufactured in the Urukian city of Susa. When Henry Wright excavated a manufacturing workshop in Susa, he found among other things "... four alabaster and calcite maceheads of a type fixed onto a handle with straps, some finished and some unfinished, perhaps for social coercion or display.'" To which anthropologist K. Otterbein adds an aside: "I doubt," says K., "they were for display..." (Otterbein 2004: 148).

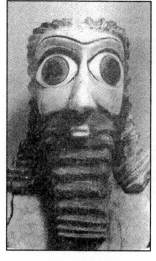

Fig. 6.6. Although it's not known for certain, many think this is the head of the war god Ninurta. It comes from a statue found at Tell Asmar, Iraq, that dates to ca. 3000 BC (Courtesy of the Oriental Institute of the University of Chicago).

Mr. C. Lamberg-Karlovsky of Harvard University thinks that even though Urukians invented a lot of what looks like impressive stuff, the main reason they invented it was so they could bully better. So for example, although the Urukians invented "writing..., standardized units of measure ... and cylinder seals..., [t]he above ... are best viewed as the invention of a technological complex devoted to social control. All ... were invented ... to monitor the production, consumption, and redistribution of ...

Fig. 6.7. Clay Figurine from Babylonian Era, possibly the war god Ninurta. Found near the ancient Babylonian city of Nippur. 116 mm tall (4.6 inches) (Courtesy of the University of Pennsylvania Museum).

labor and commodities" (2002: 975). In other words, the Yukkians … er Urukians … invented writing so they could keep track of how many slaves they had doing what jobs in what buildings, and to keep track of how much food each slave was allowed to eat each day.

Even the art of the day shows the switch from a guiding-goddess- to war-god package. Archaeologist Mitchell Rothman sees the art shifting in the early Urukian period from scenes of nature, animals and ritual, to increasing signs of bully-boy domination in later periods: "The seal designs of LC1-3 [c 4250-3900 BC] emphasize natural and ritual scenes or animals. Later LC4 and 5 seals [c. 3400-3000 BC] show 'commanding figures in charge of ritual, judgment, battle and other aspects of life' and also scenes of large-scale craft and storage activities, presumably under central control." Sealings, by the way, were our ancient ancestors' tear-off receipt books: "The comptroller who broke the sealing would keep one piece, and the other piece would be sent to its allotted destination" (Rothman 2004: 12 of 33). Kind of like when FedEx delivers a package to your door. The FedEx bloke gives you a receipt showing you paid, but he keeps a copy of the receipt, too.

Not only were the Urukians bully boys, they were snooty-snobs to boot. "The Uruk period," says anthropologist Maisels, saw the beginnings of "social … stratification." Right behind Mr. Maisels is anthropologist Keith Otterbein, agreeing: during the

Uruk period "social classes" shot up all over the landscape like poison toadstools (Maisels 2001: 146; Otterbein 2004: 144).

Worst of all, unlike the goddess-focused Ubaidians and Halafians, Yukkians were totally into war. As early as 3200 BC, says Otterbein, they were battling each other in southern Mesopotamia in full-scale warfare. And plain old warriors weren't good enough for them — they kept an "elite warrior" class armed with "maces, bows and arrows, and spears." Possibly, says Otterbein, the first armies were "upper-class followers of chief-priests," with warriors wearing body armor "of capes and copper helmets." Urukian cylinder seals show war captives bound with their hands behind their backs, and kneeling in front of authority figures. Behind them stand guards wielding — what? Maybe clubs. Or, offers Otterbein, maybe "open devices — like tennis racquets without strings — that can be placed over the heads of captives for leading them." Were these captives made into slaves, or were they executed? Although we don't know, says Otterbein, we do know that "centuries later both fates awaited them" (Otterbein 2004, 144, 148-149).

Fig. 6.8. Scimitar-armed, 82-mm-tall figurine (3.2 inches), possibly the Babylonian war god Bel-Enlil. Found near the ancient Babylonian city of Nippur (Courtesy of the University of Pennsylvania Museum).

What we don't know about these early sterling representations of human flesh would fill the Titanic. We know only a few bare-bones facts about their towns and houses. It seems that in some periods, Yukkian towns had "neatly planned residential, industrial and administrative quarters." Inside these, certain Yukkians at certain times lived in large, three-part homes, each apparently housing a slew of people. Also, after 3500 BC they had "an evolving settlement pattern of dominant city states surrounded by politically subordinated towns and villages" (Bower 1990: 5 of 9; Lamberg-Karlovsky 2002: 975).

One thing we do know for certain, however, is that "dramatic landscape change" happened during the centuries before, during and after the Urukians stepped onto stage. The massive flood that pummeled Ur and many other Tigris-Euphrates-Valley cities was just one part of the wild climate-change ride that was pounding Mesopotamia when the Urukians came to power. In the melee, many towns disappeared. Others blew up like Topsy into the world's first cities (Fagan 2004; Maisels 2001: 175).

It was as if people were banding together for safety, or as if food and water could be found only in certain places. The city of Uruk itself blew up from 70 hectares at the beginning of the Uruk period to 600 hectares at the end. Six hundred hectares is about 2.3 square miles. This is huge. Even in its heyday, ancient Rome measured only about 1.3 square miles (360 hectares) (Maisels 2001: 175) — and Uruk existed four thousand years before ancient Rome.

Fig. 6.9. Carrying five curved scimitars, a double-thonged whip, and a hatchet, half of this Babylonian war god (possibly Ninurta) is visible above the center rail of his war chariot. Found Near the Babylonian City of Nippur (Courtesy of the University of Pennsylvania Museum).

As for religion, if the Urukians made goddess or god figurines, no one's talking about them. According to British Museum curator and leading authority on cylinder seals Dominique

Collon, the Urukians were "slow to evolve a depiction of deities." The first ones they do finally show, around 3400 BC, are on seals and come from Susa in southwestern Iran. These seem to be not goddesses but gods. One such deity wears an elaborate headdress and holds a bowl in the air. Even though this deity wears a skirt, Collon says he's probably male not female — he's minus breasts, hips, and that extra layer of body fat that women carry compared to men.

At the very end of the Uruk period, says Collon, Uruk art begins to show symbols that would later be paired with the Sumerian Goddess Inanna. One such symbol is a bundle of reeds with streamers attached (1990: 44). Inanna herself, however, fails to appear in Yukky Urukian art. Although we can't tell for certain, this evidence would fit nicely with the idea that the goddess of the Halafians and/or Ubaidians was trying to make an official comeback at the end of the Urukian period, and then did so — as the Goddess Inanna — after the Urukians gave way to the Sumerians.

Fig. 6.10. Babylonian God Enkidu holding what may be a colossal club. Found near the ancient city of Nippur 67 x 60 mm (2.6 x 2.4 in.) (Courtesy of the University of Pennsylvania Museum).

When the first written records begin to speak about religion, they do indeed speak about the Goddess Inanna. They also, however, burble on and on about a war-god named "Ninurta," with whom Inanna had to share the stage. At first just the god of thunder in the form of a thunderbird, Ninurta later morphed into a deity boasting a man's body. One cylinder seal shows him holding a bow in one hand and an arrow in the other. The arrows represent lightning, and you can almost see thunder roaring out of the mouth of the lion crouching at Ninnie's feet.

Leeming tells us that "Ninurta … wage[d] a preemptive war against his enemy Azag." The ancient Sumerians wrote "hymns" to him. One the translator calls "To Ninurta as a God of Wrath." This holy song "exalts Ninurta as a god of wrath who roams about in the night, and is dedicated to battle …; he … crushes the … rebellious lands;… he brings about the destruction of the enemy and of the … disobedient" (Leeming 2005: 289; Pritchard 1975: 124).

The Rascals Run Roughshod Over the Indus Valley

Time now to tango on, east to South Asia, to territory currently encompassed by the countries of Pakistan and India. By the time the switch from guiding goddess to war god sashayed into India, the great Indus Valley civilization had long since withered away (we're not sure why). At switchover time, the Indus people were living not in large cities, but in small, peaceful villages again, about which we don't know a whole heckuva lot. And when the war-goddites rode into town, being nomads they brought next to nothing with them but the clothes on their backs. So's there's not much in the archaeological record to account for either side in the battle that took place in India at some point in the second millennium BC (Bamshad et al. 2001: 2).

However we're fairly certain that the dudes who rode in to do damage were the same Indo-Europeans who hit Europe around 4300 to 3500 BC — or at least cousins to those dudes. Archaeologist Brian Fagan talks about a "conquest" of the Indus peoples by the Indo-Europeans (actually in India, Indo-Europeans are usually called Indo-Aryans). Anthropologist Charles Keith Maisels too says "there can be no doubt" that the incoming Indo-Aryan pastoralists "imposed themselves as dominant classes" onto the East Indians (Fagan 2004: 419-20; Maisels 2001: 249).

It's likely that these Indo-Aryan rascals invented the Indian caste system: "The conventional conception of the advent of caste ... is through a form of conquest theory. In it the Aryans, who arrived at the Indus region around the middle of the second millennium, were characterized by three social categories: warriors/aristocracy, priests, and the rest, which became a four-caste system on subjugation of the indigenous population" (Maisels 2001: 250).

Chances are, when these Indo-Aryan doodle-bugs got to India, they ripped people's lands away from them, and then shuffled the people off into slavery. A few native Indians, however, were probably too wily for the doodles to mess with. And once the Indo-Aryans discovered they couldn't beat the wilies, they joined 'em — by making up a club called "high caste" and plopping themselves and the wilies in it together: "'Indo-Aryans placed themselves and those they could not dispossess of their land, in the elite castes — those in the three 'twice-born' varnas at the top of the hierarchy — appropriating to themselves the land and labor of those they dispossessed'" (Maisels 2001: 249 quoting from Berreman 1983: 242-43).

Actually there's strong genetic evidence that Indo-Aryans were indeed the proud authors of India's plug-ugly caste system. Since past genetic studies dealing with this issue have come up with confusing results, the researchers of this latest study (Bamshad et al.) used five different tests to compare the genetic makeups of East Indians, Europeans, Africans and Asians. What they found was a lot of European genes in India — old ones too, not ones from say when the British ruled India in the 1700s and 1800s. What's more, these genes didn't come from European women, they came from European men: "...admixture with West Eurasian males was greater than admixture with West Eurasian females, resulting in a higher affinity to European Y chromosomes." What this suggests is that "the majority of immigrating West Eurasians may have been males" (Bamshad et al. 2001: 3, 7-8).

Now the bombshell: Bamshad's study shows that although Eurasian genes are scattered all over India, they're not scattered all over the various Indian castes — not equally anyway. In the lower castes they appear hardly at all, in the mid-level castes somewhat, and in the upper castes most of all: "...five different types of data (mtDNA HVR1 sequence, mtDNA RSPs, Y-chromosomes STRs, Y-chromosome bialleic polymorphisms, and autosomal *Alu* polymorphisms) support the same general pattern: relatively smaller genetic distances from European populations as one moves from lower to middle to upper caste populations" (Bamshad et al. 2001: 7). What this shows, think Bamshad and his research partners, is that Indo-Aryan bully boys created the caste system and plunked themselves into the top caste. How they did it is a complete mystery. Was it by sweet talk, or assault and battery? I'll let you place your bets on that one.

What about Indo-Aryan religion? We've already learned a tad about this religion from our trip to switchover-Europe. Remember the God of the Shining Sky, alias Dieus, who raped his daughter Usas? In India this same god pops up in the earliest written religious records — the Rg Veda — alongside the same daughter, the ill-used Usas. Heather Elgood, Course Director in Asian Art at the British Museum, says the Rg Veda has not even one major goddess in it. However, she says, Usas is the "most significant" of the ones who do show up for dinner. Usas is goddess of dawn. Why am I not surprised — if your pop tried to rape you, wouldn't you be up at the crack of dawn every morning too?

Not surprisingly, another god who crops up in the Rg Veda is the infamous Indra, Vedic god of war. "Indra of the Rig Veda is the ... old Indo-European warrior god Zeus/Jupiter/Odin, the god of the warrior class (*ksatriyas*).... He is the destroyer of cities — the conqueror" (Leeming 2005: 202). Jolly good, jolly good.

Myce or Min?

Winging our way west again, we drop down now on the Mediterranean island of Crete. As they do in Europe and the Indus Valley, on Crete too the Indo-Europeans make it to the switchover party from Goddess to war god. On Crete the baddies are called Mycenaeans — or "Myce" for short. In general, the Myce are unremarkable. Even most of their "large" towns measured only a few hectares (a hectare is about 2.5 acres). Despite the impressive looking Lion Gate at their town of Mycenae, Mycenaean architecture in general is "not impressive" and their houses are crude (Dickenson 1994: 78, 80).

Nevertheless, around 1450 BC the Indo-European Myce brought to Crete a package similar to the one other Indo-Europeans brought to Europe and the Indus Valley: one bristling with snooty snobbism, domination, traces of a war god, and if not war, at least the threat of it. Take snooty snobbism for starters. Among the Minoans the palaces are gorgeous, but the peoples' homes aren't bad either. And in the grave-goods department, everyone looks more or less equal. With the Myce, however, it's a different story altogether.

First there's the matter of Myce homes — the ones on the mainland of Greece, where the Myce came from before whomping Crete. They're pretty poor — only a couple of rooms (and not very nice ones at that). Myce palaces, on the other hand, are grand. So there's a "considerable gap," as Dickenson puts it, between palaces and the peoples' homes. Also, a big gap yawns between the ordinary peoples' graves and what Dickenson calls Myce "princely tombs," the latter being stuffed with gold, silver and all kinds of pricey gee gaw, baubles and such. In other words, the Myce seemed to have a "ruling class" that "celebrated its status with lavish burials." In short, says Dickenson, "all sources imply" that snooty-snobbism ran thick as thieves among the Myce (Dickenson 1994: 79, 85, 302, 304).

But the Myce were not only snooty, they were also bullies. Just

Fig. 6.11. Clay seal impression of a probable Mycenaean god. He seems to be mocking the Minoan Goddess of the Mountain, who appears in a scene very similar to his (Courtesy of the University of South Carolina Press).

like the Indus-Valley Goddessites, the Minoans showed absolutely no sign of having a dominating power-over ruler. The Myce, however, put an end to that in a hurry: they brought a do-as-I-say "monarch" to Crete with them — the "wanax." When he came to Crete, the wanax burned all the Minoan palace-temples to the ground — except for the fab one in the city of Knossos, which he kept for himself. And while he ate like a piglet in the palace, he apparently starved the Minoans: "...signs of malnutrition, especially the markings in tooth enamel that indicate periods of arrested growth, are found in Crete ... but in the Late Minoan III cemeteries," i.e. Myce-time cemeteries. It seems they are "absent from the Middle Minoan contexts" (Dickenson 1994: 305, 88).

The Myce also brought dominator gods, including Zeus, descendant of Dieus, same delightful god who raped his daughter Usas, Goddess of Dawn. (We know, because Zeus is listed in the Linear B records the Myce kept; unlike the Minoan's Linear A script, we've deciphered Linear B.) Although the Minoans had a few male gods, they seem like mentally healthy, peaceful beings. But the Myce — once again — are another story. In addition to dirt-bag Zeus, they dragged over other gods too — most of them worth their weight in fleas. For example in their art we see what are called "smiting-god figures," figures similar to ones found in the Near East after the war gods hit. And there's evidence of a Myce god named "Enyalios" — "a name that

Fig. 6.12. Minoan Goddess of the Mountain, shown
standing in front of a key religious symbol — the
Minoan horns of consecration (Courtesy of the
University of South Carolina Press).

survived into Classical times as an epithet of" the Greek War God
Ares.

But the most sinister god (Fitton 2002: 178) of all is one archaeologists call "the Master Impression." The Master was found on
Crete and dated to the era in which the Myce hit the island.
Menacingly and over the top of what appears to be an entire
Minoan city, The Master stands with a staff at the end of one stiff,
outstretched arm — as if he owns the place. He seems to be
mocking the Minoan Guiding Goddess, who appears earlier in a
scene in many ways identical to the one The Master's in (see Ch.
3, "Great Mother of the Mountain").

Both god and goddess stand on top of a thin, triangular object.
Both hold their bodies almost impossibly erect. Both hold one
hand at the waist and the opposite arm jutting stiffly into space.
Both hold staffs into space and perpendicular to their bodies. But
that's where the similarities end, and the powerful differences
take over. While the Goddess stands in nature on a mountain, the
God stands over a city on a people-built construction. At the
Goddess' feet are wild animals, and in front of her a male

worshipper. In the god picture, on the other hand, other than The Master himself, there's not a hint of anything alive or breathing.

Then there's the matter of religion. Most archaeologists consider the Master a god. There's not, however, a whole heckuva lot of religion going on around him. The Goddess on the other hand, not only has a worshipper paying Her homage, behind Her are three sets of a universally accepted sign of Minoan religion: the "horns of consecration."

Fig. 6.13. Horns of consecration at the palace-temple at Knossos, Crete, south end of the central court. Unlike the Minoan Goddess of the Mountain, the probable Mycenaean god above appears without any accompanying religious symbols (Photograph by the author).

So what's the message here? I suggest it might be this: the invading Mycenaean god is saying, "I'm here first and foremost to control you. None of this namby-pamby, horns-of-consecration stuff. They're not consecrated to me. I know you're all hiding in your houses because you're afraid of me. And you should be. I'm here for one reason and one reason only: to crush you into dust."

Considering all of the above, you won't be surprised to hear that the Myce "loved war." "Battles and hunting scenes appear very often on gems and other objects found on the mainland and on wall paintings.... The age was such that a war deity was sorely needed." The Myce have "warrior graves" and they made warrior art. And finally, on the Greek mainland the Myce hid their cities behind mammoth "Cyclopean" walls (Nilsson 1949: 412; Fitton 2002: 146, 180, 189, 191; Dickinson 1994: 162).

Even the Myce goddesses carry swords and wear helmets — (Minoans never show their goddesses wearing war parapher-nalia): "the Mycenae Room of the Fresco ... shows two goddesses facing one another, one with a ... sword." Nearby in the Tsountas House is a "'shield goddess' on a painted stone tablet" and "two frescoes ... show females, who may be goddesses, wearing helmets." Several centuries later, one of these goddesses could well have become the Greek Goddess Athena, patron of the Greek city of Athens and often shown weighted down under war gear and carrying weapons. On the Greek mainland, archaeologists have found Myce goddess figurines – but in the graves of the poor only (Nilsson 1949: 305, 307, 321). Did the poor stay loyal to the Guiding Goddess while the rich upper classes abandoned Her – for their masters' vicious gods of war?

In Japan: the Jomon Jump Ship

Time now to swing east across Asia to the Pacific Rim and Japan. Remember the gentle Neolithic Jomon? With them it's the same story: guiding-goddess utopia stomped into the ground and replaced by a goddess-less dystopia. Almost overnight we make a giddy journey from peace, free will, and equality, to war, domination, and snooty snobbism. Here in Japan the people responsible for the switchover to Hell are called the "Yayoi." After the Yayoi paddled over on boats from Korea around 400 BC, things in Japan were never again the same. As a matter of fact Jared Diamond calls the switch from the guiding-goddess Jomon period to the war-ridden Yayoi not "a" striking feature of Japanese history, but "*the* most striking feature of Japanese history..." (Diamond 1998)(emphasis the author's).

First thing that strikes you about the Yayoi is they were snooty snobs. Koji Mizoguchi of Kyushu University says the Yayoi period is "widely accepted" as a time of "rapid development of social stratification." The Yayoi even had separate cemeteries for snoots, while everyone else had to go somewhere else to rest in peace. After they came in and routed the Jomon, it took only a couple of centuries for the Yayoi "to show the first signs of social stratification, as reflected especially in cemeteries. After about 100 BC separate parts of cemeteries were set aside for the graves of what was evidently an emerging elite class, marked by luxury goods imported from China, such as beautiful jade objects and bronze mirrors" (Koji 2001: 173, 185, 190; Diamond 1998).

But the Yayoi weren't just snoots, they were violent snoots to boot: archaeologists have found all the telltale signs: armor, weapons (stone, bronze, and then iron), combat injuries on skeletons, moats, and so forth (Koji 2001; Kazuaki 2000). As the Yayoi period progressed,

> war became more and more frequent: ... evidence includes mass production of arrowheads, defensive moats surrounding villages and buried skeletons pierced by projectile points. These hallmarks of war in Yayoi Japan corroborate the earliest accounts of Japan in Chinese chronicles, which describe the land of Wa and its hundred little political units fighting one another (Diamond 1998).

And what about the Jomon? Apparently the Yayoi "drove the Jomon north and south" (Stanley-Baker 1986: 19), and more or less out of business (although many think the tiny populations of Ainu living today up in northern Japan may be living descendants of the ancient Jomon). These days in Japan there's lots of fuss and feathers about who the Japanese descend from. Jomon? Yayoi? Both? Not surprisingly, most Japanese seem to be rooting for the Jomon.

About Yayoi religion we don't know much. But when the area's first written records appear in AD 300, at the end of the Yayoi period, and document religion in Japan, they're about the Shinto religion. Although Shinto is a religion with more than one war god, the best-known is Hachiman, worshipped at Yahata Shrine. Another Japanese war god is Sumiyoshi Myojin, who is worshipped at Japan's Sumiyoshi Shrine (Hardon 1968 Vol. 2: 223; Carpenter 2001; Reider 2005: 214, 228).

What Twisted Them into Monsters?

By now some of you might be asking how Hachiman, the Yayoi, the Yukkians and the Indo-Europeans got to be so mean and mucky. The answer again is, no one knows exactly. There are theories out there, however. According to Miriam Robbins Dexter, the proto-Indo-Europeans were "wolf boys" kicked out of society in their homeland north of the Black and Caspian Seas (Dexter 2005: 146). According to Dexter's theory, these boys ran wild in packs, losing all culture, and then gradually creating a brand, spanking new culture based on the dog-eat-dog and dominance-hierarchy behavior of the wild pack animals they ran with. How Dexter came up with her theory is interesting:

> I heard a lecture at UCLA ... by the Irish Celticist Kim McCone. McCone discussed young warrior heroes such as the Old Irish Cu Chulainn, 'the hound of Chulainn,' theorizing that such young male heroes (and groups of not so heroic warriors who lived as outlaws) reflected a social reality in Indo-European culture: the Männerbund, groups of young men who live at the edges of society and are connected in legend and myth to wolves, dogs or other animals.... Information about these young male groups is found in ancient Germanic, Gaulish, Celtic, Greek, and Roman myth and probably society as well.... Perhaps the ... violence and warrior mentality which we see in conquering Indo-Europeans was the produce of ... a surfeit of testosterone, as it were (Dexter 2005: 148).

To me this theory packs a snappy punch. According to Dexter, DNA evidence shows it was not women, but Indo-European men who rode a-conquering into the areas they molested — and only a handful of men at that (148-49). And remember the Indo-Europeans/Indo-Aryans who made mincemeat out of India in the second millennium BC? There too, DNA points to men, not women, riding in and doing the mischief. Unfortunately, these possibly testosterone-challenged dudes were some of the first to transform metals into war weapons. After that, it was all downhill for most of the folk they ran into.

So much for Indo-Europeans. What about the Urukians in Mesopotamia? What bee bit under their bonnets to make them so surly and sour? If you want typical answers, type "the origin of the state" into your favorite computer search engine. Since Mesopotamia boasts the world's very first "states," everyone and her brother has theories about how and why the switchover from the Nice Neolithics to the (many say Sinister) State took place.

These "origin of the state" theories tend to run in circles. Mostly they begin with father-god notions that humans are just itching to be bad, and if you give them half a chance, they will be. So for example, one says that right before the Urukians appeared on the scene, the climate got bad, food got scarce, and people invented war as a way to grab food from each other. A variation on that theme says the population grew, food got scarce, and (again) people invented war as a way to grab food (Otterbein 2004; Melleuish 2002). As we've seen earlier, however, populations bursting at the seams aren't a cause of war.

Another origin-of-the-state theory: talented people were able to grow more food — and then they hoarded it all for themselves. The less talented got hungry. Thus social classes were born, with the talented plopping themselves into the high class, and everyone else into the lower-rung, stomach-growling class. Then when fights broke out (surprise, surprise), bully-boy government was invented — someone hadda break up the fights for gosh sake! Then the bully boys took sides — with the rich and talented: "[P]eople were able to produce a surplus, which gave rise to the cleavage of society into social classes. Government emerged to suppress open conflict between the classes, but government sided with the rich..." (Otterbein 2004: 100). Even though this theory was first snapped out years ago by Friedrich Engels, the twenty-first-century anthropologist Keith Otterbein swears by it too.

According to archaeologists John Clark and Michael Blake, social classes happened because certain men were born more "ambitious" than others: "'The development of social inequality was ... a long-term unexpected consequence of many individuals promoting their own aggrandizement. Ambitious males compete for prestige" (Otterbein 2004: 105).

Anyway, once you get to social classes and government sidling up to the rich, then you have to explain how the Really Bad states started — you know, the ones who went out and slew a zillion Zeblamites and turned survivors into sorry slaves so the pyramids could be built? For these big bruisers here's a sample of the kind of explanation running around out there: Once you get bully-boy government, then the government has to get mean. Then you'll get Egypt, slaves and the pyramids: "'Political legitimacy theory' ... argues that emerging or recently formed states use a wide range of cruel and repressive sanctions, including torture and capital punishment, to subjugate and control the population. After control is obtained, repressive sanctions are no longer needed; the governing body can rely on consensus for social regulation" (Otterbein 2004: 107).

Excuse, please: Cruel governments are born when governments get cruel? I mean, there had to be something with more of a punch than this to explain why, after 400,000 years of fully modern human culture, humans suddenly switch 180 degrees backwards into snooty snobbism, bully-boy rule, and constant warfare. About one thing, though, I think these theories might be right: the climate was probably a key factor in the switch from utopia to dystopia.

Where'd All This Dust Come From?

About 500 years before we see clear archaeological signs of the yukky Urukians, the Mesopotamian climate began having the dry heaves. As University of California archaeologist Brian Fagan puts it, "the landscape" didn't just change, it "changed dramatically.... Rainfall became more irregular, the environment became drier, and agricultural populations were dislocated. Some areas were abandoned altogether, as many groups dispersed into nomadic life ways" (2004: 360).

In fact, according to geographer James DeMeo it wasn't just Mesopotamia having a climate crisis. DeMeo says there was "global warming" going on all over, so that a gigundo corridor of land running from North Africa, across Saudi Arabia, Iran, Afghanistan and all across central China — DeMeo calls it "Saharasia" — began turning from green to shades of beige and grey:

> Climatologists ... have demonstrated that Saharasia was once wetter and greener prior to around 6000 years ago. The Arabian and Central Asian cores of Saharasia began to dry up around 5000-4000 BCE. Other parts of Saharasia began to dry up shortly thereafter, in an oscillatory manner. Whole regions were devastated and abandoned as desiccation set in, Droughts, famines, and starvation occurred, and mass migrations ensued (DeMeo 1998: 8).

Look at your technicolor world map and see for yourself: a gigantic brownish-yellow finger of land stretches from Africa's Sahara Desert all the way across Asia, and ending at the Pacific Ocean (DeMeo 1998). This enormous finger covers almost a fourth of the world's land mass. Notice too that it takes in the land north of the Black and Caspian Seas — the area many consider the original homeland of the Indo-Europeans.

The hit-the-jackpot question is, what caused this finger to dry up? Some, like DeMeo, think it was climate change, while others think it was the world's first farmers overfarming the land. If the latter are right, starvation would be a heckuva lot less extreme: once he killed his farm land, all a farmer would need to do would be move over and farm the next plot. But if the others are right, then Eurasian people in the fifth millennium BC could have starved on a scale hitherto unknown to humankind.

Like DeMeo, German culture historian Heide Goettner-Abendroth also thinks it was not overfarming but climate change that led to a dramatic shift in the natural environment over Europe and Asia, beginning in the fifth millennium BC. What's more, says Heide, this wasn't just a matter of happy, rosy-cheeked farmers waking up one morning and discovering their barley and green-bean fields turned to dust. The change would have been a dragged-out, complicated and painful affair:

> Catastrophic migrations are caused by wide-ranging natural catastrophes that do not necessarily happen suddenly, but rather creep forward slowly with devastating effects…. It is quite likely that with every step these people took in this shift towards arable land, they tried to till the soil again, to set up a new settlement. But the expanding steppe caught up with them again and again. This fight for survival in a land that became more and more inhospitable must have lasted for generations and centuries….

"But it was hopeless," says Heide, "and so it must have slowly led to the breakdown of the existing social order" that Heide, too, believes had been organized in many areas around goddess religion (Goettner-Abendroth 2005: 34).

But how specifically did this catastrophic change make peaceful, egalitarian, and civilized goddess peoples morph into their mirror image, i.e. devils from Hell? For the answer, let's check out what goes on among modern starving peoples. Basically it's this: if the starvation goes on long enough, the group suffering it becomes grossly psychotic.

Take, for example, the Ik, or Teuso, of East Africa. Forced in the mid-twentieth century into a region with little food or water, the Ik began to starve:

And as they starved, their social structure broke down entirely. A passive indifference to the needs or pain of others manifested itself, and ... feeding of the self became their all consuming passion. They sat in the midst of great heat and drought ... losing interest in the pleasures of life.... Brothers stole food from sisters, and husbands left wives and babies to fend for themselves. While the maternal-infant bond endured the longest, eventually mothers abandoned their ... children. Older children gathered into gangs dedicated to stealing food, even from their own younger siblings, or older, weakened kinfolk (DeMeo 1998: 77).

Eventually mothers even eat their own children: "'Interpersonal relationships may be broken down so completely that parents devour their own children; cannibalism has been reported ... in almost every part of the world.... Animals may attack humans in broad daylight without apparent fear. Social chaos is evident everywhere...'"(DeMeo 1998: 78 quoting Carlson 1982: 7-8).

What's That Spider Web Sitting on Your Head?

Besides climate, another thing we need to check out before we can understand where the yukky Urukians might have come from is another force that probably played a key role in their origin: 'culture.' Stay with me on this, because culture's a biggie. Never sneeze at the thing anthropologists call culture. In every corner of the world it's not genes but culture that makes us different from any other group in the world. Like a giant spider web, culture sits on top of all our heads with miles and miles of silk-road rules and warnings, stories, traditions, cautionary tales, myths, parables and so forth, about the proper way to do things, make things and even think about things.

Oh sure, there's a little wiggle room. We all have a little freedom to spin our own lives in our own directions — but the directions we get to choose from are all laid out in advance on our particular culture web; mostly you just pick and choose from what's already there. Culture is why you speak English instead of French or Farsi. It's why, while you turn white at the thought of blood soup, certain Inuit people up in the Arctic can't imagine life without it. If you'd been adopted at birth by Inuit people, you'd be laughing your fool head off at anyone who'd blanch at blood soup.

When it comes to what makes you different from others in the world, genes barely show up on the radar screen. What counts is your New England, Zulu, Russian or Inuit culture. From how to hold your hands while speaking (in the pockets? Open palmed? Behind the back — or is this a super no-no signaling possible concealed weapons?) to whether, how loudly, and in what pitch to burp after a meal to show gratitude to the chef, your culture has rules for everything. Culture silk-road rules can be so taken-for-granted we barely notice them. Are there a hundred rules in Western culture for how to walk down a sidewalk? You betcha! "Don't walk down a sidewalk backwards." "Don't stop on a sidewalk, face a brick wall, and just stare at it." And how about, "When you walk down a sidewalk, keep your tongue in your mouth."

As you can begin to see, there are possibly a cold trillion rules in our giant silk-road culture webs. And at birth, none of us know any of them. Unlike other animals, we humans are born morons. About all we're born knowing, is how to cry, take in food, and push it back out. While other animals get instincts, all we humans get are big, fat brains — for learning culture.

Two final things about culture, and we're done with it: First, just as Jehovah is a "jealous god," your culture spider-web is a jealous web: it wants no other webs before it. In other words, we all think our own way of doing things is better than the Chinese way, the Chilean way, or even the Chesterfield's way across the street (jiminy critters they rake their leaves into the street gutters! They give gifts at the drop of a hat including Halloween and May Day!).

Second, that culture web hovering over your head is stubborn as a mule when it comes to major change. Take the French and the English. They've lived side by side for hundreds of years, and yet the French remain stolidly French, and the English, English. To make a culture truly change at its core takes a series of major psychic earthquakes.

Help! I Can't Stop Eating!

Getting back, however, to the peaceful goddess peoples starving in what may have been the rapidly forming deserts of Mesopotamia and the Saharasian corridor, you can see that it would take something darn drastic to make them morph into their mirror images. Now you might say, "Duh! You starve in a desert, you get ugly! What's the big deal?!" But remember what you just read about culture: a culture would never morph into its opposite simply because something bad happens. During bad times we might behave badly, but once the bad times pass, we return to being Danish. Or Australian. Or Inuit. Or what have you.

So to explain why around 4000 BC the peaceful goddess people had morphed into monsters — and stayed that way even after breaking free of their impoverished environment and living with plenty again — we need to scope out the scene for something highly unusual. What was it? In a nutshell I think it was this: the original Urukian culture was crushed and erased, and a brand new culture was shoved into its place — one based on human psychosis and animal behavior.

This could have happened in more than one way. If DeMeo and Goettner-Abendroth are right about major climate change blasting Europe, Asia and Africa six millennia ago, what goddess groups suffered was so extreme they either died out immediately, or became severely and permanently brain-damaged, lost culture altogether, and then died out. As the behavior of entire groups became the random, irrational behavior of the highly disturbed, most of these groups went belly-up. In a small handful, however, the offspring of brain-scrambled adults would build brand new cultures — ones based on all the offspring had to go on: their parents' mentally deranged behavior — and the behavior of wild animals that came hunting in packs sniffing around their doorsteps for food.

So the next act in the drama "Where Did the Urukians Come From?" is the hypothetical birth, probably somewhere between 5000-4000 BC, of what I call "starvation culture." Based on the psychotic, mentally-deranged behavior of starving people, starvation culture was a new way of life, set into stone and trans-mitted from one generation to the next down through the centuries.

To understand the radical shift that was starvation culture, you need to understand a few key phenonmena: 1. The extreme isolation of people trapped in the middle of a desertifying area that blanketed possibly up to one fourth of the earth's land-mass; 2. the role of the desert oases in the shift process; and 3. the fact that children's brains are gigantic information sponges.

1. Alone on a Desert. Since the land area that began drying up in the sixth millennium BC was monstrously large, unless you eventually stumbled upon a major oasis, you and your group very likely went belly-up in a hurry. Major oases formed on the banks of the Tigris, Euphrates, Nile, Yellow and other large rivers, but for most caught in the withering landscape, these oases would be hundreds or thousands of miles/kilometers away.

2. At the Oasis. One situation in which a long-term starvation group might have survived, however, is this: The rabid, starving adults in the group bumble onto a small, empty oasis — one that formed around, say, a large water hole. Here the women get good nutrition during and after pregnancy, and a few of their babes

manage, even, to survive the brutal abuse and neglect of the adults around them. At the waterhole along with the people would be, of course, many local wild animals — come to soak in the only pond for miles around.

3. Gigantic Sponges for Brains. Although in order to learn culture children come equipped with giant sponges for brains, our desert kiddies have no culture to sponge up. For miles around all they spy is humans showing bumbling, random, psychotic behavior, including snatching, hacking and killing for food. (Remember, since we're on a mammoth desert, there are no other human groups for up to hundreds of miles/kilometers in any direction.)

Although starving people are pathetically common today (DeMeo 1998: 77 ff), modern starving children have other cultures nearby to sponge up. In contrast, our sixth-millennium-BC waterhole kiddies had nothing to sponge but psychosis and wild-animal behavior. Although neither psychosis nor animal behavior are culture, a few of our big-brained kidlets would combine them to make a core — think of the plastic spools sewing thread's wrapped around — for a brand new culture. After they added thread to the spool (i.e. culture rules spun off from their new core values and beliefs) — voila! The birth of starvation culture.

But this isn't the end of the story. After all, these are possibly the people who pummeled paradise into the ground. If so, they're the worst enemy the human race has ever faced. Before we can pitch them off the planet, we need to know as much about them as possible.

After the starvation-culture kids wove a complicated map of thousands of silk-road rules onto their culture core — with political, economic, religious and social-rules roads all meshing — what they had, turned out to be pretty odoriferous. The economics system, for example, not only allowed stealing, thievery, filching and pillaging (behavior the starvation-culture kids watched their psychotic parents do daily) — it handed out big, fat, brownie points for them. While under the healthy old goddess systems, everyone worked together to *produce* goods, under the new starvation-culture system, small groups worked together in coordinated packs to *steal* goods gathered or produced by others.

Like those of your typical, garden-variety wolf- and wild-dog pack, the starvation-culture social and political systems were built on the twin towers of social dominance and social hierarchy. Hey! At least wild dogs work together! The hypothetical parents of our starvation-culture kids were too divorced from reality to work together, period. For their ideological system, the starvation-culture kids' new number-one rule was simple: "all pleasures bad (except eating), all pain good." So if my theory is right, this is it folks: the birth of bully-boyism and snooty snobbery, all in one fell swoop.

While under the healthy old goddess systems everyone was equal, under the new, upstart, animal/psychosis-based starvation-culture, everyone suddenly found themselves teetering on different rungs of a power ladder. High at the top was perched a glorious alpha male. A lot of 'nothing'-people crowded together on the bottom rungs, while somewhere in the middle sat everyone else. A pecking order was popped into place: everyone barked and pecked at the person on the rung below — and in turn got barked at by the person above. Under the goddess, decisions became decisions only after everyone agreed they were. But in starvation culture, decisions are made by the "Top Dog" perched on the top rung of the new power ladder.

Evidence suggests that the glue that held starvation culture together was a brand new deity: "god" aka weapon. Remember earlier in the chapter the Scythians making sacrifices to their holy dagger that represented — or in their minds actually was — the god Akenakes? And for an economy synonymous with stealing and theft, what better god than a weapon? Just like Mother Earth, god aka weapon fed and clothed his people. But while Mother Earth said "I will help you birth what you need from my body," god aka weapon said "I will help you steal what you need from others."

When the starvation-culture kids first tried their hands at forcibly taking things from the goddess peoples (those who'd survived without starving first — at, say, the Tigris and Euphrates River oases, or the Nile oasis), they were no doubt miserable flops. First, the starvation-culture kids would have been vastly outnumbered. Also, the goddess peoples, even though non-violent, would probably have tried to defend themselves against what looked and smelled more like wild animals than humans. But when the starvation-culture kids begin to organize their new starvation culture around weapon-god religion, that's when they were able truly to realize their core culture value: pilfering and pinching life's necessities versus working for them. My guess is that the starvation-culture religion was devised by a few starvation-terrified con men and women, who saw it as their chance to form their fellows into a biomass weapon potentially useful in easing their own knee-shaking fears of starvation.

And — ta da! — now we have the Urukians, the war-god people who, around 4000 BC, took over the Goddessian Ubaidians in Mesopotamia. I suspect most everything about the Urukians was born out of starvation culture: women, childen, the sick and the elderly probably dominated and abused by packs of young males, the world's first insitutionalized warfare, and violent war gods. Oh, and arising out of a constant need for more warriors/war fodder, institutionalized population booms, eventually leading to insitutionalized overpopulation.

It didn't take long for the Yukky Urukians to morph into the not-quite-as-bad Sumerians. Somewhere in between the two peoples, everything about starvation culture — economics, social structure, politics and all the rest — was converted into weapons or weapons-support systems. Even individuals morphed into weapons ("warriors"). Women morphed into warrior-production machines. And the group's clot of young men morphed into a brainless biomass weapon controlled by a "top-rung" con man (today we call this biomass weapon an "army" or a "navy").

At this point, a "miracle" whirls into view: the world's first city-states, the first "civilization." Popping up first between the Tigris and Euphrates Rivers, these are not in fact marvels of good, but of evil — the beginning of the starvation/war-god nightmare that has plagued us ever since. Whereas the old goddess peoples had spread out evenly across the landscape in decent-sized communities, the new cities were simply people packed like sardines in a can, and then transformed by starvation-culture overlords into biomass weapons and biomass-weapons support teams. We now recognize that these first cities

> tended to be disease-ridden places, with high death rates.... Dense population, class systems, and a strong centralized government created internal stress. The slaves and the poor saw that the wealthy had all the things that they themselves lacked.... The poor did not have enough space in which to live with comfort and dignity... Evidence of warfare is common.... As time went by the rich became richer and the poor poorer.... Given the problems associated with civilization, it is perhaps not surprising that a recurring phenomenon is their collapse" (Haviland 1997: 305-06).

Birth of Daddy War God

At first, starvation-culture "religion" might have looked simply like a vague, fuzzy reverence for weapons. After all, weapons translated into the food, water, shelter, sex and almost anything else the starvation-culture kids needed (or had even half an interest in). Gradually, however, this reverence would morph into full-blown religion, with weapons as the deities worshipped, adored and spit-polished daily. Just as the Scythians would later make sacrifices to their beloved god/dagger Akenakes, the starvation-culture kids too might have bowed down in front of a special battle axe, with a name such as "the God Axeynasty," or "His Holiness, Himdugoodstuff." In most places these deities eventually took on the physique of a male warrior. In Mesopotamia this god shows up in early historical records as Ninurta, who we've met before, and who evolved from the god Im-du-gud — a name meaning "slingstone" or "ball of clay" (some sling "stones" were actually made of clay)(Jacobsen 1976: 128). Although at first Imdugud looked like a giant thunderbird with a lion's head, when he morphed into Ninurta he took on human shape.

On the other hand, the starvation-culture religions could have been consciously manufactured — not to meet the spiritual needs of the people, but to manipulate the people into meeting the material needs of a few. At some point it might have dawned on some scared but smart starvation blokes that if they could just invent the right 'religion,' they could sucker others into licking their sandals, etcetera. At this point, you need to remember the psychology of the starvation-culture man. His central core is empty of everything but an overwhelming dread of the bottom falling out of things — a dread he's learned at the feet of every adult he grew up with (who learned it at the feet of *their* elders). This is a knee-jerk fear of suddenly not having enough. Enough food. Water. Enough pairs of Gucci shoes. Whatever.

Con Dude Goes to Town

So anyway, our ancient starvation-culture man says to himself, "Hm. If I could just get everyone to work for me for nothing — and work like the world's coming to an end — I'd be home free. They'd kill and pillage for me, and I'd store all the goodies in my zillions of fortified storehouses, and I'd never have to worry again — about anything.

"Hm. So how to con them into working for nothing....

"I know! I'll tell them this: 'The Earth She dried up, see, and let us starve. Why? Because there's a new god in town who's smacked Her down. He not only lives in our weapons, he *is* our weapons. He can bag us anything Mother Earth could — and more.'

"'But here's the thing: I alone can speak to this god. He chose me. He told me to tell you about him. Says he won't talk to anyone but me.

"'Says he's a warrior.

"'Says if you don't do exactly what he says, when you die, he'll fry you for eternity.

"'Says you can't have any other gods except me — uh *him* — or when you die, he'll fry you....

"'Says you have to go smite the Elamites and Canaanites, the Ickymites and Itchymites and bring me all their gold, or he'll fry you.

"'He says since I'm his appointed one, I get all kinds of stuff the rest of you don't — 1000 wives; a giant palace you all have to build for me; I get to wear purple....

"'Sorry! Hey! I didn't decide this! He did!'

So the others say, "This sounds bleak. We kill ourselves working so you can have it all, and we get — nothing? Are you sure that's what this new god says?"

Con Dude (nodding): "Yeah, that's it. Sorry."

Others: "Well, we might as well go jump off a cliff."

Con Dude (thinking fast): "Uh ... see, this god, he says if you don't jump off that cliff, he's got this great place you can go to after you die. Called heaven."

Others: "Heaven?"

Con Dude: "Yeah. All your wildest dreams come true up there — fab food, wild women, diamonds dripping off the clouds, prop your feet up all day long...."

In sum, my theory is that in more than one place around the

globe, the switch from guiding-goddess utopia to war-god dystopia happened because starvation culture crawled its ugly way into the human species. Starvation culture could have risen independently in various places around the globe, or it could be that, though time, the first starvation-culture gradually diffused from the Near East. Since She was at complete odds with this new culture, the Guiding Mother Goddess didn't stand much of a chance against it. On the other hand, the perfect symbolic guide, the one that condoned and rewarded the violent, me-first, pilfering dominance-hierarchy at the core of starvation culture, was the war god. Just as gasoline keeps a car engine running, I suggest that the war gods have kept starvation culture in full throttle.

Here's the really scary thing: If you're reading this, you're probably reading it in a modern starvation culture. If you live in one of the world's larger countries — America, Australia, Brazil, Canada, China, England, France, Germany, Iraq, Iran, Japan, Russia, South Africa, etctera — you live in a starvation culture. The reason is simple: starvation cultures are war cultures. They pump massive amounts of energy into war machines. Therefore over the past 6000 years, starvation cultures have crushed most of the world's non-psychotic, non-starvation populations. Not that starvation-culture countries haven't done a few good things — for example topple a genocidal dictator or two for the neighbors — but that doesn't excuse the fact that for millennia they've also trampled and flattened their neighbors, and forced their neighbor's children to learn starvation-culture ways.

Although starvation culture is only a theory, suspicious-looking evidence stands behind it. First, "dramatic" climate change did actually sweep over Mesopotamia in the centuries before the arrival of some of the first true snooty-snob, bully-boy war-mongers the planet had ever seen (Fagan 2004). Second, unlike bonobos and the handful of sane, non-violent societies still left in the world (see chapter two), most nations today behave just like a happy combination of pack wolves and long-starving social groups. Today most of the world's business is conducted by wolf- and dog-like dominance hierarchies peopled by packs of young men headed up by top-dog alpha-males.

Like a bunch of starving psychotics in a small sandbox, the world's major nations today spend most of their energy violently snatching food and other resources out of the hands of "weaker" nations. From our constant wars and interpersonal violence (if you never have enough you "need" to take from others) and our rape of women, their children and the environment (deep down we feel Mother Earth abandoned us) to our obesity, overpopulation and propensity to hoard, starvation culture supplies explanations for almost everything about ourselves we deeply despise. As a matter of fact, when you finally realize it, it's hard to see why we didn't see it before. Almost everything we loathe about ourselves looks suspiciously like the behavior of wild dog packs, wolf packs, or the unhinged humans we keep locked up in mental and penal institutions.

Third, although your pastor possibly hasn't clued you in on this, the Bible often focuses on parents cannibalizing their kids (In Appendix J see Deuteronomy 28.53; Deuteronomy 28.55; 2 Kings 6.28-29; Jeremiah 19.9; Lamentations 4.10; Lamentations 2.20, and Ezekiel 5.10). Eating kids for lunch happens among long-term starving peoples whose altered biochemistry is betraying their brains, but it certainly wouldn't seem to be something added to the behavioral rule-books of psychologically healthy societies.

Amazingly, in spite of the six-millennial reign of starvation culture and its starvation/taking gods, the Guiding Goddess has nevertheless managed to retain Her hold on human consciousness. So even though She suffered severe damage back in the BCs, that wasn't the end of Her. No way, Jose. As we'll see in the next chapter, the Great Guiding Mother Goddess is one tough cookie. Don't let anyone tell you She's not still in the race, because She is.

7

Fight

To anyone who's been keeping track of the situation, it's obvious that the Great Guiding Goddess is as indestructible as Superwoman. For the past 6000 years, the starvation/taking gods have tried every trick in the book to take Her down, but She just keeps bouncing back. For those paying attention, the past 6000 years have been a giant see-saw, with the taking god knocking Goddess down, then the Goddess bouncing back again in his face, making him look a total fool, then he's at Her again, and so forth. She's like one of those life-sized, toy-balloon clowns with the smile on its face: no matter how many times you pop it, it just bounces up again, in your face, grinning at you. So let's take a gander at a few of these smackdown-bounceback sessions, beginning with one of the first, in the fifth millennium BC, when the first starvation war gods charged into town on their Harleys.

Bounceback #1. The Return of Tiamat

In the last chapter, we learned that soon after the war-based Urukians roared into Mesopotamia around 4000 BC, the peaceful Ubaidians and Halafians disappeared — and took their goddess figurines with them. We also saw that the Yukky Urukians didn't make figurines of either sex, and didn't even show many signs of having deities at all. When they did begin to depict deities, these appear to be not goddesses but gods. It appears likely, in other words, that the Yukky Urukians smacked down both the Ubaidian/Halafians and their guiding goddesses as well.

But the Guiding Goddess wasn't gone — She only ducked underground for a while. When the Urukians gave way to the

Sumerians around 3000 BC, the Goddess made a comeback in Mesopotamia. Although She went by different names and forms in different places, one of Her most popular forms was as the Goddess Inanna.

Like the old Guiding Goddess, Inanna was a powerful deity. Unlike the Guiding Goddess, however, She wasn't all-powerful. Not only did she have to share the stage with a number of sassy sky gods, she also (as we saw earlier) had to move over and make room for the Sumerian war god Ninurta. Neither does Inanna seem to be a mother goddess. She's more like a powerful version of Usas of the dawn, daughter of the big-daddy god of the Indo-Europeans we've talked about in earlier chapters. The Guiding Goddess also made a comeback as the Sumerian Mother Goddess Tiamat, although a lot less info's come down to us about Tiamat than about Inanna. What we do know, however, is that the early Sumerians considered Tiamat the sacred mother of all their deities (Leeming 2005: 382).

Bounceback #2. Anything You Can Do, I Can Do Better

One of the first things the new starvation/war gods learned about the Guiding Goddess was, She refused to go away. They therefore decided to try to trick Her into leaving town. Their first trick was kind of silly (well, very silly, but that's the war gods for you). One of the most radical things about the Goddess is, She births stuff from Her own body (the world, cosmos, us, other deities, etc.). So the war gods decided that to win the hearts and minds of the people, they'd first have to birth something. If they could just learn to give birth, well then, the people would forget all about the Great Guiding Goddess and turn all their attention to them, the starvation/war gods.

In one way, the starvation-culture gods were right. Birth giving from your very own body is powerful magic. Thing is, the Mother Goddess not only births, She feeds everything She births, too. From Her own body. Behind female deity, the double-punch is birth *and* edible provisions. What did you think your body's made of? Rocks? Minerals? Air? Clay? Water? Something else? What else is there? Your own body not only comes from Mother Earth, it *is* Mother Earth. And your peas, potatoes and Pete's Pale Ale don't really come from the earth, they *are* the earth, Mother Earth (Her soil, minerals, moisture and so forth).

In other words, it's really the Great Mother, and nothing else, that stands between you and starvation/annihilation, i.e. returning to dead dust. And of course women are similar: through their bodies they not only give birth, they feed whatever's birthed. You have to admit, there's no greater magic on earth than what women can do with their sacred bodies. The Earth-our-womb-'n-food is female simply because it's only women who possess the magic to birth and feed through their flesh-and-blood bodies. The male body can do neither.

What's extra sad about the starvation/war gods of the Bronze Age is, they actually thought they could con us into thinking they — just like Mother — could birth us directly from their own flesh, muscle and bone. They wanted this so badly they could taste it. "[U]surpation of the feminine power of birth-giving seems to have been the distinguishing mark of the earliest gods," says award-winning goddess scholar Barbara Walker. And poor dears, they tried so hard. They 'gave birth' through slits in their heads and bellies, stolen ribs, masturbated penes, and sweaty armpits. And they actually thought we'd fall for this stuff! (Oh. You did fall for it? ... Um, sorry.)

Figure 7.1: And the Dude Bore a Nine-Pound Blond

The God	*Where*	*How He Gave Birth*
Ra	Egypt	From his mouth.
Zeus	Greece	From his head, but only after he swallowed the real mother, Metis.
Atum	Egypt (Heliopolis)	In 2000 BC created the first

		two humans by "masturbation and self-fertilization through his mouth." (But "the oldest traditions" said these first two humans were "born of the primal Mother, Iusaset").
Kun	China	By "Caesarian section." He was "slain and cut open so Yu, founder of the Hsia dynasty, could emerge from his stomach."
Ymir	Norse (Europe)	From his "sweaty armpit" gave birth to the first woman and man.
Loki	Norse (Europe)	"Gave birth to Odin's horse after making himself pregnant by eating a woman's heart."
Rg Vedan	India	"Gave birth to the Mother of Creation, then impregnated her, so she brought forth the rest of the universe."
Kumarbi	Hittite (Near East)	Became pregnant "by eating his rival's penis…. [H]aving no vagina he was unable to deliver [the babies]. Finally the sea god Ea took them out through his side" just like Jumping Jehovah did later for Mr. Adam.
Apollo	Greece	"A Greek carving showed the god Apollo sitting on a pile of eggs, trying to copy the life-giving magic of his mother

> Leto ... who gave birth to the
> World Egg."

*Sources: Walker 1983; 106-08; Hassan 1998: 107.

After noticing that birthing through their mouths, penes, sides and armpits didn't impress people, the starvation gods switched to Plan B: downsizing the Goddess. Since She was so beloved by the people, however, this was a slow job — one that slid along in stages that were different in different places. In some places, the starvation-culture god first played the role of the Goddess' admirer, son or lover. In other places She "agreed" to marry him but at the same time stayed the prime mover and guide for the people. In stage two, the starvation-culture god gets grabbier and sassier. Maybe he declares himself co-creator. Maybe he says although the Goddess can guide women, he's going to guide the men from now on.

Stage three: The ultimate sassiness and grabbiness. The god takes over completely and the Goddess is shunted off to a corner.

Stage four: The goddess is hurt, humiliated, raped and/or cut up into little pieces and strewn all over the cosmos (temper, temper).

Stage five: Eventually, among some people (the Hebrews come to mind), the Goddess says sayonara altogether (although only in the official records).

The Mesopotamian goddess Tiamat is a good example of stages one through four. To the ancient Sumerians, Tiamat at first was "'Goddess Mother' (Dia Mater), from whose formless body the universe was born." Later, however, when the Babylonians took over Mesopotamia they adopted Tiamat — whereupon their god Marduk promptly murdered Her, "his mother," dividing Her in half to form heaven and earth. When she labels this a "mythological incident marking the early struggle between the sky gods" and "the older earth-based goddess religions" goddess scholar Karen Tate is right on the money. "Modern scholars tend to ignore Tiamat's maternal Creatress nature" sighs goddess scholar Barbara Walker, "describing her as nothing more than a 'dragon of chaos' slain by Marduk. It is seldom emphasized that this was a myth of matricide" (Walker 1983: 998-99; Tate 2006: 150).

But as always, the Mother Goddess bounced back. Take for example the Near East around 2000 BC. As the well-known Jungian analyst Eric Neumann puts it, the Near East at this time enjoyed a rebirth of the Great Mother Goddess: "At about the year 2000 BC there took place in the Mediterranean region a renaissance of the Mother Goddess, who would seem to have been the dominant deity two thousand years before. An early Babylonian fragment contains a childbirth incantation in which the primordial traits of Aruru-Ishtar as potter and creatress have been preserved from a much earlier period yet. In one version of it we read:

> [...they kis]sed her feet,
> [saying: 'The creatress of mankind] we call thee;
> The mistress of all the gods be thy name!'
> They went to the House of Fate,
> Ninigiku-Ea [God] and the wise Mama [Mother Goddess].
> Fourteen mother-wombs were assembled
> To tread upon the clay before her.
> [...] Ea says, as he recited the incantation.
> Sitting before her, Ea causes her to recite the incantation.
> Mama recited the incantation; when she completed her incantation,
> [...] she drew upon her clay.
> Fourteen pieces she pinched off; seven pieces she placed on the right,
> Seven pieces she placed on the left; between them she placed a brick.
> [Ea] was kneeling on the matting; he opened its navel;

[... He c]alled the wise wives.
Of the seven and seven mother-wombs, seven brought forth males,
Seven brought forth females.
The Mother-Womb [Mother Goddess], the creatress of destiny,
In pairs she completed them,
In pairs she completed before her.
The forms of the people Mami forms.
In the house of the bearing woman in travail,
Seven days shall the brick lie.
... from the house of Mah, the wise Mami.
The vexed one shall rejoice in the house of the one in travail.
As the Bearing One [Mother Goddess] gives birth,
May the mother of the child bring forth by herself" (Neumann 1991: 135-36).

At about this same time, Sumerian records talk about "reforms" that tore fruit and other food grown on temple lands out of the hands of priests, and placed them into the mouths of the poor. Over and over the tablets say this was the way things were done in the past. It's no accident that the name of these reforms, "Amargi," has a double meaning: "freedom" and "return to the mother" (Stone 1993: 41).

Bounceback #3. 180 Degrees Backwards
Despite trying to embezzle Her birth-giving talents and drop Her to low slot on the company organizational chart, the old starvation/taking gods still hadn't buried the Guiding Goddess. The people just kept right on loving Her. But the gods weren't done. They still had a trick or two up their sleeves, the next one being turning everything about the Goddess 180 degrees backwards. In the West at least, many starvation-god traits are simply goddess traits turned upside down and backwards — in what appears to be a thinly disguised attempt to

drag the Goddess' good name through the mud. Just a few examples:

Since goddess was moon, the starvation/war gods became sun (and moon became somewhat flawed, as in "moonstruck" and "mooning around").

Since the Goddess' womb and fertile soil are black, the war gods began swearing black is a bad color (and white, which some say the old goddess societies considered bad — it's the color of bones after all — the war gods began calling good).

Since to certain goddesses the numbers 666 and 13 were holy, the war gods began calling them "unlucky" numbers.

Since goddesses were of the earth and therefore reachable by humans, the starvation/taking gods became of the sky — and unreachable.

Since the Goddess makes men born from women, Jehovah made Eve, the first woman, born from a man.

Since Goddess creates life through Her womb, the war gods created life through anything but (heads, ribs, penes, armpits, slits in stomachs, mouths and so on; see above).

Since Goddess sees sensual pleasures as sacred, the war gods made them sinful, even kicking Eve out of the Garden for eating the apple (which Stone says symbolizes sexuality)(1993: 220-22).

Since under the Goddess, women interpreted divine will, the starvation/taking gods twisted women into people who became doubted and ignored.

Since for millennia the serpent helped women interpret divine will, the war gods twisted the serpent into a symbol of the downfall of the human race.

Since the old Norse were born from the warm womb of the Goddess Hel, the starvation-culture gods twisted Hel's womb into a fiery pit of eternal torture (Stone 1993; Walker 1983).

This last one really pickles my liver. They took a gorgeous goddess of warmth, love and hugs, and tried to con us into believing She was really an underground torture chamber. This trick was so below-the-belt that it was what finally shook me loose and opened my eyes to what a stunning con job the war- and sky-god religions really are.

Hel: Goddess Who Couldn't Be Conquered

What? Hel used to be a Goddess with a warm loving womb to whom we all returned at death?!? You got it. Hel, especially, shows up the war-god perpetrators for the sneaky, conniving crackerheads they really are. What they did to this goddess was a smear campaign to beat all smears. This was spin at its height.

Actually, Jehovah wasn't the first to come up with the idea of Hell. As far as we know, the snaggers of that award are the ancient Egyptians. After hurting you for a while, however, the ancient Egyptians let up. Leave it to Jehovah to invent pain that goes on forever and ever, i.e. "perhaps the most sadistic fantasy ever conceived by the mind of man" (Walker 1983: 387).

Anyhow, what really, really makes me see red is this: not only did this sack of shame invent one of the most vicious, pernicious and downright skanky concepts in the history of human religion, he named it after a guiding goddess probably sacred to the peaceful, healthy Neolithics of Europe. This goddess's name varied from Hel, Hella, Helle and Ella in some places, to Helga,

Holle and Holde in others. As Jehovah tried to twist Hel/Ella/Holde and Her love for us into the exact opposite — unending, unbearable pain — he was also aiming to strip us of one of the few healthy deities we've ever had.

Originally Hel was anything but hellish. All humans returned to Her loving womb for "rebirth after death." By placing them in the bodies of newborns, She resurrected the souls of the dead, and "the early 'Hell' seems to have been a uterine shrine or sacred cave of rebirth, denoted by the Norse *hellir*." Jungian psychologist Eric Neumann refers to Hel/Holde as one of the "Great Mothers" of ancient Europe and the Near East, along with Isis, Athene and Neith (Walker 1983: 380-81; Walker 1988: 251; 462; Neumann 1991: 228).

Hel was especially linked to children. While Jehovah callously pitched unbaptized kids into his vast underground torture chamber to burn in fire forever, Hel welcomed the souls of unbaptized kiddies back into her womb. Children who died unbaptized were called 'heimchen,' or 'little-ones-going-home' (to Mother). Hel, "as universal mother, was the patron of all newborn children and had charge of naming them — which used to be the symbolic equivalent of giving the child its soul" (Miles 1976: 242; Walker 1988: 466).

Archaeologist and mythologist Marija Gimbutas believes Hel was one of the old guiding goddesses of Neolithic Europe, and that She represented the entire life cycle: "The images of Freyja, Valkyrie, and Holla witness the continuity of the Old European goddess as life giver, death wielder, and regeneratrix. She can be young, beautiful and strong or old, ugly and powerful, representing a full cycle from birth to death to rebirth." Like the Basque Goddess Mari we met in the first half of this book, Hel too was a shape shifter: She "brings out the sun, and as a frog, she retrieves the red apple, symbol of life, from the well into which it falls at harvest. When ice melts in the spring, Holla sometimes appears as a beautiful nude woman bathing in a stream or lake" (Gimbutas 2001).

No wonder the starvation-culture gods felt forced to turn Hel into a torture chamber. How else could anyone rout such a fabulous goddess? Actually, rout Her they have not — even after 6000 years of clanking around trying. Even today Mother Hel/Holle stands among us. All over Europe Her name is preserved in places like Helsinki, Holland, Hollingstedt, Holderness, Holstein, Helgo, Heligoland and others. "Iceland still has a traditional 'home of the dead' in Helgafell or 'Hel's Hill,'" while Germans used to believe that all the world's newborns came from Dame Holle's well. (Walker 1983, p. 381).

Hel/Ella also smiles back at us from our fairy tales. It's likely that Cinder-ella is actually the Goddess Hel/Ella biding time, disguised and hiding from Indo-European war gods until it's safe to return. Some think the tale is a coded message from the Great Goddess Herself, with Cinderella symbolizing the Goddess after the gods have violently reduced Her and Her regenerative fires to cinders. Playing the part of the Christian Church would be the evil stepmother. Starring as the "church's twin darlings" the military aristocracy and the Christian priesthood, are Cinderella's evil stepsisters. The prince plays the part of humankind — forever seduced by physical beauty and fine clothes.

Finally, Ella's "fairy godmother" must be none other than the GodMother Herself, Mother Earth come to rescue Her child from evil. The coded message? Not to worry: one day the Goddess Ella/Hel will rise again from the ashes of her cinder life and reclaim Her monumental abilities to hold us in Her warm, loving womb. There we'll rest a while before waltzing into future earthly incarnations (Walker 1983: 168).

Hel appears also in a book settled in on my living-room bookshelves. In *Grimm's Fairy Tales,* the Brothers Grimm retell the tale of "Mother Holle," in which another evil stepmother forces her good and lovely stepdaughter to retrieve a loom shuttle dropped down a well. At the bottom of the well, the daughter discovers an awesome land full of green meadows overflowing with flowers in all the colors of the rainbow. She lends a hand to an apple tree in need of shaking (apples are sacred to Hel) and to a loaf of bread about to burn (bread is also sacred to Hel). By and by she makes her way to "Mother Holle," and for some time bustles around working for the Goddess. Before the girl leaves, the Goddess leads her to a doorway where a "heavy shower of golden rain fell, and all the gold clung" to the girl "so that she was completely covered over with it."

After the daughter climbs back to the earth's surface and the evil stepmother sees her covered in gold, the evil mother's eyes glaze over with greed. In a flash she sends the lazy daughter down the well to claim her share of the gold. But after turning up her nose at the tree, the bread and the Goddess, the lazy daughter drags home covered not in gold, but in tar (Grimm 1972: 133-136).

Finally, linked to the Goddess Hel/Holle are certain figures who appear at European midwinter festivals: the Holly King, the Holly Knight, the Green Knight and the Wild Man. Holly berries were Hel/Holle's life-giving blood. Holly and mistletoe represent the Goddess and God at Yuletide, and as such the 'sacred marriage.' Although Jumping Jehovah tried like the dickens to stamp out the hanging of mistletoe and holly in Christmas homes, Europeans have stubbornly clung to this reminder of their Goddess Hel/Holle, and do so even to this day. Nevertheless, even today scholars misjudge and underestimate the great Hel. Apparently many have fallen hook, line and sinker for the spin the war gods stuck on Her long ago. For example, in his recent 417-page encyclopedia of world myth, Leeming throws Hel only a scant paragraph. Obviously buying 100 percent of the war-god spin, Leeming labels Hel the "half-dead monster offspring of the Norse trickster Loki..." (Walker 1988: 466; Walker 1983: 406; Leeming 2005: 174).

Stealing Her Magic

If turning the Goddess 180 degrees backwards wasn't entirely successful — and it wasn't — "Then by golly" said the starvation/war god one day to himself "I'll just pilfer Her magic powers lock, stock and barrel. Maybe then the people will like me better." So those Goddess traits he couldn't con people into giving up, the war god stole for himself — claiming original ownership. For example, Jonah and the whale, Noah's ark, Moses parting the Red Sea, Adam and Eve, Easter, the fish, the dove, the trinity, Lent — all were property of the goddess long before they were filched and pilfered by the Abrahamaic starvation gods. Not only did the starvation/taking gods filch and pilfer, they also lied about it, revamping history to hide the fact that Jonah, Noah, Moses and the others were originally Goddess men (Walker 1983).

Let's start with Adam. In pre-Biblical myths an 'adam' was simply "a man made of blood." He was an entity formed by the Goddess out of clay (adamuh) and given life via her blood. Not only that, "the idea of Adam's rib was taken from a Sumerian goddess who formed infants' bones from their mothers' ribs" (Walker 1983: 8-9). This goddess, of course, existed a thousand years or so before Jumping Jehovah ever saw the light of day.

And how about Moses parting the Red Sea? Original with the Hebrews? Again, not. Long, long before Moses, the ancient Egyptian Goddess "Isis ... parted the waters of the River Phaedrus on Her journey to Byblos." The Goddess Bindamati did the same when She crossed the Ganges.

Surely "the Pearly Gates" is an original? No. Long before the Bible was put to paper, pearls were sacred to the goddess Aphrodite Marina, whose body served as the gate to the afterlife.

Father, Son and Holy Ghost? Nuh-uh. Way before the Hebrews, goddess people all over Europe and the Middle East saw their major Goddess as a shape shifter like Hel, who could and did represent the life cycle — as Mother, Daughter and Elder

Woman. In Greece, She was Hera/Hebe/Hecate. In Rome She was the three Fates. To the Druids She was Diana Triformis, to the Irish the Triple Morrigan (Walker 1983: 1018-19). For more see Figure 7.2 below.

Figure 7.2. The Bible: Pinched from Pagans

Element	Stolen From:	Original Purpose
Jonah and the whale	Ancient Babylonia	The God Oannes ("Jonah") was "reborn from the mouth of a great fish" — symbol of the Great Mother.
Noah and the Ark	Ancient Egypt, India, Sumer, Babylonia	Many had flood myths and flood heroes. Ark = arc = crescent moon = Goddess
Jacob's Ladder	Ancient Egypt	To climb to heaven Egyptian kings and prophets used the "ladder of Set."
Moses and the Bulrushes	Ancient Akkadia	As an infant, Sargon of Akkad (2242-2186 B.C.) was "set ... afloat on a river in a basket of rushes" as were many other ancient heroes.
The Ten Commandments	Ancient Near East, Greece etc.	Deities delivered commandments on mountaintops in many ancient pre-Christian religions. Zoroaster got his on a mountaintop from Ahura Mazda; the

		Goddess Rhea got hers on top of Mount Dicte.
Samson	Ancient Greece	"Samson's lion-killing, pillar-carrying and other feats were copied from the Labors of Heracles."
Crucifixion, twelve disciples, communion	Ancient Greece	Heracles, who traveled with twelve "archer companions," was crucified on an oak tree. Adonis too was sacrificed on a tree and his blood drunk as wine, his flesh eaten as bread.
The Resurrection	Ancient Neolithic cultures	Some ancient cultures thought the moon died each month, stayed dead three days and then resur-rected (Christ was in the tomb three days before resurrecting.)
The dove	Pagans in general	To most Pagans the dove was the symbol par excellence of the "Great Mother's all-giving love."
Eve	Ancient India, Assyria etc.	In ancient Assyria, Eve created the first males and females, "in pairs she completed them." Genesis 1.27 is directly lifted from the Assyrian scriptures — with the "she's" changed to "he's."
Easter	Ancient Saxony etc.	During the Goddess

		Oestre's festival (celebrated long before the Christian era) the god died, was placed in his tomb and then rose again.
Eden	Ancient Persia	Purloined from the Persian Garden of Heden. Heden was an earthly paradise where the first couple was joined together.
Isaac and the ram	Ancient Boeotia	Probably pilfered from a myth about a prince about to be sacrificed on the alter; in the nick of time the ram of the Golden Fleece appeared to take his place.
Fish	Roman Empire	The fish as goddess symbol "was so revered throughout the Roman Empire that Christian authorities insisted on taking it over."
Lent	Ancient Rome	The Roman "Feast of Mothers" involved fasting and the performance of various religious rites.
Easter lily	Ancient northern Europe	The lily was a symbol of the Goddess Oestre/Easter.
The word	Ancient Greece	In ancient Greece one theory of creation said that words carry such power that deities can use them to

		create matter.
Paradise	Ancient Persia	In ancient Persia the magic garden "Pairidaeza" held the Tree of Life — source of immortality.
Love your neighbor	Ancient Egypt etc.	2000 years before Christians saw the light of day the Goddess Ma'at gave ancient Egyptians forty-two Admonitions, along the lines of love your neighbor, feed the hungry etc.
Christ the Savior	Ancient Pagans in general	In the ancient world among groups too many to mention, annual sacrifice of a god on a tree or cross insured rebirth of life in the spring.
Christ, Son of Man	Ancient Hindus	To con people into thinking male gods can give birth Hindus called their god Vishnu "Son of Man."
Abraham	Ancient India?	Abraham "…seems to have been a Semitic version of India's … god Brahma."

(Walker 1983: 478, 524, 676-78, 888, 288, 267-69, 312, 314, 535, 542, 768, 950, 5; Sjoo and Mor 1987: 170, 121, 101)

Bouncing Back All over the Place
Despite all this whomping, people still clung to their goddesses.

Especially in out-of-the-way places like the Greek and other Mediterranean islands, goddesses promenaded back into town and prospered. Of course, the starvation-culture war gods doing the whomping, dictated all the books back then, and rarely were they truthful about who was getting worshipped and who wasn't. Fortunately we have archaeologists to dig up the "truth." According to archaeologist Mary E. Voyatzis, for example, the Greek goddesses were a lot more important in eighth century BC than the Greek poet Homer let on in his written works (Voyatzis 1998: 147).

Around 1000 BC, big-daddy Yahweh was among the first to boot all goddesses out of town totally (Condren 1989: 12-14). Officially, that is. Just reading the records you'd think that by 1000 BC the goddesses had totally vanished in the land of the Hebrews. What archaeologists dig up, however, tells a different story. Despite the official booting, most Hebrews still stuck to their goddesses: "We know from the Bible that the official deity" in Israel "was male..., but the common people persisted in worshipping ... deities such as the goddesses Asherah and Astarte. In Judean houses down to the destruction of the Temple in 586 BC, we find Astarte images" (Gordon 1966: 31).

In Japan, the Goddess made a comeback around AD 500 with the erection of the Ise shrine to the goddess Amaterasu on land that later became the city of Kyoto. As Goddess of the Sun, Amaterasu seems a curious combination of a guiding goddess and a shyer lass. Although she's "considered to be the prime ancestor of the Japanese emperor," she nevertheless gets yanked around considerably by what could very well be descendants of old Yayoi starvation-culture gods. Take for example her storm-god brother Susanowo. In a drunken rage, Suse once smashed his sister's home — along with most of the rest of heaven and earth. All this sent Amaterasu into deep hiding, after which it took major effort to coax Her and Her sunshine out again. My guess is that Amaterasu is a guiding-goddess makeover, with credit for the conversion due primarily to Yayoi or later war gods (Tate 2006: 235; Leeming 2005: 13-14).

In seventh-century-AD India, a temple was built to the goddess Lakshmi, who some see as a direct descendant of the Guiding Goddess of the old second-millennium BC Indus Valley Civilization. And during the Greco-Roman era, the two-millennia-old Egyptian goddess Isis began to shake the dust off Her gown, set Her sails, and take off for stardom. By way of "Roman legions, merchants, sailors, and missionary priesthood," Isis spirituality spread "to Greece, throughout the Roman empire, as far north as Britain, west toward France and Germany, and northeast into Turkey, and the Middle East." Some think she got to India on the coattails of Alexander the Great (356-323 BC). Others even "believe she traveled the Silk Road into the Far East, where her aspects can be seen in the beloved Buddhist Goddess Kwan Yin" (Tate 2006: 196, 121).

Why was Isis so loved by so many? Goddess scholar Karen Tate thinks it's because She is

the quintessential mother, sister, and wife.... She searched the world for her murdered husband.... Using her ... magic, she breathed ... life into his lifeless body, resurrecting him.... Humankind recognized Isis as a ... Goddess who had experienced the pain ... mortals must endure.... They saw her suffering, and knew she would understand theirs (Tate 2006: 121).

But then came the smackdown. Isis was just too popular for the starvation gods to bear. "More than any other Goddess, Isis was a challenge to the emerging patriarchal religions, her worship coming close to superseding that of Christianity." And so, during the reign of the Emperor Justinian, AD 527-565, Isis' temples were slammed shut for good (Tate 2006: 121-23).

Bounceback #4: A Bit of Goddess Back to the Christians

So popular was Isis in the Roman world, that whenever the war god Jehovah thought about Her, he turned beet red with rage. J. had come up with a new angle on the old Hebrew religion. He thought this angle made the old religion sexier than ever before. Imagine: a guy dies on a cross to save the world....

Okay, so the idea wasn't ripping new. Jehovah had filched it from every other religion afloat in the Roman world at the time. But J. could see the utility in the idea, and he was determined to lay it down on territory being hogged by the Goddess Isis. Of course, before he could, he had to get rid of Isis — and all those other pesky sects floating around making his life pure misery.

Well, to make a long story short, Jumping Jehovah won this battle. "Though many centuries of transformation" had taken a toll on Goddess religion, "the worship of the female deity survived into the classical periods of Greece and Rome. It was not totally suppressed until the time of the Christian emperors of Rome and Byzantium, who closed down the last Goddess temples" in the 500s AD (Stone 1993: 18).

Actually, however, even then the adoration of goddesses wasn't "totally suppressed" as Stone puts it. It still chugged along, in large part in the form of adoration of Jesus' mother Mary. The people just could not — and would not — surrender their Guiding Goddess. Jumping J. was blown away by the power Mary had over the people. To them, Mary mother of Jesus was simply a "composite of Mariamne, the Semitic God-Mother and Queen of Heaven; Aphrodite-Mari, the Syrian version of Ishtar; Juno the Blessed Virgin; Isis as Stella Maris, Star of the Sea ... and many other versions of the Great Goddess" (Walker 1983: 603).

It didn't take Jumping Jehovah long to see he had to sit on Mary just as he had Isis. And sit he did. As a result, for the first 500 years of Christianity, Mary was forbidden to wear a halo. Even the three wise men got to wear halos, but not Mary — she'd been demoted to the lower rung of the war-god ladder. But for all the good it did him, Jehovah might as well have sat around sipping frozen margaritas. To the people, Mary went right on being a totally awesome goddess, as shown by this story told by Caesarius of Heisterbach: The Devil met up with a certain knight who needed money. So the Devil said, "Renounce God and I'll see that you get plenty." The knight agreed and immediately renounced God. Then the Devil said, "Renounce Mary." Whereupon, aghast, the knight refused with a vengeance. Later on, goes the story, Mary "intervened" to keep her knight free of Jehovah's vast, underground torture chamber (Walker 1983: 611, 608).

And then J. saw that people were threatening to walk off his ball court altogether. So after grumbling and spanking the wall a few times, in the sixth century he invited Mary back into his Church. The way he did it was by giving temples belonging to the Pagan goddesses to Mary, and by giving Mary fancy new titles like "Ecclesia (the Church)." So in the sixth century, for example, Jehovah turned the temple of Isis at Philae and the sanctuary of Aphrodite on Cyprus, into churches of Mary. Whereupon the Cypriots, at least, just went right on worshiping Aphrodite in what was now supposedly a church of Jehovah. Mary may have been lower than Jesus at first, but when the goddess temples closed, the "Goddess herself was not so much ousted as absorbed" (Walker 1983: 609, 455).

Bounceback #5: God Dark Ages, Goddess Renaissance

Another smackdown-bounceback comedy of errors rolled onto stage after Jehovah plunged Europe into what some still call "The Dark Ages." Although there's no shortage of theories as to what dumped Europe into the Dark Ages roughly around AD 500, some lay the blame squarely at Jehovah's feet, seeing as how at exactly that time his followers trashed and burned almost every book on the continent. And did I add that they threw a few scholars into the fire along with the books?

Well they did. So of course anyone who knew anything ran for the hills, emptying Europe not only of its libraries and books, but of its brains to boot. "Suppression of the teaching priestess or *alma mater* led to an eclipse of education in general. Many scholars fled from Christian persecutions eastward to Iran ... the world's intellectual capital for two centuries." As goddess scholar Barbara Walker puts it, even though historians have offered scads of theories about the cause of the downfall of the Roman Empire, "the one cause that may have had more to do with it than any other" is Christianity (Walker 1983: 210, 208).

First, Jehovah's followers burned all the books they could lay their hands on:

Christians said one of the diabolic symptoms of the oncoming end of the world was 'the spread of knowledge,' which they endeavored to check with wholesale book-burnings, destruction of libraries and schools, and opposition to education for laymen (Walker 1983: 208).

Second, Jumping J's followers burned whole libraries, including the library of the Palatine Apollo, for example, and possibly even the great library of the classical world, that of Alexandria in Egypt. Not only did they burn books and libraries, they even banned learning. For example they actually nixed the study of medicine, "on the ground that all diseases were caused by demons and could be cured only by exorcism" (Walker 1983: 208, 210).

Third, just to make sure they drove their point home, Christians burned a few book readers too: In sixteenth-century Spain, the penalty for owning a Bible in the everyday language of the people was toasting and roasting over a slow fire until your spirit departed your body (Walker 1983: 212). In the fifth century AD, one of the world's outstanding scholars was the philosopher and mathematician Hypatia. Jehovah the so-called 'heavenly' god reserved a special death for this professor: a posse of Christian monks "dragged her from her chariot, carried her into a church, stripped her, scraped the flesh from her bones with oyster shells, then burned what was left: all by order of St. Cyril, the city Patriarch...." Cyril somehow managed to prevent any official investigation into the murder, and in 1882 was dubbed a Christian saint (Walker 1983: 420).

Fourth, once they got started, Jumping J's followers just couldn't seem to stop. They burned anything they could get their hands on: "Contrary to the conventional mythology, Christians were not prosecuted ... for being Christians but for committing civil crimes...." It was Christians, for example, who set the Great Fire of AD 64 in the city of Rome, and at least one Christian was later dubbed a saint for no other reason than having a talent for setting fires, i.e., for burning to the ground a temple dedicated to "the Mother of the Gods" (Walker 1983: 209-210).

With all this burning going on, things were not good. Europe sank from a center of culture and learning, to what today we'd call a third-world sink hole. It plunged from knowing the earth was round, to "knowing" that dried, powdered duck produces frogs. It sailed from knowing how to build a Coliseum, to knowing how to build — well, next to nothing. "The widespread literacy of the classical period disappeared. Aqueducts, harbors, buildings, even the splendid Roman roads fell into ruin.... [C]enturies of devastating war could hardly have shattered Roman civilization as effectively as did ... ascetic monotheism" (Walker 1983: 210-12).

The Christians jumped so hard on science it became a field of gibberish, with the best books in the land teaching that mice could be "generated spontaneously ... from 'the putrefaction of the earth.'" These books taught that "wasps produce themselves" out of dead horses, and bees out of cow carcasses. Since Christians had banned the scientific method, ideas that in the past could have been tested and found — well, just plain silly — now became the law of the land by fiat. Long before the first Christian ever saw the light of day, Pagans had determined that the earth was round. They'd even calculated its circumference within a very small margin of error. But Lactantius pooh-poohed the notion, and used the Bible to "prove" the earth was flat (Walker 1983: 211-212).

Is it any wonder that "the greatest of English historians," Edward Gibbon, author of *The History of the Decline and Fall of the Roman Empire*, laid the blame for the fall of the Pagan world squarely on the twin devils of barbarians and Christians? Finally, "after years of vandalism and destruction, St. John Chrysostom proudly boasted, 'Every trace of the old philosophy and literature of the ancient world has vanished from the face of the earth.'" But it wasn't just the plundering of knowledge that plunged Europe into the Dark Ages. Walker thinks just as deadly was the shredding of the Goddess: "By denying women's spiritual significance and forbidding Goddess worship, the church alienated both sexes from their Pagan sense of unity with the divine through each other" (Roberts 1997: 79; Walker 1983: 208).

Calling the climbing of Western Europe out of the Dark Ages a "miracle," historian Hugh Trevor-Roper admits that he and his colleagues "seldom agree" on how this miracle happened. Maybe that's because Mr. T-R and the others haven't studied goddess history. Soon after the Goddess rode back into Europe (on the coattails of the Crusaders in the twelfth century), Europe began getting "vigorous and creative in a new way." Remember — as Europe tumbled into the Dark Ages, the Goddess escaped to the Near East to wait for safe days to come home again. So not only did the old Pagan learning return to Europe with the Crusaders, but along with it goddesses as well, toting romantic love, song, dance, troubadours, fine art, King Arthur and his Round Table, Guinevere, courtly love, and all the rest of the beauty in life. (Trevor-Roper 1989: 24; Roberts 1997: 219).

Europeans were tickled and thrilled.

Music, dance, poetry and "erotic love songs to Venus" got big in a hurry, erasing starvation-god notions that if it felt good it was a fast track to Hell. "Europeans were 'backsliding' into their indigenous Paganism. Gnostic beliefs were circulating *sub rosa*, and communities of medieval 'hippies' were springing up everywhere" (Sjoo and Mor 1991: 299). In other words, life was getting good again.

Beneath all her war-god makeover, Guinevere was actually the ancient goddess of Britain, the Welsh "Triple Goddess, Gwenhwfar, 'the first lady of these islands.' "Since no king could rule Britain without her, she was always getting abducted: Guinevere was appropriated by Malwas, Meleagant, Arthur, Lancelot and Mordred. On the other hand, losing Guinevere meant losing the throne too, and being pitched back out onto the streets again." (Walker 1983: 357, 352).

Well this boiled down to Jehovah seeing a red-suited matador whipping a red neon flag in his face. Time for another smackdown. This time old J. did an outstandingly odoriferous job. The stench left was so bad that even school textbooks won't talk about it. As a result, most modern Christians don't know what mischief their daddy dearest did, for "five solidly sadistic centuries," to hundreds of thousands of innocent men, women and children (Sjoo and Mor 1991: 310). Below is a passage from one of thousands of chilling Inquisition-torture cases. One is just about all I have the stomach for (don't read it if your stomach's shy). It's about a girl named Erzebet, who lived somewhere in Europe during Jehovah's Inquisition.

JUDGE: Do you confess that you made love potions and let the young men from Csongrad [sic] drink of it so that they all became enamored of you?

ERZEBET: No. I know nothing of such a drink.

JUDGE: Do you confess that sitting on a wand you flew up and became a bird?

ERZEBET: No, I don't.

JUDGE: Do you confess that you spat upon the wheatfields and thereby caused a great drought?

ERZEBET: No.

JUDGE: Do you confess that you gave birth to twins and then buried them alive?

ERZEBET: It is true that I gave birth to twins, your Honor, but they were dead. I had to bury them, otherwise I would be suckling them, since my milk is oozing after them.

JUDGE: You had better admit to the rest of the charges or you will be tortured.

ERZEBET: I cannot, your Honor, because I have not done these things.

Erzebet was then given over to be tortured.... The priests were eating lunch and dinner while the poor woman screamed from pain. The torturers poured hot water into Erzsebet's mouth through a sieve, and she finally confessed to everything....

Erzebet had to dig her own grave. Then she was put in a casket that had the head-end sawed completely off. When they placed her in the casket, her face was looking through the hole into the ground, and the rest of her was buried alive. Then the men poked at Erzebet's face with hot irons until she felt no more.... All in the name of Jesus (Budapest 1980: 184-85).

Jehovah's Christian Inquisition was creaming and crushing non-Christians all the way up and into the twentieth century. In 1928 in Hungary, for example, an elderly woman, because her religion was not Christian, was brutally murdered: "In January, 1928, a family of Hungarian peasants beat an old woman to death, claiming she was a witch. A court acquitted them, on the grounds that they acted out of 'irresistible compulsion'" (Walker 1983: 1087).

"But," you protest, "couldn't Christians just as easily cough up evidence of Pagan 'Devil-worship' wrongdoing?" It's true that Devil worship, or "Satanism," seems to have been a problem for a while — among American teens at any rate (Emerson and Syron 1995). Devil worship, however, is not a Pagan, but a Christian phenomenon. The Devil is a Christian, not a Pagan deity. And Devil worship — a serious problem — is with us only because Christians are. I mean, if they had no picture of Satan already sitting in their heads, put there by Christianity, how could people dance around as "Satanists"? As for the ugly things done in Satanic cults, most seem to have been invented by Inquisition priests in order to scare Christians into "staying in line."

Twenty-First-Century Bounceback

At the dawn of the twenty-first century, the world is witnessing the birth of another Goddess comeback. Today, all over the globe, goddess conferences and festivals are held annually: in UK, the Glastonbury Goddess Conference (www.goddessconference.com) and The Goddess in Cornwall Conference (http://www.goddessincornwall.co.uk/); in Turkey, the Goddess Conversations Conference; In the US, Wisconsin's Everyday Goddess Conference and Seattle's Women of Wisdom Conference; in Australia the Ariadne's Thread Goddess Conference; in Hungary the Budapest Goddess Conference (http://www.goddessbudapest.com/); and many, many more (*Radical Goddess Thealogy* weblog 10 February 2007).

In 2000, people all over the globe celebrated the Goddess 2000 Project, and organizations such as the Fellowship of Isis now have members worldwide. Founded in the 1970s by Lady Olivia Robertson and her brother Lawrence Durdin-Robertson in their family castle in Ireland, the Fellowship "is thriving — with more than 20,000 members across the world." In 1993 it "was one of two Goddess-oriented religions to be represented at the World Parliament of Religions ... in Chicago." And in Glastonbury UK, the Goddess Temple is the first goddess space in modern history to be officially "recognized as a place of worship" (www.goddesstemple.co.uk and www.kathyjones.co.uk). Since June 2003 it has been acknowledged in the UK "as a registered place of worship" (Tate 2006: 65, 39).

In California USA, the Goddess Temple of Orange County was built in honor of the Goddess, as was the Tien Hau Temple in San Francisco's Chinatown (according to its literature this temple was dedicated in 1852 to the Goddess Tien Hau, but is "associated by some with" the Chinese Goddess Kwan Yin and with Isis)(Tate 2006: 349).

In Nevada USA, the Temple of Sekhmet was built to an Egyptian goddess whose real nature was twisted by starvation/war gods. Rather than being an "impulsive, deadly and heartless" goddess, Sekhmet is actually, according to Her devotees, "an entity of power and strength that enables manifestation and transformation." Since this temple was built on Western Shoshone Indian territory, it houses, across from the lion-headed woman-bodied statue of Sekhmet, the 'Madre del Mondo'" (Mother Earth Goddess) — a statue sporting "the features of a Native American woman" (Tate 2006: 355-56).

In southwestern Wisconsin USA, the Circle Sanctuary Nature Preserve, rambling over 200 acres (81 hectares) of prairie, forest and wetland, is a nature-spirituality site with indoor and outdoor goddess shrines, nature walks, a "large archival library," regularly scheduled events, and Spirit Rock, an ancient Native American sacred site connected to Indian vision questing (Tate 2006: 371).

And increasingly the Goddess is carving out a media presence for Herself — in journals, periodicals, books, films, music and on the Net. A growing gaggle of goddess weblogs are penned on the Internet on a regular basis, by both men and women alike. In sum, here we are in the twenty-first century with Goddess on the upswing. Although for the past 6000 years the war god's worn himself out working to waste the Goddess, he's failed —

miserably I might add. As author and goddess devotee Tim Ward puts it "We can't destroy you, goddess, can't flee you, can't even desecrate you, because you are the indestructible thing alive in us" (Ward 2006: 346).

8

The Fix

A Vision

In my vision, the world has become a peaceful and fiercely environmentally conscious set of communities sharing a Mother Goddess who preaches loving every person on earth the way healthy mothers love their children.

Because all communities are organized around one or more Mother Goddesses, this is a world without starvation-culture gods, war gods, or taking gods. Although the goddesses look different in different communities, they all guide their devotees into the kinds of societies our Neolithic ancestors enjoyed: playful, risk-taking, sensual, creative, wealthy, non-violent, egalitarian, self-ruling, peaceful, and exhilarating. Instead of being foisted on communities from the outside, these goddesses mostly come from communities' ancestral pasts, pasts which in many cases included, at some point in time, one or more guiding goddesses — who to one extent or another should be retrievable.

When we oust our war gods and the starvation-culture that birthed them, we won't need large nations to protect us from, well — war gods. In other words, we can return to living in smaller, more sustainable communities. With new guidance from the Mother, women, and oxytocin, world organizations will be aces at using more tend-and-befriend behavior (versus the fight-or-flight behavior that now helps prevent the world from living in peace).

In my vision, on top of its new warlessness, the world has also made a dramatic shift out of another deadly sink-hole: human-caused global climate change. Children reared to sense on a deep level that the Earth is Mother, will fight like banshees to keep even one hair on her head from being harmed. Children reared to see the sacred Goddess' breath as the wind, her hair as the fluttering leaves of the forest, her skin as the bare earth, her blood flowing in the earth's rivers, her bones as rocks and boulders, and her body as the curves of the hills — these children might even fight to the death to stop anything from fouling their Mother's breath, pitching sludge into Her lifeblood, or carving into the hills that form Her body. If we need to hustle the world in a hurry onto the same page about global climate change — and we do — nothing could be as quick or powerful as shifting the world from a distant, Earth-besmirching sky god, to an unconditionally-loving Mother Earth Goddess, who actually *is* the Earth under our feet.

With a Little Magic, The Fix Would Be Simple

In one sense, the fix is simple. Let's say "A" is war-god dystopia, and "B" is Mother-Goddess utopia. If by some magic in the next split second everyone on earth suddenly grasped the basic truths in this book, we might zoom from A to B in as few as five or six years. When everyone "gets" it, few will be able to do much of anything but two-step toward the switch. It's like spotting a $100 bill or a 50-pound note on the sidewalk. Are you going to do anything else before diving for it? Probably not. Of course since a few are getting rich as Rockefeller from the status quo, we can probably count on some of them to gun monkey wrenches into our two-stepping. However, after the other 95 percent of us get moving in earnest, this tiny bunch will have almost no chance against us.

Anyhow, gazing into my crystal ball, here's what I see in the weeks and months after the world grasps the situation: I see think tanks all over the world busily tackling the task of getting from A (war-god dystopia) to B (Mother-Goddess utopia). I see international development organizations across the world grasping the fact that boosting girls, women and mothers will make men and their whole community a winning team. (Some sustainable development organizations already know this; for example, Heifer International won honors recently from the

United Nations for their work in "Gender Justice"). In my vision I see that several international organizations — for example Earth Charter (www.earthcharter.org) and the UN (www.un.org) — have adopted the Goddess (Gaia maybe?) as their central "world organizing principle."

Still gazing into my crystal ball, I see that in the industrialized nations, social scientists are pushing certain research projects into overdrive: the link between starvation/war-god religions and criminal behavior, for example; the birth and personality of starvation culture; and the absence of any human predisposition for war. Worldwide, galloping over the Internet via thousands of websites and weblogs, I see a grassroots "Mother's Whispering Campaign." Mothers are taught they have not only the right but the duty to whisper to their children from birth to avoid war gods like the plague.

Around the World, Nations Switching

Still peering into the future, I see that everywhere nations are beginning to understand that putting starvation- and war gods in charge of the world is like putting foxes in charge of the chickens. I see nations uncovering the glorious old Guiding Mother Goddesses of their free, peaceful and egalitarian ancestors. In Europe, my crystal ball shows Bridget, Freya, Gaia, Holle, Isis, Mari of the Basques, Sovereignty and hundreds of other local Goddesses standing tall for inspection as Europeans try to piece together the old guiding systems these goddesses pumped into their veins.

Depending on their preferences and backgrounds, I see Americans too checking out a bevy of ancient Goddesses: Spider Woman, Thinking Woman, White Buffalo Woman, Ala of the Nigerian Ibo, the ancient Minoan Goddess(es), the ancient British Goddess Sovereignty (Matthews 2002), and many more. Among others, Middle Easterners are resurrecting the goddesses Nut, Astarte, and Tiamat. India is breathing new life into Devi-Shakti, and China into older forms of Kuan Yin (after scouring off Her war-god tarnish). For goddesses other countries might return to, see Appendix D: Possible Guiding Goddesses We Can Return To.

In my crystal ball I see that all over the world people are seeking out those hit least and last by the war gods, people who might still remember the Guiding Goddess, and be able to teach about Her. The Japanese are turning to the Ainu, Americans to the Pueblo Indians, Europeans to the Basques and Scandinavians, the Chinese to their Moso.

Around the world, I see countries beginning to realize that their starvation- and war-god "religions" are really only political control systems, akin to cults, dangerous to adults and deadly to children. As governments yank tax-exempt status for starvation-god churches and institutions, I see them gifting it instead to guiding-goddess organizations focused on peace, non-violence and egalitarianism. After ditching their war gods, moderate Christians, Jews, Hindus and Muslims are turning to their own radical sects and helping them follow suit. In my magic crystal ball I see that one by one, war-god seminaries are either closing their doors, or morphing into guiding-goddess seminaries.

Still gazing into the future, I see media mogols going into overdrive searching for media on the switch. I see artists, writers, musicians, publishers and producers all panting to keep up with the demand for media showing the starvation war gods for the primitive disasters they really are, and the guiding goddesses as the new path for world peace and plenty. TV and films are awash with the switch. On drama channels, after becoming trapped in war-god cults, children are rescued and deprogrammed. On talk shows I see experts explaining how to use the Mother Model to help yourself and others climb out of difficult life situations. I see news documentaries covering the rapid shut-down all across the planet of the starvation war gods, and the resulting increase in global and environmental health, and in wealth, freedom and good times for all.

On cable TV the history channels are crammed with documentaries on the starvation war gods and the guiding goddesses. In my crystal ball I see documentaries about our Neolithic ancestors fashioning thousands of otherworldy female figurines, but never doing war. On the TV screen I see spellbinding documentaries about the awesome Minoan and Indus Valley Civilizations, both Goddess-centered and neither doing war. I see documentaries about the Goddess-society oecumene or commonwealth, discovered recently among both the ancient Goddess-centered Halafians and the Indus Valley peoples. The TV commentator is explaining that no evidence has ever been uncovered for either group holding any truck with centralized, top-down government, brutal rulers, or dweeby dictators.

My crystal ball also zeros in on audiences being blown away by gripping documentaries on the mysterious and explosive "rise" of the first states, in Mesopotamia around 4000 BC, then in Egypt, then across Eurasia to China, and then down the left coast of the Americas. The commentator explains how the first states always galloped in toting the world's first starvation/war-god packages (institutionalized warfare, conquest, torture, slavery, etc.). Less than a millennium after the war-god state hit China, it popped up across the Pacific along the west coast of the Americas. These documentaries explain how, contrary to our old views, the state proved a giant and grotesque leap backwards for humanity — from peace to perpetual war, from freedom and dignity for all to slavery for many, and from the good life for everyone, to grinding poverty for the masses.

I see in my ball chilling documentaries exploring the dramatic climate change that swirled over North Africa, Europe and Asia immediately before the rise of the first state; in these shows narrators muse about the possible consequent birth of something called starvation culture. Gazing deeper into the crystal, I also see documentaries about the first written records, and how they speak about powerful Guiding Mother Goddesses. As the starvation gods climb to higher and higher heights, however, these Great Mothers begin to dim. Although most of them drop underground for periods of time, through history they've also made periodic comebacks. Finally I'm seeing fascinating documentaries about the sexy, peaceful and egalitarian bonobo, the power-packed hormone oxytocin, and about the Moso, Hopi, Basques and others who over the millennia have managed to preserve their ancient Guiding Mother Goddesses.

In my crystal ball I see psychotherapists in special training programs learning how to help people recover from war-god religions and starvation culture. In both men and women, the terrible wounding of our sexuality brought about by war-god religion and starvation culture is taking time to heal. But as it does, a wide range of social problems are softening up: rape, incest, child porn, child molestation, hate crimes, divorce, STDs, prostitution and more.

Around the world I see goddess groups organizing around the Mother Model, and pitching any war gods they might have been harboring, replacing them with gods like the pre-Olympian Apollo, the Anasazi-Pueblo's Kokopelli, the British Good Man (also known as Robin Goodfellow and Robin Hood), and the pre-Christian King Arthur, who at one point seems indeed to have been a god (Walker 1983: 858-59, 60-61).

Switching at Home

Still hovering over my crystal ball, I see that around the world in local communities too people are demoting war-god religions to cult status, and dumping the tax-exempt status and community-involvement rights of these cults. Parents are warning their children against these pseudo-religions the way they warn them against child molesters. I see former war-god worshippers selling their churches and building beautiful structures in wilderness areas, allowing easier connections with nature and Goddess. Some are giving their old buildings to the homeless. Areas of the world without wilderness are setting aside land for wilderness to develop.

Since the starvation/war-god religions have been redefined as cults, the images in my crystal ball show schools now helping children steer clear of them. Also, schools are teaching the biochemical tendencies of females toward "tend and befriend" behavior and male tendencies toward "fight or flight." I see students grasping the fact that if humans are to survive, women as well as men must use their special talents for the good of all. While boys are being specifically trained to respect girls, girls are being taught to earn and demand respect.

Switching Hearts and Minds

After the world grasps the basic truths in this book, people will begin to rise on a personal level too. Everyone will begin practicing the Mother Model. We'll all aim, in other words, toward treating others the way a healthy mother treats her children. While men check out their attitudes toward women, polish them up, and begin treating women like guiding goddesses, women will check out their attitudes toward themselves, and begin to give themselves more credit. Above all, mothers will understand that to be strong guiding goddesses for the world, they need to heal in a hurry from their starvation/war-god wounds. In order to make these mammoth changes ASAP, both men and women will work in circles, as suggested by Jungian analyst and internationally known lecturer Jean Shinoda Bolen of the University of California Medical Center (see *The Millionth Circle: How to Change Ourselves and the World*, Bolen 1999).

Everyone will check out their attitudes too toward snooty snobbism, bully-boy behavior, war, violence, domination, and sex-as-power. Like drug addicts, most of us are deep-down addicted to war-god programming on these things. We'll begin to understand that, to one extent or another, we all need de-programming.

Switching for Men

Among the more difficult aspects of the switch to Goddess will be helping men move toward modeling themselves after mothers. Recently, Gandhi-King Peace Award recipient Amma, "best known in the West as the hugging guru," defined motherhood like this: "It is not restricted to women who've given birth; it is a principle inherent in both women and men. It is an attitude of the mind. It is love — and that love is the very breath of life." Going on, Amma describes the monumental power of this "attitude": "With the power of motherhood within," people "can influence the entire world. The love of awakened motherhood is a love and compassion felt not only toward one's own children, but toward all people, animals and plants, rocks and rivers — a love extended to all beings" (Bolen 2005: 15).

Of course most men in starvation/war-god cultures today are afraid of doing anything the way women do it. For the past six millennia, the starvation gods have used every trick in the book to make sure men feel this way. After turning them into emotional cripples, the starvation gods found it easy to plop men exactly where they are today: in manipulatable spaces where they can be talked into doing almost anything against their own best interests, including dying in wars to make a few rich, and dying of stress from working too hard.

Unfortunately for everyone, all across the planet now, men are disliked by possibly up to millions of women (sometimes even their own lovers and spouses). Why? Because they've become emotionally crippled from trying to get along without the help of women. Of course since many women can't face these negative emotions in themselves, they try to hide them — even from themselves. Doesn't matter. In a hundred little ways the negativity bubbles quietly to the surface. As a result, everyone suffers. And all the while the war gods are sitting back laughing their fool heads off over how they've conned men, now seriously ill from a lack of healthy woman-love.

Men are right where the war gods want them: crippled so badly they're putty in the war gods' hands. Because they've been denied the use of the Mother Model, men are riddled with internal fears and doubts, which they try to mask in destructive ways. Jean Shinoda Bolen gives helpful information to Western women about Western boy-culture, and the way it cripples men. In her section "Why Men Don't Ask Directions," Jean explains how older boys often deliberately humiliate younger ones asking questions:

> Men learn in childhood how painful it is to be made fun of when they don't know something that the other boys do.... They also learn that when they ask a question they can be deliberately misled. The other male might not know the answer and yet acts as if he does. He makes up an answer rather than reveal his ignorance. Or he may have fun at the younger boy's expense and give him a wrong answer on purpose (2005: 85).

When they're goaded into fighting a boy larger and stronger, boys stand in a double-bind. Whatever they do, they lose. If they refuse to fight, they're jeered at. If they fight, they may, and sometimes do, get seriously hurt. And if a boy spots a picked-on boy, he's in another bind: if he helps the boy, he's lumped in with him from then on, and physically hurt along with him; if he doesn't help, he feels guilty (Bolen 2005: 85).

Part of the answer, says Bolen, is for women to take a greater role in shaping community values: "Until women are equal partners in setting values, it is not safe for boys and men to be feeling and nurturing people without suffering from patriarchal judgments that they are not man enough." Like Bolen, many men are beginning to get it. Says Archbishop Desmond Tutu, recipient of the Nobel Peace Prize, "Our earth home and all forms of life in it are at grave risk. We men have had our turn and made a proper mess of things. We need women to save us" (Bolen 2005: 97, front matter).

Switching to What?

But when we talk about the switch, what exactly are we switching to? Since the starvation/war gods spent six millennia working like dogs to destroy Guiding-Goddess spirituality, we need to work like dogs too, to recover as much as possible of what was lost. Like mystery-novel detectives, we need to uncover the clues as to what it was exactly about guiding-goddess societies that enabled them to live free of snooty-snob dominance hierarchies, institutionalized warfare, and oodles of social violence of all shapes, sizes and stripes.

I believe a major tool in the arsenal the guiding goddessites used to keep their societies free of war, snootiness and all the rest, was the Mother Model. This model was described earlier in this book. According to the Mother Model, we treat each other the way healthy mothers treat their children. That is, with unconditional positive regard, with teaching preferred over punishment, and with an instantaneous protective response when that child faces danger. In a guiding-goddess society, boys as well as girls, of course, are all taught to follow the Mother Model.

A second tool the guiding goddessites might have used to keep their societies free of war and other social sludge, was something called the "gift economy." Instead of distributing goods and services by trading them for money or other things, the goods and services are distributed through a society via gift giving. And instead of the kudos going to those who can hoard the most (starvation-culture style), they go to those who can give the most away. So while society's talented are still motivated to produce in spades, the least able are never left to starve or sleep in the snow (or in "cardboard condominiums" in the city park). For more on the gift economy, check out Genevieve Vaughan's *For-Giving*, Lewis Hyde's *The Gift*, or Lietaer and Gerloff's

"Creating a Giving Culture."

According to economist and author Bernard Lietaer, not only does gift-giving build community, the word "community" itself actually comes from the words for gift giving. So even our language clues us in on how vitally important gift giving is. And yet we in the West don't get the things we need through gift giving. As true starvation-culture refugees, the spider web sitting on our heads tells us to hoard money — to grab as much as we can, and then sit on it.

The end product, says Lietaer, is misery. Even our wealthy — actually especially our wealthy — are missing a basic ingredient in the happiness recipe: trust. When people have lots of money, says Lietaer, they find it hard and sometimes impossible to trust anyone — even themselves: "If I were no longer wealthy, would this person be my friend?" And, lately my brother's being awfully nice to Gramps. Will that mean Gramps'll give him more inheritance than me? Even trusting themselves can be hard for the wealthy. Am I more than my bank account? Is there anything about me that goes beyond my money? (Lietaer and Gerloff 2003).

By creating connections between neighbors, giving builds community. Say you're on your way to the store to buy some lubricating oil for your lawn mower. As you walk by, your neighbor says, "Hey, I have some oil, let me get it for ya." So now "you have a connection to your neighbor that, as a human being, you are not likely to ignore." Maybe next time your neighbor runs out of milk, he'll knock on your door and borrow some. "A relationship has been formed or strengthened," says Lietaer. Although he doesn't think we can or should chuck our money system entirely for a gift-giving economy, Lietaer thinks we could soften it a bit with systems like time-dollar networks. In a time-dollar system if I do an hour's worth of work for someone, I get a credit plunked into my account, while if someone does an hour's worth of work for me I get a debit.

A third thing that might help us revive pertinent parts of the old guiding-goddess societies is to reverse the 180-degree turns the starvation/war gods foisted on them over the past six millennia. As we've seen earlier, much of war-god society seems to be a deliberate turn-around of what came before it. In the Goddess world, black symbolizes good, so black becomes bad. Since to Goddess, Nature is sacred, Father makes it scary. Since Goddess says sex is sacred, Father says it's sin. Since Goddess says the Body is Her gift to us, Father calls it evil. The Mother says humor's a gift, so Father says humor's disrespectful. So wipe that smile off your face! In short, to aim at recreating the old guiding-goddess world, we need to turn many things backwards, to where they were before the war gods roared in on their Harleys and blasted everything to bits. For this we need packs and packs of bright, think-outside-the-box minds.

A fourth thing that might have kept guiding-goddess societies free of war, snootiness, etc., were their relatively small, sustainable communities. As painful as it sounds, goddess scholar and culture historian Heide Goettner-Abendroth thinks perhaps one of the few ways to save humanity is by breaking it up into smaller communities. When she says the world is "facing an extremely difficult future" Heide certainly isn't alone. On 17 November 2007 a US cable-TV history channel aired the program "Global Warning [sic]." In a truly frightening segment, the narrator said the greenhouse gases humans are pumping into the air are releasing methane gases from lakes, permafrost, and probably the ocean too.

Methane, said the narrator, is 20 times more potent than carbon dioxide. And if we can't stop cramming our atmosphere with carbon dioxide, the real danger will be giant, global methane explosions. It would be like striking a match in your house after pumping your house full of gas (see Lovett 2006 and Gallessich 2006). Even more frightening: we now know that in another period of abrupt climate shift millions of years ago, the shift was so fast it took only 20 years for most life on earth to become extinct. Could the trigger have been giant, global methane explosions?

"So," asks Heide, biting her nails, "what can be done?" And then, sighing, she answers her own question: " [T]he only sensible thing … would be to break up … industrial patriarchy … in order to create small, humane units such as affinity groups, clans, communities, and regional networks. This means a definite departure from the level of wealth we are used to and adopting a much simpler way of life. This dissolves the superstructures from below" (Goettner-Abendroth 2005: 40).

Speaking of small, sustainable communities, one trait of starvation/war-god religions probably helping to keep them alive today is their maintenance of small support communities called "congregations." In the West, the congregation (not the Church) fills a black hole. For most Westerners, the small communities of the Neolithic have gone poof. Even the extended family is a rare bird. Unless they join a starvation/war-god congregation, many have no community, period.

It's not easy finding the one-stop combination of stuff the war-god congregation offers families, especially: more-or-less guaranteed social acceptance in a relatively small group; guaranteed psychological and other kinds of support in times of need and crisis; guaranteed help with childcare and child rearing by people whose values you trust; eldercare; and so forth. It isn't easy to find this nice salad-mix of goodies any-where else anymore, all in one location, and all at the same (low) price.

It's important to see that the congregation is a unit that can be looked at as totally distinct from the Church, i.e. the war-god hierarchy. Although they don't often do it, most congregations would be perfectly capable of flying off on their own, cutting themselves loose from any "higher" church organization. They are, in other words, separate and potentially removable cogs in the starvation/war-god Machine. If they'd fly, most over time at least would probably be able to shuck off their damaging baggage (war gods, war songs, fear of women and the human body, etc.). At the same time, however, they could hold on to all the benefits of congregations – the promises of love and support to members, of help to members in need, of help in socializing tots, toddlers and teens; the knowledge of group dynamics and small-group financial systems; and so on. In the West at least, my guess is that what replaces war-god religion needs to offer something to replace the congregation and all it offers, not only spiritually but socially, psychologically and kid-caringly too. Really, there's nothing else like it. Figure 8.1 tosses out a few big things people get from congregations they get from few other places.

Figure 8.1. Congregations: In a League All Their Own (How congregations differ from, say, bridge clubs, country clubs, botanical clubs, the library volunteers, or your Friday-night drinking buddies)

The War-God Congregation	Non-Congregation Groups
People are obliged to come visit you in the hospital.	In many social groups people aren't obligated to visit you in the hospital. As a matter of fact, in many groups this would be a no-no.
People are supposed to try to be kind, loving and supportive of you.	In most social groups, people are under no mandated obligation to be nice to you.
You are totally expected to get along with everyone, and show kindness and concern – or at	In most social groups, you're not expected to go out of your way to get along with

least give it your best shot. There's often an expectation that one gives without expecting anything in return.

people you don't like. In most social groups not so much as in the congregation.

There's a group leader — the pastor/rabbi/priest — who gets mucho training in leadership. Also s/he collects a salary for leading. Congregants are expected to help pay this salary.

In many non-church groups, the leader leads without collecting a salary. (But not in all: a paid librarian may lead the library volunteers; ditto for hospital volunteers).

In addition to the pastor's salary, you are expected to give money to support the group in other ways: i.e. re: building expenses, help for the less fortunate, etc.

Except for the country club, most other groups ask for labor, not money. (Or maybe just a turn taking up the bar tab every once in a while.)

Usually you are entitled to free personal counseling from your leader.

Very few other groups offer this service.

You are entitled to help in times of crisis. Death in your family? Many congregations bring food, help with the funeral.

Nuh-uh.

When you go to this group, there's often someone to watch your children.

Usually no, although bowling allies used to offer this — but can you really trust that bowling-alley sitter?

You get help rearing your kids the way you want them reared.

No. Even Scouts let in kids with 40-piece artillery

Other adults tell them the same behavior rules you're telling them. Your kids whose behavior you generally like.

collections and the habits of trolls.

Of course in many respects, a guiding-goddess "congregation" would look like the mirror image of a starvation/war-god congregation. (First, though, let me confess: I hesitate to use the word "congregation" — it smacks of the old war Lords. So I'm going to use "GoddessGathering" instead.) At any rate, while war-god congregations worship mostly indoors, Goddess Gatherings prefer outdoor, natural settings. And while starvation-culture congregations worship in rows facing a leader with superior training, GoddessGathering attendees sit in a circle with everyone facing everyone else, equals among equals. Goddess Gatherings involve more physical activity — dancing, drumming, chanting, guided meditations and so forth.

Nevertheless, if the guiding-goddess congregation could offer the same support system the war-god congregation does (Figure 8.1), it wouldn't hurt. Other good stuff to save from the war-god congregation would be the best of the volunteer service in local and international development organizations. For example, even today some US churches in Maine are helping communities work toward local economic sustainability, by setting up farmer's markets in their church parking lots. Sellers have full use of the churches' parking areas, kitchens and bathrooms (See Goldfine 2007).

But the GoddessGathering should move beyond the congregation. Social ranking of any kind should be mixed altogether. Ongoing Swedish study circles could advise on the Mother Model, non-violence, conflict management, encouragement of healthy risk-taking, and encouragement of playfulness, creativity, sensuality, generosity, self rule and riches for all. For information on study circles, check out Oliver's *Study*

Circles: Coming Together for Personal Growth and Social Change.

Within the GoddessGathering, regular gift giving could serve as a type of magic super glue to bind the group together. For financially-stressed members, time-dollar networks could be set up. Maybe some Goddess Gatherings could try to emulate the small, sustainable communities of our guiding-goddess Neolithic ancestors. Eventually, could the GoddessGathering even serve as a model for the "small, humane" political/economic units Heide Goettner-Abendroth wants the world to return to?

Another question: Would it be possible for all of today's war-god congregations to switch to the Goddess? If they could, it would be fantastic. Why reinvent the wheel? To start and keep a congregation going takes a heckuva lot of work. Besides a physical location and an agreed-upon set of operating instructions, you need a group of people willing on an ongoing basis to donate money and sweat equity. And that's just for starters.

On the other hand, starvation/war-god congregations bristle with bad habits. Not only do they worship indoors, some even shut out nature altogether (nature, they say, takes their minds away from "true" worship). To many, much about the human body is offensive. Deep-down, both men and women dislike women; even now in the twenty-first century, male ministers, rabbis, priests and deacons outnumber women two to one — at least. War-god congregations sing holy songs about war: *Onward Christian Soldiers, The Battle Hymn of the Republic, A Mighty Fortress Is Our God, Christian Dost Thou See Them* ("Christian up and smite them..."). And could starvation congregations really abandon their Bibles, those manuals for living that are chock full of cruelty, violence and references to war?

Although some won't be able to make the necessary changes, others probably will. If congregations kept the following in mind, it would help them make the switch to Goddess: with a well-built, guiding-goddess congregation, you should be able to get all you get in a war-god congregation — and far, far more.

As soon as possible, we need to trumpet the call for war-god congregations to break free of the Church, Temple and Mosque, and switch to the Guiding Goddess. If a substantial number at least break free of the war gods, it will, as Heide Goettner-Abendroth puts it, "dissolve the superstructure from below." Even if a congregation finds the switch impossible, if it at least breaks free of the Church, it will have accomplished some small part in destroying war and dystopia. Undoubtedly it will be the strongest congregations who will be able to make the switch. And those are the ones we want anyway.

"When God Wants War"

At this stage in the game, it might be good to remember that the Christian Church is not totally a war-god enterprise. When Christ came, he softened the war Lord Jehovah up a bit. What's more, the Bible mentions peace about as often as it does war. And today at least, many Christian congregations — and even entire denominations — work against war.

On the other hand, the majority of Christian churches do not actively work against war. And from the Warriors for Christ Ministry (http://wfcministries.com), The Faith Force Multiplier, and BattleCry, to the Quiverfull movement that pushes women to bear as many children as possible, to spend their entire reproductive lives "birthing God's Mighty Warriors," Christian churches today — in America at least — are rife with militaristic language and sentiments. In Quiverfull, the "language reflects the church's 'constant state of war'; the husband a 'commanding officer' and his wife a 'private' below him" (Joyce 2006).

For most of us reared in Christian cultures, Christ is not strong enough to neutralize his father's weakness for war. When the going gets tough, we fall back on the Old Testament, with its twin crutches of war and violence. Here's just one example: six months before the 1941 bombing of Pearl Harbor, the editor of the Christian rag *Bible Banner* wrote the following:

Purity first, then peace. We ought to be anxious for peace, but not so anxious for it that we would compromise the truth or unite with those who do. In the days of Jeremiah the prophet, the ancient people of God had rejected him ... Of them it is said, "from the least of them even unto the greatest of them every one is given to covetousness; and from the prophet even unto the priest every one dealeth falsely." And ... there were appeasers who were wanting peace. Of them the Lord said: "They have healed also the hurt of my people slightly, saying Peace, peace, when there is no peace" (Jeremiah 6.13, 14; 8.10, 11). *There are times when God wants war*, not peace — opposition, not submission — separation, not unity (Wallace 1941)(italics mine).

But We *Haven't* All Gotten It Yet

Of course the problem is, most of us haven't heard the drumbeats in this book — not yet at any rate. So the true trick will be getting the word out to ordinary people *before* it leaks out to those scoring big from the status quo (those reaping riches from war, violence, political oppression, and social inequality, and who wouldn't mind if the flow into their coffers continued). As we spread the word, three rules apply: First, one way to move forward is to clean the war-god warts off peoples' old goddess myths. Second, since they're our guides into a utopian future, mothers around the world must become strong and fit. Third, the world must move together on the switch — or the switch won't work.

Rule 1. Revive the Old Myths. Around the world, many peoples have much-loved and magnetic old myths and legends that just won't go away — many with goddesses hidden inside. In addition, some people have rich archaeological records showing glowing pasts, many including goddesses. One way to quicken the switch is to clean the gunk off these myths (put there by starvation/war gods to besmirch the goddesses), and then shoot both the myths and the archaeological records with a power boost. For example, evidence shows that Robin Hood was not a man but a god (just one clue: he's depicted by the Church in a 1639 London pamphlet as a Pagan god). At the same time, Maid Marian seems to have been "the Goddess Maerin, or Marian, or Mari-Anna, the Saxon wudu-maer, literally the Mary or the Mother of the Grove" (Walker 1983: 858; Graves 1991: 396). So why not revive Robin and Marion's true identities?

King Arthur too seems to have been a god, demoted by Jehovah the Jealous to mere mortal status. Likewise, before Jehovah trotted into Great Britain and sank his hooks into the Emerald Isles, many of the women in the Arthurian legends were goddesses too. And while our old gods Robin and Arthur push truth, beauty and justice, Jehovah, who stole their lands, pushes — what? — mostly himself. Mostly all Jehovah appreciates is allegiance, the licking of his boots ("Do not worship any other god, for the lord, whose name is Jealous, is a jealous God." ~ Exodus 34.14). So the upshot is, we with British heritage are hiding our shining, superior deities under a barrel — simply because this green-eyed dud named Jealous tells us to.

In the Arthurian and Robin Hood legends both, men's purpose was to help and protect those who needed it. Period, end of story. Why don't men today see this as their primary, sacred, solemn and awesomely important role in life? Men are nature's way of providing backup protection for women and children. Making tons of money, winning the Olympics, becoming famous for X, Y or Z, or fighting wars so others can get rich, are not men's destined roles. Their destiny lies in protecting women, children, the elderly, the sick, the poor, the disadvantaged and any other human on the planet who needs help. And not with knives and guns but with brains, brawn, and sometimes just pounding on doors for donations for the Down-and-Out Foundation. Of course as I've mentioned before, many men are also wicked good at entertaining people, getting us to laugh. And although laughing is one of the Goddess' greatest gifts, we usually need a little expert prodding before we can fall into it.

But getting back to the protection piece. The Robin Hood legends are all about the role of men, the old role under the Guiding Goddess. As mentioned earlier, the Goddess in the Robin Hood legends is Marian, who the Christian war gods, when they got their hands on Her, demoted to a mere "maid." Don't buy it for a second. Marian is the Guiding Goddess Herself, the "Mother of the Grove" (Walker 1983: 858). And it's no accident that Robin lived in the forest. Since She's the earth and everything on it, the Goddess *is* the forest. As the Lady of the Lake chose Arthur to become Grand Protector of the Land, so Marian chose Robin to take on the same role in Sherwood Forest. And like Arthur, Robin's role is active protector of any and all who need protection — which is almost everyone, considering the extent to which war gods have hog-tied almost everyone in Robin's time period.

Several early Disney movies were based on fairy tales seen by some as old coded messages from the underground Goddess. As we saw in an earlier chapter, Cinderella has all the makings of such a coded message. If you want to take a break from modern life and travel back to a place closer to the old Goddess world, go see Disney's *Bambi*, *Cinderella*, *Pollyanna* or *Davy Crockett*. Says Neal Gabler, author of *Walt Disney: The Triumph of the American Imagination,*

Disney's ... values are not traditional conservative American. On the contrary, Disney's films challenged authority, disdained the acquisition of money, abhorred hypocrisy (including religious hypocrisy), promoted tolerance and community and celebrated rebelliousness. (Just see how Davy Crockett challenges Andrew Jackson in the 1950s TV programs, or how Pollyanna scolds her own minister for his intolerance.) In his own life, Disney denounced what he called 'billboard patriotism,' and he looked askance at organized religion (Gabler 2006).

Although Disney's world isn't perfect — feminists see it as chock full of chauvinism, for example — it still, overall, tilts in the direction of the old Goddess ways.

Rule 2. Women Must Be Strengthened. Quite a while ago, the highly-rated international development organization Heifer International grasped the fact that helping women helped everyone else become winners. Says Martha Hirpa, director of Heifer's Gender Equity Program, "We believe that families and communities are strengthened when men recognize and support women and girls in all aspects of their lives, especially their education, health, access to resources and decision-making opportunities" (Heifer International Website). Former UN Secretary General Kofi Annan also promotes educating girls as the key to ending poverty ("UN Secretary General Kofi Annan Calls for Girls' Access to Education" 2000).

For millennia, the starvation/war-god religions have whomped women all over the world. If we want them to coach us again, it's in our best interests to strengthen women, girls and mothers until they rise to meet the stars in the sky. First and foremost, women themselves must wake up and see clearly where they are. When the American heroine Harriet Tubman was asked how she managed to smuggle so many slaves out of the South via the Underground Railroad during the Civil War, her reply was, "I could have saved thousands—if only I'd been able to convince them they were slaves." Women must relearn how to love and support one another, and how to work together as teams.

Rule 3. The World Must Move Together. Why? Because unless the countries of the world disarm their war gods at roughly the same time, the war gods left will skewer the disarmed. On the other hand, if Jehovah and Yahweh countries begin the process of retiring their gods first, it might move Allah countries toward dipping a toe themselves into the god-retirement waters. After all, not everyone in the Islamic countries is in love with Allah. With some encouragement from the West, these ex- or anti-Muslims might become bold enough to try to begin the process of dragging their countries out of the grasp of their hoary old desert gods.

These three cornerstone rules of 'turning on the switch' are shown in Figure 8.2 below:

Figure 8.2: Turning on The Switch: Three Cornerstone Principles

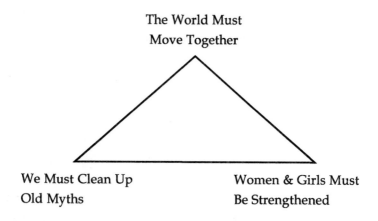

The World Must
Move Together

We Must Clean Up
Old Myths

Women & Girls Must
Be Strengthened

Beating the Talking Drums, Getting the Word Out

So how do we broadcast the word so people all around the world ditch their starvation/war gods simultaneously (more or less)? Here one of the thorniest challenges are countries barring open communication. How do we spread the word to people in China, Russia, the "third" world, and the land of radical Islam? I believe it's somewhat like being on a plane and hearing the stewardess say, "Put on your own air mask before helping others with theirs." If we in the industrialized world — Europe, North America, Australia, South Korea and Japan — begin the switch first, we might be able to reach out and pull the rest of the world along with us as we go. Interestingly, most of today's industrialized nations represent world areas lambasted last and least by the Bronze-Age starvation and war gods. Not only do we have the most freedom, resources, and best communication systems to bring about the switch, but compared to the rest of the world we are also closer in time to our guiding-goddess utopian pasts.

To turn on the switch, we in the industrialized world would be wise to launch a two-pronged attack: First, we need to conduct massive research into all areas covered in this book, including the following:

oxytocin
bonobos
ancient goddess figurines
other ancient pre-war goddess representations
early ancient texts shedding light on pre-war-god goddesses
Neolithic utopian societies around the world
the origins of the first starvation/war gods
the origins of the first war-god societies
starvation culture

Second, we need to launch a gigantic mass-communications assault to broadcast information about the switch and the necessity of making it. We need to churn out stories, plays, soap operas, weblogs, e-zines, documentaries, fiction, non-fiction, poetry, music, films, holiday cards, greeting cards, photography and other art to explain the switch and to spell out our understanding of and magnificent attraction to the Goddess. Beginning immediately, both prongs of this attack should be turned on at full throttle.

After we begin the switch in our own countries, one of the best ways to reach people in closed societies is through the Internet. According to InternetWorldStats.com, China in 2007 had 162,000,000 Internet users — 12.3 percent of the Chinese population. What's more, from 2000 to 2007 Chinese Internet use jumped 620.0 percent. Russia in 2007 boasted 28,000,000 Internet users, 19.5 percent of the population. On the other hand, only 3.6 percent of Africa was using the Net, representing a 643.1 percent jump from 2000 to 2007. In contrast, 39.8 percent of Europe and 69.5 percent of North America were using the Internet in 2007.

According to InternetWorldStats.com, 19,539,300 Middle Easterners, or 10.1 percent of the population, were using the Internet in 2007, with a 494.8-percent usage jump over the seven years since 2000. In the same year in Iraq, only 36,000 were Internet users. Although this is only 0.1 percent of the population, many Iraqi ex-pats use the Net in the countries they've hustled to since the American invasion. Iran, on the other hand, boasted 7,600,000 Internet users in 2007 (10.8 percent of the population) and from 2000 to 2007 witnessed a whopping 2,940.0 percent increase in use.

Even though repressive governments try to block parts of the Internet in their own countries ("Censorship 'Changes Face of Net,'" 6 June 2007), at this point all-out blockage doesn't seem possible — and probably won't be for some time. As long as sites like the-infoshop.com keep Internet users up to date on ways to bypass blockages, governments will be hard pressed to rope in the Internet. Also, since repressive leaders concentrate on crushing political sites, religion sites may not even make a blip on their radar screens — especially since many countries that formerly nixed religion are now softening about it (e.g. China, Russia). So we need to write articles in online magazines and journals, about pre-war-god societies in all nations, and articles clapping on the back any with enough courage to challenge their community's modern starvation/war gods.

Weblogistan
Tucked inside the Internet is another good vehicle to reach out and touch the hard-to-reach: weblogs. Since most webloggers write their "blogs" at the grass-roots level and work hard to get

their readers to respond, blogs are great for reaching lots of ordinary folk. Also, blogs are often run and read by students and other young people — a group often more open to new ideas. China, the Middle East and Africa are spawning lots of blogs of all kinds, many in English.

Despite their restrictive or poverty-stricken governments, for now at least, China, the Middle East and Africa are allowing bloggers fairly free and open communication. In the Middle East, for example, according to Dr. Liora Hendelman-Baavur of Tel Aviv University, "along with satellite television and mobile phones, weblogs have irretrievably changed the way people in the entire Middle East interact with one another and with the rest of the world."

Since the establishment of the Islamic Republic in 1979, Iranian printed and broadcast media has been strongly controlled by the state. However, the state's authority has been compromised due to online publishing and the free flow of information, especially through "Weblogistan" — the Iranian cyber-sphere of online self-publishing journals.... Beyond redefining personal connectivity in the Islamic Republic, Weblogistan has also been an outlet through which unmonitored contents have made their way into the country. The free flow of information, along with foreign cultural invasion — mainly from the United States — has slowly diminished the cultural isolation imposed on the local population by the state (Hendelman-Baavur, 2007).

In China, too, if they know how to skirt around government blocks, blog authors channel information flow both in and out of the country. Recently, for example, a Chinese blogger scoffed, "There's too much Western media emphasis on Internet censorship in China. Experienced bloggers know how to use proxy servers to get around the government firewall and access

Google's main English language site" ("Chinese Bloggers Debate Google," 26 January 2006).

According to Dave Sifry at Technorati.com (the widely acclaimed blogging statistics keeper), although English and Chinese are the top two Internet-usage languages, the top two blogging languages are Japanese (37 percent) and English (33 percent), with Chinese coming in a distant third (8 percent) — but third nevertheless (Sifry, 5 April 2007).

Although not as common as Chinese and Iranian webloggers, bloggers are blogging away in Africa, Iraq and Russia too. For example, someone in Sudan keeps a blog called "Black Kush," while someone in Iraq regularly updates "Iraqi Atheist." Although weblogs are booming in Russia, most are written in Russian. I did, however, dig up a few in English, including "Neeka's Backlog" and "Mikhail Khodorkovsky." For more examples of weblogs blossoming in relatively closed countries, see Appendix E: Weblogs in the Closed Countries.

In addition to the World Wide Web, a second way to reach people in closed societies is by inviting students and workers into your country temporarily. When they return home, in their back pockets they carry with them exciting new ideas about how to make their own countries crackle and pop. When in your country, of course, these visitors should mingle first and foremost with groups trading in starvation/war gods for guiding goddesses. Unfortunately, in the US at least, Catholic and Protestant organizations are two of the larger sponsors of incoming refugees. As a result, many refugees get zipped immediately into American war-god homes for sponsorship. Ideally, in the future such funding would bubble up less from the war-gods and more often from goddess organizations. Refugees and permanent immigrants can also help their birth countries make the switch to Goddess, since even after becoming citizens of new countries, refugees often still correspond with and visit friends and relatives in their old home countries.

Whadda We Say? How Do We Say It?

Since chances are good they've never heard of them, we need to clue our closed-society cousins in to their wicked-cool, pre-war-god ancestors. First, of course, we need to find out about these ancestors ourselves — when they lived, their peace records, their lack of violence and political repression, their religions. For some countries this will be a piece of cake. Iraq for example is simple: archaeologists have dug up tons of ancient people in Iraq, so we know lots about the pre-war-god Halafians and Ubaidians and the early Sumerian goddesses.

China on the other hand will be less of a cakewalk, since Chinese governments throughout history have rarely seemed bothered by the truth. The great mythographer Joseph Campbell is astonished at "how little we know of the writings of the Chinese before the period of Confucius (551-478 BC)" and by "the fact that from the period of Confucius onward there was such a doctoring of texts that even the most learned scholarship ... has been at a loss, up to now, to reconstruct with assurance even the work of Confucius himself — not to mention whatever wisdom, mythic, philosophic or other, may have gone before" (Campbell 1962: 379-380).

On the other hand, we do know that before Buddhism sashayed into China, Chinese mythology was chock full of goddesses. If these goddesses could shed the starvation/war-god muck they've picked up, we'd have some idea of what the Chinese could return to. Also, within the borders of China live the fabulous Moso, with their shining Mother Goddesses. The Han Chinese could certainly learn much from both the Moso and their deities (see chapter two).

Second, we need to tell our cousins how cool we think their goddess-society ancestors were. This helps them focus on these ancestors. What's more, it gives them an ego-boost — and a healthy ego never hurts when you're taking on a hefty job like rebuilding your ancestral goddess society. Also, whenever we can, we need to heap kudos, support and encouragement on closed-society cousins who move away from their war gods. For example, when people like medical doctor and Muslim reformer Tawfik Hamid say "It is well past time that Muslims cease using the charge of 'Islamophobia' as a tool to intimidate … those who … rightly criticize current Islamic practices and preachings," we need immediately to shower them with praise (Hamid 2007).

Congregation Revolution

Getting back to congregations — we need to urge closed-country war-god congregations, too, to yank themselves free of their war-god superstructure and switch to Goddess. By using congregations to help fire up the switch, we're tapping into already-formed organizations spread over much of the world like peanut butter and jelly on a sandwich — even into closed countries like Russia and China. All over the world, Christian, Islamic, Jewish and Hindu congregations must be encouraged to morph into guiding-goddess groups, based on their pre-war-god Guiding Mother Goddesses. The best of the congregational structure already in place can then be jettisoned into the new guiding-goddess congregation (or "GoddessGathering," or whatever any particular group wants to call itself).

Above the congregation level, starvation/war-god Church structure is likely to be set in stone. Without chipping away from the bottom up, we may never be able to move the Big War Daddies off their pedastals. I believe our best bet is to work directly with individual congregations, encouraging them to switch to their old Mother Goddesses. If enough individual congregations revolt, the higher war-god structure will wither away from lack of meat to chew on.

Don't Believe in Goddess. See If I Care.

To back the views in this book there's no need to believe in supernatural goddesses, gods, Tinker Bell or Santa Claus. You do, however, need to agree with the following:

1. Not only are starvation/war gods bogus, they're deadly — especially now that the world community's shrunk to the size of peas in a pod.

2. If people are going to follow supernatural religion — and judging from everything science knows, most will — it's far healthier for everyone if believers believe in deities unconnected to war, violence or cruelty.

3. And if our deities are not only strangers to war and violence but are also pushing for peace, psychological health, and reverence for the earth and everything on it — well, we're in even rosier shape.

On this small planet, there's no more room for primitive desert gods naming themselves "Jealous" ("...the lord, whose name is Jealous, is a jealous God." ~ Exodus 34.14). There's no room for gods calling themselves "warriors" ("The Lord is a warrior; the Lord is his name" ~ Exodus 15.3) and who happily provoke their followers into fighting wars on a basis regular as clockwork. And there's no room anymore for a holy book holding so many acts of cruelty that even a "short list" runs into several, long pages (See Appendix J: Cruelty in the Bible: Short List).

Goddess historian Barbara Walker puts it this way: "Some ask how, if both god and goddess are constructs of the human imagination, can one be any more ... valid than the other? The crucial point ... is that the validity of the image depends on its effect on human behavior.... There is no doubt that the goddess image has induced more tolerant, peaceful, kind, and caring societies than the god image." God societies, she continues, have "always tended toward war, violence, Puritanism, and hierarchy" (Walker 2000: 39).

Calling All Manly Mother-Men

According to Jean Shinoda Bolen, women around the world are beginning to pummel the war gods. But women need manly "mother-men" to back them up. The following examples should fire up all of us, suggesting ways we too can help begin the switch.

In California USA, women bought an old-growth forest to keep it from being logged "in perpetuity." In Nigeria in 2002, six hundred women took part in a sit-in that shut down a mammoth Chevron Texaco Terminal. Since 1977, the Argentina group "Mothers of the Disappeared" have marched every Thursday to protest the kidnapping of their children by the military dictatorship that ruled their country from 1976 to 1983. In the US, the friends of a raped woman marched into the rapist's office with "signs and chants" to let his coworkers in on his secret. In 2004, mobs of East Indian women retaliated against men who were raping women "with impunity." When five of the protesters were arrested, over 400 women blocked the courtroom door.

And in Rwanda after the Hutu-on-Tutsi genocide, it was Hutu and Tutsi women who met together to rebuild the country. Their first concern: the orphans left by the violence. Both Hutu and Tutsi women adopted the orphans — without asking which background any adoptee claimed. Bolen labels these women's actions "women as peacemakers." I label them "women as Goddess heroines." Most women, says Bolen, are able to listen and talk to each other "with empathy, bonding, and an increase in oxytocin." (Bolen 2005: 101-08, 114-15).

We Can't Lose

Because the Guiding Goddess is such a mighty archetype, we can't lose. Now that the important data is emerging — on oxytocin, bonobos, the worldwide Neolithic goddess-utopia connection, the blaat-blaat-blaat of dystopia as soon as the starvation/war gods step on stage — the world can't help but be swept off its feet by the Goddess and Her promise for us, Her world family.

If a picture is worth a thousand words, an intoxicating archetypal symbol like the Great Guiding Mother will spin off an infinite number of pictures worth an infinite number of words. Once artists around the world hear of Her, they'll automatically be captivated, just as artists were before the starvation gods plunked themselves down onto the earth. And the pictures, paintings, songs, statuettes and stories our modern artists create will glow like neon lights all the colors of the rainbow, capturing the hearts, minds and souls of people everywhere.

The Mother Goddess is old, and She runs deep. She's not an abstraction most can't grasp — like "secular humanism" or "the phenomenology of spirit." She's a deeply personal, loving, colorful and graphically dazzling archetype. According to the best evidence, for many if not most of our ancestors She was the center of life and the cosmos. As a worldwide symbol, She, as nothing else can, will pull us all together in our twenty-first-century global village into one, united human family.

And that's good. Because if we're going to all live in the same village, it could be dicey if we don't share at least one thing in common.

But Time Is Running Out

You know it and I know it: time is running out. At the very least we need to finish the switch from starvation/war god to Guiding Goddess by 2035. I don't need to tell you the dangers the world faces today because we've let war gods trample the Guiding Mother Goddess. It's as if we've stuck pokers in our eyes while racing toward the edge of a six-story cliff. Unless we yank out the pokers, at least three things threaten to kill us off as a species: overpopulation, weapons of mass destruction, and climate change (Pearce 2006). Mother-Goddess guidance would have nipped all three of these threats in the bud. While the first stems from a lack of respect for healthy human mothers — all of whom intuitively understand how many kids to have in one lifetime — the second two stem from a lack of respect for Mother Earth and Her creations, both of which the starvation/war gods said we could and should rip to shreds anytime we please.

We Can Do It by 2035

Chaos theory teaches that social change can happen in the flicker of an eyelash. Even though switching from endless warfare, deep-rooted cruelty and violence, snooty snobbism and bully-boy rule may seem like a six-century housecleaning job, chaos theory clues us in on how fast such change can actually happen: "An idea can become contagious and spread like a virus, through geometric progression, by doubling and doubling again, and again and again, until it reaches a critical mass, which is the tipping point. If we are talking about viruses, the result is an epidemic." But with social systems we're talking about social transformation. "When a critical number of people accept a principle, it becomes the new standard, an 'as if it always was so.' Like voting rights for American women, for instance, which we now take for granted" (Bolen 2005: 135).

Although as I've pointed out throughout this book, cultures don't change easily, the Goddess is already a deeply buried part of many if not most world cultures. In the West She hangs out as Mother Earth, Mary "Mother" of God, CinderElla and her GodMother, Maid Marian, Mother Goose, Mother Holle, mistletoe and holly, the Goddess Oestra (Easter) and Her sacred hare, and in myths, legends and holiday traditions too many to mention. All we need to do is slide Her out of hiding, ditch the disguises She's cloaked Herself in, and restore the brilliant old magic that made us the peace-loving, non-violent, earth-revering, sensual adventurers we all long to be again.

Money Can Be Part of the Mix in the Fix

Of course money isn't the only solution to the switch, but it wouldn't hurt, either. With money we could fund think tanks and other research on how to pull off the switch before it's too late. We could fund media organizations to educate the world about the Guiding Mother Goddess and how She can save us. These media organizations could tell the world about the true nature of the Abrahamaic and other starvation/war gods, about starvation culture, and about the urgent need for the switch. With funds we could hire and train consultants to help congregations make the switch.

According to Jean Shinoda Bolen, the greatest shift of money in the history of the world is about to take place, with most of it dropping directly into the hands of women:

> According to the Federal Reserve, women control 51.3 percent of the private wealth in the US, with more on the horizon. The largest wealth transfer in history is about to take place as the Baby Boom generation inherits from their parents. Forty-one trillion dollars are expected to pass from generation to generation in the next fifty years. Since women generally outlive their husbands, the family assets will become concentrated in the hands of Boomer women... (Bolen 2005: 113).

First and foremost this money can and must go toward neutralizing the war gods and bringing the Mother Model in to replace them. Before we collect much of this money, though, we should set up organizations to receive, handle and distribute it well. If we do this early on, our financial organizations will have time to develop track records. We want donors and recipients too to trust our organizations to handle their money honestly and wisely.

If you're looking for a place now to give your money to help promote the switch, one good place is the Ms. Foundation for

Women. Jean Shinoda Bolen, who was on their board, says they support "many national and international efforts to improve the lives of women and girls" (Bolen 2005). Another good place: Heifer International, the award-winning international development program that obviously understands the role women play in keeping communities healthy. Sorely needed too, however, are organizations to help men recover from their starvation-god-instilled fear of using mothers as behavior guides, and organizations to help all of us recover from starvation culture. And it would be nice to have a few national and international umbrella organizations for if and when Goddess Gatherings need support of any kind.

Get Ready for the Big Daddy of All Backlashes

It won't be long now. As soon as the Guiding Goddess gets a little stronger, the starvation/war gods, as they've done for six thousand years now, will slam back at Her — and hard. So hold on to your socks. This time we need to come super prepped for this fear-based backlash. We need to begin now funding efforts to plan ahead what our response will be this time around. We need many women and men with good strong backs to stand up to these primitive desert gods and defeat them once and for all. We need people good with money — raising it, asking for it, minding it, and discharging it to worthy arenas — to help strengthen us in all the ways money can. Because if we can't beat the bad daddies this time, we may be done for as a species.

Home Again

"Deep in my heart,
I do believe,
We shall overcome
One day"
American civil rights movement song

In a Nutshell

In a nutshell, when we stuck to guiding goddesses, life was great, and when we let the upstart starvation/war "Lords" trump the goddesses, we lost — big time — and have been losing ever since. As Figure 9.1 shows, in only a few millennia we've gone from being relatively peaceful, non-violent, equalitarian and prosperous risk-takers, to a twenty-first century in which galloping overpopulation, climate change, rapid plant and animal extinction, and weapons of mass destruction all threaten to wipe us off the face of the earth.

Figure 9.1: A Generalized Look at History, Goddesses, Gods, and Society

Time Period	Religion	Society
c. 10,000 BC — 1000 BC	Around the world, many of our ancestors fashioned female figurines by the boatload, many "other-worldly"; most agree that many if not all of these figurines	From the archaeological record, we know these female-figurine fashioners were mostly peaceful, non-violent, equalitarian risk-takers. (Although some had written languages, we

were symbols of powerful goddesses.

(haven't decoded these yet.)

c. 3000 BC–AD 500

From the Eastern Mediterranean to China and Meso- and South America, war gods always accompanied the birth of "the state," as does a sudden exploding volcano of war, violence, loss of egalitarianism, loss of popular rule, etc. In many other corners of the globe, however, Guiding Mother Goddesses linger as commanding creatrixes of the cosmos and everything in it.

From archaeology and written records, we know these war-god societies as violent, non-equalitarian politically repressive and at war constantly. (Since the war-god languages are ancestors of the major languages spoken today, we've been able to translate them.)

c. 1000 BC-AD 1000

In many corners of the world, goddesses plummet from creators of the universe, to wives of male creators -- who make life out of stolen ribs, cracks in their heads, masturbated penises, and sweaty

For roughly 500 years the Eastern Mediterranean huddled in a Dark Age. The starvation/war-god Greco-Roman world followed, after which Europe plunged into another Dark Age, c. AD 500 -1000 (some today say it wasn't so Dark; I armpits.

say when the entire light of Classical-Age Greek and Roman learning packed up its bags and left town, what was left, if not Dark, was very, very Dim.)

c. AD 000-Present	By warring against and smashing all other religions, starvation/war gods increasingly take over the planet. In many places, Goddess is pushed further and further underground (but remains always with us -- even to this day).	Crusades; Inquisition; decimation of Native Americans; Atom Bomb invented; constant warfare among starvation-god nations. In countries outlawing religion, massive people-exterminations by god-like dictators named Stalin, Mao and Pol Pot.
AD 21st century	Two-thirds of the world is enslaved to Jehovah (33 percent), Allah (20 percent) and Vishnu (13 percent). Overall, these three have spread themselves via war and/or violence. Today, three of the world's most repressive regions — Russia, the Middle	It's as if we've stuck pokers in our eyes while loping briskly in the direction of a six-story cliff. Unless we pull the pokers out in a hurry, one of three things will kill us: overpopulation, climate change, or weapons of mass destruction.

East and China — are
the original hornet's
nests of most of the
world's first
starvation/war gods.

Today the war gods do their dirty work through Big Money, Big International Business, Big Oil and Big Religion. Under Big Religion I include the Christian Church and its enormous real-estate holdings, most snatched gratis centuries ago from those tortured and murdered by the Inquisition. Also included are America's fabulously rich and corrupt televangelists (Walker et al 1985: 309; Sjoo and Mor 1991: 302; Oldenburg and Gundersen 2006; Boston 2006).

In one way, since they're all inescapable results of starvation culture, none of these Big Things can be blamed. Remember starvation culture, that monstrosity born out of the actual behavior of some of our long-ago-starving ancestors? Since everyone in starvation culture has an unconscious fear of never having enough, hoarding and getting too Big is as natural as breathing. Also only natural is that starvation culture handsomely rewards those who are aces at stealing, lying, cheating and conning those with less power (for starters, women, children, the poor, the disabled and the elderly).

All Signs Point to Switching

But it's not just history that shows the switch to Guiding Mother Goddesses will save us. Evidence that this switch is just what the doctor ordered is pouring in from all directions. Biology, physiology, primatology, sociology, anthropology, mythology, emerging metaphysics, and other disciplines all point to the same thing: the switch is the answer. We know now that when they birth babies, women receive a rush of the hormone oxytocin, which makes them fall in love with their newborns. Since this mother-love is unconditional, it can serve as a fabulous social archetype/role model, helping us treat others with the same unconditional regard that healthy mothers model for us 24/7. We also now know that oxytocin serves as a calming hormone. Whereas men under stress lean more toward "fight or flight," oxytocin helps women bat back with "tend and befriend" behavior. So for this reason also, mothers would seem awesome societal role models.

Bonobos too suggest the switch will serve us well. As close to us genetically as chimps, bonobos were the final primates discovered. But unlike chimps, bonobos do little "war," violence, or social ranking. What's more, bonobo females do not allow males to push them around. Recently someone quipped that if we'd discovered the bonobo before the chimp, we'd all be talking less about human violence and male dominance, and lots more about human empathy, caring and cooperation.

From anthropology we know that the Hopi, Basques and Moso are three modern societies that until recently, at least, circled around strong Mother Goddesses. Among its neighbors, each stands out for its various utopian ways. And mythology too suggests that if we're to survive as a species, women need to be cajoled back in to lending a helping hand in our power structures: "Myths of leadership forcibly wrested from women occur throughout the world and cannot be overlooked.... In some ways, it may have meant the downfall of all humanity from a basically peaceful social order to a hierarchical structure established and maintained by aggression" (Walker 1983: 687).

War to End All Wars

In 2007, Robert Kagan, author and senior associate at the Carnegie Endowment for International Peace, reminded us that after the Cold War many of us thought war would disappear forever. "The years immediately following the end of the Cold War offered a tantalizing glimpse at a new kind of international order, with nations growing together or disappearing altogether, ideological conflicts melting away.... But that was a mirage.... It is no longer possible to speak of an 'international community.' The term suggests agreement on international norms of behavior, an international morality, even an international conscience...." (Kagan 2007).

No longer can we afford to be this dim-witted. Unless and until we recognize and then get to know the foggy, half-hidden forces driving us toward greed and violence, war will never end. Since many human groups throughout history have been far more functional than the major world nations are today, these smoky forces obviously can't stem totally from "human nature." I believe what's driving us to dystopia are starvation culture and the war gods that have locked that culture into place. Not until we ditch our war gods and the starvation culture they've cemented in stone, will we end war and human misery.

We shape ourselves after our gods, our guiding stars. Many believe it's humans who create gods and not the other way around. It makes no difference: the kind of god your society creates will shape your society in too many ways to count. Unfortunately, the war "Lord" is now one of the world's guiding stars. "The Lord is a warrior; the Lord is his name," says Exodus 15.3. Mythographer David Leeming of the University of Connecticut says the god of Abraham is "a god of war who could mercilessly kill the enemies of the Israelites.... [H]e was a 'jealous' god.... He was the god who denied humans a common language — through which they might become too powerful" (Leeming 2005: 154).

Jesus the forgiving son is forever overpowered by his War Father. When the going gets tough, humans fall back on their old Devil ways. As the plane plummets at a radical tilt toward ground for the crash landing, even atheists raise their eyes to heaven and pump out prayers to one or another hoary old starvation/sky god. Likewise, when we find ourselves low on heating fuel, and winds of ice begin to circle and howl around the house, thoughts of taking oil from whoever has some, creep into our heads — along with mental images of tossing a few bombs around and offing a few hundred (thousand? hundreds of thousands?) to get mission accomplished. In starvation culture, even the best of us, in the back of our minds, think "It's us or them, what can I say?"

Have War God, Will War

When we worship violent, cruel, self-identified warrior gods who solve problems through war, is it any wonder we can't chuck war? And when these warrior gods bear sons called things like "The Prince of Peace," how schizoid do you think that makes us? While we've been turning over every stone searching for reasons we can't play nicely together in the sandbox, the answer's been staring us in the face for 6000 years: all our trophies go to fear-crazed, starvation/war gods who solve problems by smiting and annihilating entire societies at a time. And when we house war and so-called peace gods in the same pantheon, we're going to do both war and peace. To our children we say, "These are the best the universe has to offer, kids. If you could only be like this war god Jehovah and his peace-son Jesus, you'd be all anyone could ask." So which god do the kids pattern themselves after? The war god, or the peace prince?

When we force Junior to sing songs praising one of the war Lord's favorite pastimes — wiping societies off the face of the earth — I'm thinking it helps him decide. In *The God Delusion*, evolutionary biologist and popular British science writer Richard Dawkins says as a child he sang this hymn in church (Dawkins 2006: 245):

Christian, dost thou see them
On the holy ground?
How the troops of Midian
Prowl and prowl around?

Christian, up and smite them,
Counting gain but loss;
Smite them by the merit
Of the holy cross.

In church: the place we send kids for getting pictures in their heads of ideal human behavior. As long as we drop in our churches, synagogs, temples and mosques on bended knee in front of primitive desert war gods — say it with me now — we ... will ... have ... war.

Little Ones, Come Ye Unto Daddy War Lord

Our children model themselves after deities we point them to. Because most modern parents know that what children see and hear is what they become, many restrict TV, while others even direct their child's social lives. Any parent who would let a child watch a cartoon based on the real starvation war Lords would be accused of child abuse — and rightly so. Any cartoon based on the real Jehovah (versus the pruned and polished version many pastors pick for Sunday's sermon) would show him letting dads burn their kids to death (Judges 11.30-39). It would show him demanding people be stoned to death weekly, for sneezing wrong (Numbers 15.32-36; Deuteronomy 21.18-21; Exodus 21.17, Deuteronomy 22.13-21).

And if you grew up in a Christian church like I did, thinking "stoning" meant pitching pebbles at people, think again. Not long ago someone pointed me to a video of a live stoning airing on the Internet. Unfortunately, I watched. A Middle Eastern man and woman were carried out onto a barren, flat piece of land into the middle of a large, dusty circle ringed by a crowd of men. Both were tied in brown bags from head to toe. As I sat in front of my computer screen, this man and woman were buried in the ground up to their knees — so they could stand longer as they began to pass out. Their crime: they'd made love without being married to each other.

Now it's target practice time. The bodies in the bags eventually begin to weave and wave in the wind, gently bending and bowing as fist-sized stones whiz and hit their targets — "Plok ... Plok ... Plok" — the people inside slowly dying while I watch over my keyboard. This was one unlucky man — in many Muslim places in case of adultery, the woman is stoned while the man gets off scot free. This is the love of Jehovah, Yahweh and Allah. This kind of butchery goes on even today, even as the trains of print in this book pass before your eyes.

Of course the "this is the real Jehovah" cartoon would beam in on monthly massacre-a-people parties (see Appendix J or Joshua, Numbers, Exodus, the Samuels, Deuteronomy, Genesis, Judges, the Kings and 2 Chronicles for too many examples to count). Kids watching this cartoon would witness events in mommy and daddy's master bedroom, featuring daddy offering mommy to strangers (See Genesis 20; Genesis 12.10-20; and Genesis 26.1-14). And so forth. In my third ear I can hear the deafening roar of parents howling with outrage and Congress and Parliament flooded with phone calls. The cartoon creators would be lucky to leave town with their necks intact.

Why would we want to give our children the model of a bogus butcher and killer to emulate, instead of the model of the life-force, of a supplier of human needs (food, warmth, love, protection)? What do we gain by telling our children, in so many words, to become butcher-warriors like Jehovah, Vishnu, Allah, Yahweh and the other deadly daddy war Lords, when these are self-proclaimed killers and mass-murderers with no natural abilities to create or feed us, the earth, or anything on it? What would we gain if we erased all our barren, butcher role models from the face of the earth, and in their place dropped nurturing, sustainable, life-force providers? What if we pointed to these new models and said, "Kids, this is what you should become. Might does not make right — only right makes right. And over the next few decades it's your job to see that we kick Might right off the planet."

Jesus the Conditional Lover

"But Jesus," you say, "does this. Jesus nurtures, loves and protects us." Not really. Jesus' love has strings attached. For starters, you have to "believe in" and "accept" him. If you don't, you get waltzed right down into that wonderful little starvation-god invention, the gigantic, underground, eternal torture chamber (see John 3.16; Matthew 5.21-22; Matthew 5.29-30; Matthew 10.28; John 6.47, etc.). Which, last time I checked, was nobody's idea of love. Obviously no healthy mother would do anything of the sort to her child. With the Goddess, it doesn't matter what you do; at death you return to Her warm, loving womb. This is what is meant by "unconditional" love — no strings are attached to it. It's totally free.

But with no Hell to keep people in line, wouldn't we get serial killers? I don't think so. Most human societies throughout history have had neither Hell-beliefs nor serial killing. Some societies — all Hell-less — seem never even to have experienced murder at all. Murder and serial killing happen when societies and cultures are sick. Even after we switch to Goddess, it will take time to erase all the ruinous effects of 6000 years of being held hostage by primitive desert war gods. So as we heal from 6000 years of insanity, we might still have a few serial killers along the way. And if we do, the healthy response is to (1) attempt to rehabilitate them, and (2) if all else fails, restrain them.

"But," you protest again, "you need to get a grip on its historical and cultural context to understand the Bible." Nuh-uh. Not really. The important thing about the Bible is the effect it has on us. It doesn't really matter if Paul got Jesus' words right or wrong, or if back in AD 325 the Council of Nicaea pitched the wrong things out of the Bible.

Likewise, it doesn't matter whether or not the long-lost

Gospel of Mary should sashay in along with Matthew, Mark, Luke and John in the New Testament, or that the Bible is big-time inconsistent because it was cobbled together from various writers writing at different times and with different views. None of these things — or any other points about Bible context — changes the fact that the Bible is pumping us full of poison.

What matters is that the Bible, no matter where it came from or why, is chock full of cruelty, war and violence. What matters is that this cruelty, war and violence has shaped our cultures and behavior like nothing else has. In the present book, I'm concerned not with why the Abrahamaic holy books are what they are. And I'm not concerned with what they could or should be. Although I think removing all cruelty and violence from these books would be helpful, no one I have ever talked to seems even remotely prepared to do so. Perhaps that's because doing so would leave these books essentially meaningless.

What I'm concerned with is how the starvation-god holy books poisoned and still poison the human species. As they're read today, the Bible, Koran, Talmud, Bhagvad-Gita, and others poison us directly (partly on an unconscious level). They also poison us indirectly — through the various cultures they've helped shape over the millennia, cultures which in turn dictate our every behavior.

Whether you are a fundamentalist, moderate, atheist or Pagan, my firm belief is that the Bible — as is — has had a profoundly nasty effect on you, your culture and your behavior. "But if we could get back to the true Jesus," you say, "instead of the one Paul handed us, we'd have a good and beautiful religion. If we understood Jehovah's a war god because the early Jews were surrounded by enemies, then we could laugh off the Bible's cruelty, violence and massacre-a-month parties." I don't think so. This is like saying let's use the Ku Klux Klan Manual as our moral guidebook, but shut our eyes to everything in it about hate. If we don't work 24/7 warning everyone that to use the KKK Bible one must ignore almost everything in it, for many it will become a fast track to bigotry.

Or take another example. You ask a friend for her pie crust recipe. On a 3x5 card she writes, "1 cup flour, 8 cups shortening and 3 cups water." As she writes she says, "Whatever you do, don't take this recipe literally. Eight cups of shortening will give you a lard ball. Use ½ a cup instead. And using three cups of water will give you cream-of-lard-ball soup; drop down to 1/4 a cup."

Of course you scratch your head and ask what her point is in writing down bad numbers in the first place. And that's my question. Why do we pitch our kids a book that's supposed to lead to good things — but won't, unless we take great pains to explain nine-tenths of it away?

Anyway, back to Jesus. Even though Jesus preaches unconditional love, he doesn't really practice it. And even if he did, he's not a mother, so he wouldn't be as convincing a role model. Look around. How many white-gowned, bearded, 33-year-olds do you see modeling love with no strings attached? My guess is, not many. On the other hand, you see mothers modeling it regularly. Even if you're a stay-at-home couch potato, you can flip on the nature channel and watch mother-love to your heart's delight.

While in many ways Jesus is made out to be a superhero, there's just too much he fails to do. First, he doesn't neutralize Jehovah the warrior king. Jesus just never comes right out and says "Don't do war." Sure in Matthew 5.9 he says peacemakers are top-notch, but that's not the same as saying "Don't do wars in the first place" or "War makers are wicked." And yes, in Luke 6 he says Love your enemies and Turn the other cheek. But show me where Jesus says "Wicked are the warmongers," "Blessed are the peace*keepers*" or "It's easier for a camel to crawl through the eye of a needle than for a war-starter to get into heaven."

Second, none of the New Testament writers show Jesus slamming either slavery or any other snooty snobbery. He just tells you how, and how hard to pound and pop your slaves: Listen to Jesus in Luke 12:47-48: "And that slave who knew his master's will and did not get ready or act in accord with his will, will receive many lashes, but the one who did not know it, and committed deeds worthy of a flogging, will receive but few." Where does Jesus say "Wicked are the slave owners and other supporters of slavery"? Of course he lived in a world that accepted slavery, but what difference does that make? Wasn't the whole point of Jesus' coming, to clean up the world, make it abandon its sins and fly right? If so, why's he not slamming slave owners right up there along with temple moneylenders?

Third, while the Guiding Goddess wants us all rich — fabulously rich (as long as *everyone's* fab rich) — Jesus apparently thinks we should all be equally poor: "Then Jesus said to his disciples, 'I tell you the truth, it is hard for a rich man to enter the kingdom of heaven. Again I tell you, it is easier for a camel to go through the eye of a needle than for a rich man to enter the kingdom of God'" (Matthew 19.23-25). Why in the world would a deity want people to be monetarily miserable? What sense does that make? What's wrong with having plenty? As long as everyone has plenty, what's the big deal?

Fourth, Paul and the other New Testament writers don't hand us a Jesus who seems very thrilled with the opposite sex. Oh sure, Jesus has more pity on women than his dad does — he forgives the woman in John 8.1-11 who commits adultery, for example, instead of ordering her stoned to death as Dad would have done. But he doesn't have that many women friends. He doesn't seem to enjoy the company of women. And as far as I can tell, he never marries, dates, kisses, or even hugs a woman. What's more, he's certainly not an equal-opportunity employer — twelve disciples, and not one a woman? Tsk, tsk. The Guiding Goddess, on the other hand, adores men, and wants them around Her at all times. If you don't believe me, just go check in with the Moso and ask about their Great Goddess.

Fifth, at least as Paul and the others describe him, Jesus

possesses not one fun, creative, playful, sensual, or funny bone in his body. In the Bible, Jesus laughs not once. There's no smiling. There's no joking or teasing. No parties. Where have all the flowers gone? The beauty of nature? The ball games? In the Bible, colors range from light gray to dark. On the other hand, the Guiding Mother Goddess sparkles with color, creativity and sensuality (and expects us to, too). For examples, zip back to the beginning of this book and reread about the creativity of the Hopi and Jomon, and the playfulness of the Moso and Minoans.

Or read theologian Carol Christ's *The Laughter of Aphrodite*. "People," says Christ, "usually do not think of laughter as a spiritual experience...." But laughter, she says, "can be the mediator of transformation." Laughter helped Carol Christ "to distance myself from pain, opening a new perspective on my life" (Christ 1987: 6). Or go grab a copy of Zsuzsanna Budapest's The *Grandmother of Time*. Z, one of the leaders of the twentieth-century Goddess Movement, dedicates her book "to the Goddess of Celebrations, Habondia; may she lead us back to her paradise." The title of Z's book preface? "A Life Without Celebration Is Only Half Lived" (Budapest 1989). Growing up in rural Hungary during the first half of the twentieth century, Z Budapest claims an unbroken heritage reaching back into times when her region was far less Christianized than today.

In his 1928 play *Strange Interlude*, world-famous writer Eugene O'Neill got it right when he insisted the bungling began when god was made male:

The mistake began when God was created in a male image.... That makes life so perverted and death so unnatural. We should have imagined life as created in the birth-pain of God the Mother. Then we would understand why we, Her children, have inherited pain, for we would know that our life's rhythm beats from Her great heart, torn with the agony of love and birth.

As O'Neill points out, for goddess followers, death is simply a return to the loving Mother's womb: "And we would feel that death meant reunion with Her, a passing back into Her substance, blood of Her blood again, peace of Her peace! Now wouldn't that be more logical and satisfying than having God a male whose chest thunders with egotism and is too hard for tired heads and thoroughly comfortless?" (Walker 1983: 690, quoting O'Neill 2004). And, I might add, a god who at death makes us choose between his underground torture chamber, and a pearly-gated heaven with starvation-culture streets paved in cold, hard gold?

Full of Hope

I feel full of hope. If we put all our hearts and minds into the switch back to our peaceful, gorgeous goddess role models, we can't lose. If we flood the world with speaking and writing on the switch, and singing, and gathering in small circles; if we fill it with books, and articles, blogs and websites, TV programs, movies and magazines about the health-enhancing, paradise-producing goddesses of our ancestors, and about the toxic shock that is the starvation war gods, then we can and will change.

Even if we experience disaster through climate change or a nuclear 'event,' as long as the world is flooded with information about the switch now, a new generation down the road will be able to pick up the pieces and start over again — minus the war gods next time. Of course we need to try to make the switch before disaster hits. However, we should be mindful that we may be pumping vital information into a world that will experience a holocaust, but which somewhere down the line can be revived — maybe decades, maybe centuries from now.

And just imagine those distant survivors, with the historical records laid out on a table in front of them. On the one hand stand the shining, peaceful guiding-goddess cultures of the Neolithic and early Bronze Age. And on the other lie the vacant-eyed, rotting, high-god starvation cultures, including those twentieth-century sociocultural experiments in forcing peoples to abandon religion altogether — and which lead to some of the world's bloodiest mass murderers: Stalin, Mao, and Pol Pot. Imagine the horror when our distant descendants discover which cultures finally destroyed the earth. Imagine the disgust in their eyes and hearts. Is there any question in your mind which path they'll choose for their new beginning?

Life's too short to waste on war, violence, dominance and pain. One way out of the corner we humans have boxed ourselves into, is the way of tend and befriend, of our happy bonobo cousins, of our sisters and brothers the Moso and the Hopi, and of our guiding-goddess Neolithic and Bronze-Age ancestors. Are we going to be sharp enough to grab utopia? Or will we risk allowing our species to fade away into zip and nada? As much as it is about choosing peace over war, the switch is about do we want to continue as a species. Or do we want to risk following the non-human species we're blasting off the planet, into our own extinction? Isn't it time we went home again — to Mother?

Ten Things I Can Do to Spread the Word

Okay, now it's your turn. Stop reading, go grab a pencil or pen, and in the spaces below, list ten things you could, might and will for-sure do in the next two weeks to help lead the world toward the switch:

Could do:

1. _____
2. _____
3. _____

Might do:

4. _____
5. _____
6. _____

Will definitely do:

7. _____

8. _____

9. _____

10. _____

Luke Skywalker, Where R U?

Recently, despite widespread gloom over the state of the planet, environmentalist and best-selling author Paul Hawken published an awesome and upbeat new book. *Blessed Unrest: How the Largest Movement in the World Came into Being and Why No One Saw It Coming* describes a worldwide "movement" over one million organizations strong. The purpose of this movement? Saving the environment and pushing for social justice.

What's unusual about Hawken's movement is this: its individual organizations aren't collected together under any single umbrella. All across the planet, they've sprung up independently, and have remained more or less independent. In Canada, Cree Indians meet about toxic-waste lakes on their land — lakes so large they can be seen from outer space. In India, a group takes a ten-day trek into the wilderness to look into revitalizing ancient rainwater-catchment systems that will be used to revive drought-stricken areas. In Liberia, Silas Kpanan' Ayoung Siakor plays detective, investigating the relationship between the genocidal policies of Liberia's President, and illegal logging; this leads to international sanctions on Liberia and a change in logging practices. After years of researching this "movement with no name," Hawken makes a startling claim: this is, he says, "the largest social movement in all of human history" (Hawken 2007: 11, 4).

Although Hawken insists there's no "unifying principle" or top-down management knitting his movement together, I disagree. I think the unifier is the Guiding Mother Goddess. For too long, the starvation/war gods have ordered us to "subdue" the earth. Now, in protest, Mother Earth is rising up again. Hawken even admits that "Healing the wounds of the earth and its people ... is a sacred act" (Hawken 2007: 5). But what kind of sacred act? Coming from where? Certainly not from our current major gods; instead of healing the Earth and its people, Jehovah growls at us to "subdue" and "rule" over them (Genesis 1.28).

Actually, Hawken himself edges close to pinpointing Goddess as the wellspring of his movement, a movement linked to "an older quiescent history that is reemerging, what poet Gary Snyder calls *the great underground,* a current of humanity that dates back to the Paleolithic. Its lineage can be traced back to healers, *priestesses* [emphasis the author's], philosophers, monks, rabbis, poets, and artists 'who speak for the planet, for other species, for interdependence, a life that courses under and through and around empires.'" Like Hawken's movement, the Goddess-centered Halafian, Indus-Valley and Minoan peoples seemed knit together through forces other than top-down, centralized authority (see chapter 3, "Good Times" and chapter 5, "Before War"). When Hawken says his movement "forms, dissipates, and then regathers quickly, without central leadership, command, or control," in my mind's eye I can see Halafians, Indusites and Minoans moving through time and space in exactly the same beautiful way (Hawken 2007: 5, 12).

As our Mother rises again from Her underground safe haven, She needs help. In addition to breathing new life back into Her old myths and stories, we need to weave new stories too — ones fitting our times. Imagine how much healthier we'd all be if She shone above ground, in the light of day again. We need a new kind of hero to step forward now, one unafraid to guide us through the "dark night of our soul" and back into the light of Gaia. Luke Skywalker where are you? We need you. Help us tear ourselves away from our "dying gods"; help us find the old lost paths back to the world of Gaia our Mother. We need new myths that create not "conquering heroes," but as University of

Connecticut world-mythographer David Leeming puts it

> ...seekers after the ... Gaian world.... Those who refuse the call will hang on desperately to the dying gods and ... will continue to endanger the world .... Those who answer the call will ... participate in a breaking away — as heroes have always done.... [T]he ecological hero will have to endure a dark night of the soul, a perilous journey among the demons that haunt us as a species. As it has always been for heroes, this adventure is a quest for something lost... (Leeming 2005).

Our new heroes, Luke, must be global heroes. They must be heroes who can help lead the world as one big family in harvesting the best strands of our past and our present to weave the magnificent future we all know in our deepest hearts can be ours. If, that is we have the gumption and grit to reach out and grab it.

I think we do have that gumption and grit. And whether we know it or not, I think we've already begun the switch back to our fabulous global unifying principle, the Great Guiding Goddess, Mother of the Earth and Mother of us all. But we still have miles to go before we sleep, my fellow Earth maties. So c'mon, y'all — let's rock 'n roll!

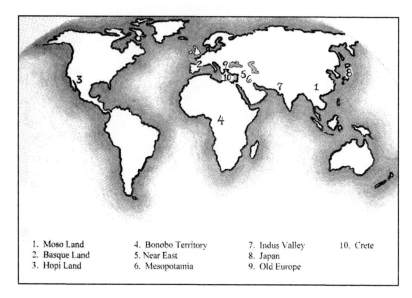

1. Moso Land
2. Basque Land
3. Hopi Land
4. Bonobo Territory
5. Near East
6. Mesopotamia
7. Indus Valley
8. Japan
9. Old Europe
10. Crete

The World

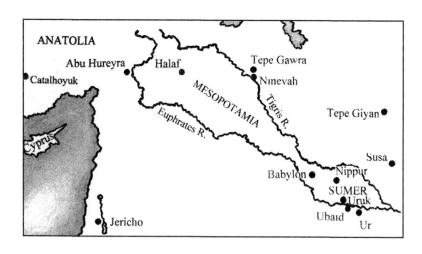

Ancient Near East

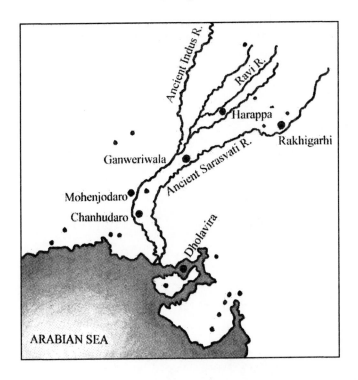

Indus Valley Civilization

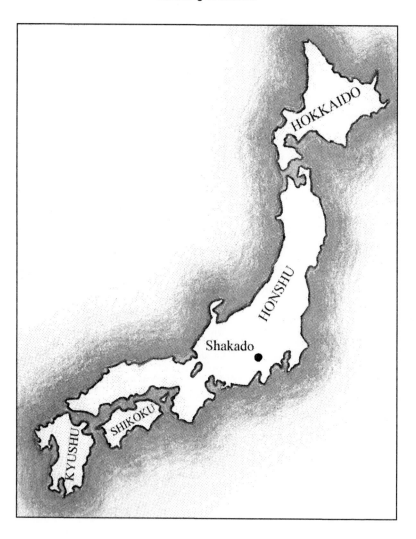

Jomon Japan

Old Europe

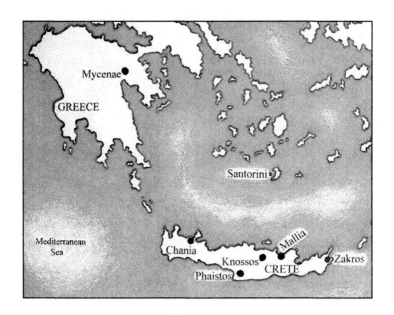

Minoan Crete

Appendix A: Origin of Starvation Culture*

Temporary Starvation Behavior	Permanent Starvation Culture
"Feeding of the self becomes the all-consuming passion."	The rise of the importance of the individual (versus the group).
"Loss of interest in the pleasures of life."	Pleasure is defined as bad, and pain as good ... ritual flagellation ... warriors undergo brutal and constant training.
"A passive indifference to the needs or pain of others."	War, violence and cruelty become culturally acceptable.
"Brothers steal food from sisters."	Certain kinds of stealing become socially acceptable. Thieving and tricking (vs. labor and production) become acceptable ways of obtaining life's necessities. War becomes acceptable (war is theiving on a grand scale).
"Husbands leave wives and babies to fend for themselves."	It becomes culturally acceptable for men to go off to war constantly.
"Older children gather into gangs dedicated to stealing food, even from their own	It becomes culturally acceptable for the strongest (young, healthy males) to assume the ace power

younger siblings, or older, weakened kinfolk."	positions and to take more than their fair share.
"While the maternal-infant bond endures the longest, eventually mothers abandon their ... children and even resort to cannibalizing them."	Anger against women and female deity becomes institutionalized.

*Column one is based on responses of the Ik to long-term starvation and on DeMeo 1998: 77.

APPENDIX B: War Gods Around the World

NOTE: For any country below, not all war gods are necessarily presented.

Country	War God(s)
America	Jehovah
Australia	Jehovah
Canada	Jehovah
China	Huangdi
Egypt	Menthu, Septu, Wepwawet, Allah
Europe	Ares/Mars
France	Teutates
Germany	Tiwaz
Greece	Ares, Enyalius (Sparta)
India	Indra
Iran	Dev, Indar, Burijas, Allah
Iraq	Ninurta/Ningirsu; Allah
Israel	Yahweh
Italy	Mars
Japan	Hachiman

Korea	Chi You
Mexico	Mextli
Near East	Ninurta; Allah
Russia & Slavic countries	Svantovit (Sventovit, Swiantowid) and Iarovit (Jarovit, Dzarowit, Gerovit, Gerovitus)
Scandinavia	Odin, Tyr
South Africa	Jehovah
Spain	Cariocienus
Syria	Reshep
Tibet	Beg-tse
UK (celtic)	Cocidius, Belatu-Cadros (aka Belatucadrus)

APPENDIX C: Questions from the Peanut Gallery

ANTI-FEMALE. "Since it objectifies women's bodies, won't goddess spirituality hurt women?"

In the past, many goddesses were imaged nude and with their maternal organs emphasized. This symbolized the Goddess' twin abilities to birth, and to feed the birthed through Her body. Only if the world continues to look at women's bodies through starvation/war-god spectacles — in which case the female body does appear (erroneously, of course) shameful — will this emphasis on the Goddess-body hurt women.

ANTI-MALE. "Isn't goddess worship an anti-male religion?"

Not at all. The Mother Goddess is nothing if not impartial. Like any healthy mother, She sees males as equal in value to females. Today, men as well as women are following Goddess spirituality.

AUTHORITY. "Who is our authority going to be? You say there

shouldn't be an authority, but there probably is going to be an authority, and it probably won't be a loving mother."

As individuals born into war-god starvation cultures (See chapter six, "Bad Times"), most of us have known nothing but life under centralized authority. That we should be nervous about living without such authority, therefore, is understandable. But nothing says humans have to endure "authority," which can be and often is autocratic, dictatorial and unpleasant for everyone concerned. The Semai of the Malay Peninsula are just one example of a human society minus "authority." Among the Semai, "the ability of one person to constrain the actions of another is limited." As a matter of fact, the Semai have a saying: "There is no authority here but embarrassment" (Dentan 1979: 68-69).

Centralized communication and leadership, yes; centralized authority, no. Of course groups with centralized authority and robot-citizens are better at war, so we need multilateral disarmament of centralized authority just as we need multilateral disarmament of war gods.

BIBLE. "Christians have a book — where can I go to find Goddess beliefs?"

There is no book containing all Goddess beliefs under one cover. In part this is because, due to war-god temper tantrums, Goddess beliefs have been zapped underground over the millennia. There's also less need for a Goddess Bible. Goddess spirituality is left-brained, intuitive, and based on the sacredness of nature and its cycles. "One book fits all" is for war-god societies needing everyone to be on the same page so a few at the top can control everyone else. For healthy, happy human beings, however, "one book fits all" is not so good.

But books on goddess spirituality do exist. See Appendix I, "Goddess Reading List."

Note: If you're in a fever pitch to write a Goddess Bible, do. Just don't expect everyone to follow it.

BLAME. "I wonder, though — can the god be blamed for what people actually do?"

Of course gods can be blamed for what people do. Gods are role models. Tots the world over are taught to love and respect starvation/war gods. Until having children, many drop out of church. Then they begin going again — to "teach our children right ways." Many of us, through our entire childhoods, are war-god indoctrinated weekly — or more.

We all know what children hear, see and experience shapes the kind of adults they become. The incidence of violence and cruelty in the Bible is greater than you think. See Appendix I: "Cruelty in the Bible: Short List." Our unconscious affects our behavior. Even though you may not remember hearing Bible verses about cruelty, if you heard them at all, they're stored in your unconscious — and undoubtedly help shape your adult thoughts and behavior.

BOATS. "Could it be there was no war in the Neolithic because navigation had not progressed to the point that one culture could sail off and conquer another?"

No. If you're dying to slash and burn, you can do it by land as well as by sea. Although the goddess-focused Indus Valley people traded regularly with the god-focused Mesopotamians, they declined to war with the Mesopotamians — or among themselves, either (McIntosh 2002: 9). In contrast, the Mesopotamians did almost nothing but war, each city state conquering its neighbors, and then in turn getting conquered itself. And mostly without boats.

BORN BAD. "But don't the bad things people do come from our 'baser natures' rather than from Jehovah or any other so-called 'war god'? Aren't people just born hateful, greedy and full of fear?"

Science has identified absolutely no 'baser nature' shared by all humans at birth. Except for a few of us who are biologically impaired, all humans can be taught to do and be just about anything. Cruel, violent, starvation war gods, however, are the wrong teaching tools for anyone, anywhere.

BUDDHISM. "For bringing peace and harmony to the world, wouldn't Buddhism work as well as goddesses?"

Like Jesus, Buddha decreed for his followers lives of sensual deprivation. Also like Jesus, he suggests humans deserve poverty, primarily. In contrast, the Guiding Goddess demands we enjoy the senses She gave us, and that we pull everyone together into abundance — the way healthy siblings might do.

And as a male metasymbol, Buddha can't function the way Mother can. In one fell swoop, "Mother" serves as a symbolic road map outlining everything we need to know, about how to treat each other (the way a healthy mother treats her child), about where we came from (Her womb), about where we go after we die (back to her womb as a way stop between lives), the relative value of men and women (in the eyes of the healthy mother, sons and daughters are equal); the value of the elderly (Mom loves you as much at 80 as when you were 8); how to treat the earth (the Earth is your Mother; treat Her like a Goddess), and so forth.

The mythographer David Leeming says Buddhism buries the Goddess in the form of Buddha's mother Maya. "In the Buddhist tradition, Goddess is submerged in the humble character of Queen Maya, whose name reveals her connection to Devi-Maya, the goddess of matter and the senses, the birth-giver of all things.... After birthing Buddha, "Queen Maha-Maya died of sheer joy at what she had accomplished" (Leeming and Page 1994: 155).

What's more, Buddhism is not always the cornucopia of peace and purity many in the West believe it to be. In Thailand, for example, the "numbers of monks are falling, ... commercialized folk Buddhism has gained the upper hand," and "monastic sexual and financial misdeeds are widespread" (McCargo 2004: 1). Some

Buddhists have turned to violent "protector" gods like Dorje Shugden, described — even "by friends — as a lightning-breathing terror with three bloodshot eyes, wreathed in the smoke of burning human flesh."

In 1997, in Dharamsala, India Shugden monks knifed rival anti-Shugden monks in a "ritual stabbing" (Van Biema 1998: 70). Dorje Shugden is only one of a pantheon of protector deities, and it seems obvious there might be a correlation between the violence of the gods on the one hand, and the violence of their followers on the other.

CAUSALITY. "But did the Neolithic Goddess cause utopia? Or were She and utopia merely twin effects of a mysterious Cause X?"

If the notion of causation in the present is tricky (and it is), it's even trickier in the past. It can't be said that a Guiding Mother Goddess causes utopia, in the sense that the occurrence of utopia depends on the occurrence of a Guiding Mother Goddess. Other forces too might produce a warless, non-violent, classless world (for example, Martians moving in and making us pitch war, violence, and social-class silliness).

Or, in order for utopia to result, it could be that in addition to a Guiding Goddess, other factors too must be present. I think such other factors include the absence of both starvation culture and war-god culture. On the other hand, other additional factors could be required, factors at present unknown.

What the evidence in this book suggests, however, is that a sociocultural "package" consisting of a Guiding Goddess in the absence of war gods and starvation culture, would go far toward pulling any society along a path toward social utopia.

CHANGE. "But you said culture is highly resistant to change. So how are we going to shift to Goddess by 2035?"

You're right, culture is resistant to change. Almost all of us, however, already live in partially-goddess societies. The starvation/war gods are simply thin overlays we've allowed to grow over far-older goddess cultures. Our job is to pull out the old goddesses from beneath the starvation/war-culture dirt layer, and dust them off again.

CHAOS. "Won't giving up God lead to social chaos?"

No. Throughout history, thousands of successful societies have lived without Abrahamaic or other war gods, and without their "keep 'em in line" concept of Hell. Furthermore, at least one recent study shows a correlation between Christianity and criminal behavior (Paul 2005; Gledhill 2005), strongly suggesting that far from preventing crime, Christianity actually promotes it.

Just like gods, goddesses too have rules for behavior. The ancient Egyptian Goddess Ma'at had 42 Commandments, including many of Moses' ten — and then some. Current Goddess scholars and theologians often write about ethics. Theologian and goddess scholar Carol Christ, for example, has offered the following 'ethical touchstones' for Goddess followers:

Nurture life;
- Walk in love and beauty;
- Trust the knowledge that comes through the body;
- Speak the truth about conflict, pain, and suffering;
- Take only what you need;
- Think about the consequences of your actions for seven generations;
- Approach the taking of life with great restraint;
- Practice great generosity;
- Repair the web (Christ 1997: 167).

The Reverend Karen Tate, of the Temple of the Goddess in Pasadena, California, has compiled the following "Goddess Perpetuations for Daily Living":

1. I strive to be in service rather than in power. With service comes humility and care. With power comes corruption.
2. I strive to live in harmony with Nature.
3. I strive to employ kindness and compassion as well as ethics and integrity.
4. I strive to be strong, tenacious and assertive, using force as a last resort, and then only tempered by wisdom, care, and discernment.
5. I strive to be accountable and responsible for my actions and expect the same of others.
6. I strive not to be influenced by power and greed.
7. I strive to be generous, supportive and nurturing.
8. I strive to work in partnership with others to create mutually beneficial relationships and associations.
9. I strive to perpetuate positive thoughts and practice life-affirming actions, knowing that what I put forth will return to me.
10. I strive to be aware I am a thread in the web of life, a microcosm of the macrocosm, and as such I affect others.
11. I strive for equality and human rights for all, no matter one's sexual orientation, race, religion or gender.
12. I strive to seek the beauty, joy and pleasures of life.
13. I strive to be grateful and know abundance, with no fear of scarcity.
14. I strive to know myself.
15. I strive to embrace diversity and tolerance, for in Goddess' many faces, skin colors, sizes and shapes, I see richness and have no fear.
16. I strive to honor all living things, including myself, and seek to harm none.
17. I strive to see the Divine in myself and all things, including the mundane.
18. I strive to recognize there is no one way to define, embrace or worship the Divine.

19. I strive to seek my own best path to the Divine.

20. I strive to be one with the Divine (personal communcation from Karen Tate).

Furthermore, the Mother Model — treating others as a healthy mother treats her children — is a powerful, observable model for human behavior.

CHICKEN OR EGG? "Isn't it likely that war came first, *then* the war gods?"

Yes. But the war gods helped, and still help, to cement war into place. They're the oil that helps keep war running smoothly in our systems. The gas that keeps the car going is, I believe, starvation culture — a nasty set of behaviors our distant ancestors fell into as a response to long-term starvation. Before we can rid ourselves of war, we need to pitch war gods and starvation culture both.

CO-EQUAL DEITIES. "Do we really have to get rid of Yahweh (Jehovah, Allah, Vishnu)? Can't we simply add the Goddess to the gods we already have?"

Please go back and reread this book.

We tried pairing Jehovah, for example, with a kinder, gentler soul — Jesus. It was a flop. In good times, Jesus and gentleness get the upper hand, while in bad times it's a fast-track race back to Jehovah's "vindictive, bloodthirsty ..., misogynistic, homophobic, racist, infanticidal, genocidal, filicidal, pestilential, megalomanial, sadomasochistic, capriciously malevolent" and war-happy behavior (Dawkins 2006: 31).

DEFENSE, NATIONAL. "Won't switching to goddesses turn our kids into sissies? And if that happens, who'll protect us from our enemies?"

The Goddess is neither wimp nor woosie. Does a healthy mother protect her children from those who might harm them?

Of course she does. The Mother Goddess demands we protect others from those who threaten them. Men must learn to be Mother Men, however, and women Mother Women. In other words, we must all use mothers as the proper model for defending others.

There's absolutely nothing wrong with men learning from a mother model. In ancient Guiding Goddess societies, men were courageous risk-takers who took part in thrilling and sometimes dangerous sports, and who sailed the high seas all over the known world. And as modern Goddess follower and author Tim Ward will tell you, they almost certainly had relationships with women 200 percent more satisfying than most men enjoy in today's starvation/war-god cultures (Ward 2006).

Speaking of national defense, all of us across the globe need to shoot for multilateral, simultaneous disarmament of the starvation/war gods. They're the gas that keeps war up and running. All across the world they're preventing us from letting go of war, violence and cruelty.

FAILED SOCIETIES. "Since all past guiding-goddess societies failed, doesn't that mean there's something inherently wrong with goddess societies?"

Absolutely not. When Hitler tried to take it over, the whole world came very, very close to "failing." This hardly makes all of us but Hitler "inherently wrong."

According to internationally-known linguist Harald Haarmann, the peaceful egalitarian ("oecumene") societies of the Neolithic disappeared through no fault of their own: "[A]re properties inherent in the ... oecumene which make it vulnerable and perhaps less viable than the social hierarchy of the state model? The answer ... is a clear 'no.' There is no element in egalitarian social structures that implies an impediment to their longevity.... It may be ... misuse of political power by the leadership in the state model which gives male-dominated society the edge to 'colonize' oecumene communities" (Haarmann 2005: 171-72).

The starvation/war-god model is wrong and bad. It's a lethal virus that's spread among humans over the past 6000 years, and considering humanity's multi-million-year history, 6000 years is a drop in the bucket. We've been sick for less than a day. We *can* conquer this illness.

GOLDEN RULE. "Isn't the Golden Rule (treat others as you'd have others treat you) as good as the Mother Model (treat others as a healthy mother treats her children)?"

Because you can see it in action, the Mother Model is better than the Golden Rule. You can look around and see how healthy mothers treat their kids (even if you have to turn on the nature channel and watch a mother in the wild with her cubs or chicklets). Healthy mothers love you unconditionally and treat you as you need to be treated to thrive. In the Golden Rule, on the other hand, is a glaring faultline: the possibility of the projection of your own wishes (and even pathologies) onto others.

JESUS. "Isn't Jesus the same as a Guiding Mother Goddess? He loves us unconditionally."

Jesus' love is not unconditional. See "Jesus the Conditional Lover" in chapter nine.

MEN, ROLE OF. "But what role will men play in a Guiding-Goddess utopian world?"

Men will play the same roles they play now: teachers, doctors, dads, lawyers, lovers, comedians, candlestick makers, etc. Furthermore, I believe there will always be a role for people with more testosterone than the rest of us have. In a shrinking global village, however, there's more need than ever to carefully train testosterone, via the Mother Model. But for a long time to come I think we'll desperately need law enforcement — to help clean up the world from a whole variety of starvation-culture ills that will need extra work to fix, including but not confined to the following:

Drug addiction.

The one percent who profit heavily from a war-god world.

Violence stemming from poverty and the lack of basic necessities.

The criminally insane and others unable to learn from a Mother Model.

MODERATES, RELIGIOUS. "Instead of switching to goddesses, isn't the solution simply to get religious radicals to turn into religious moderates?"

No. At first glance, radical Christians, Muslims and Hindus seem more dangerous than their moderate cousins. But the mere presence of the latter legitimizes the former. Since they preserve the radical's roadmaps (Bible, Koran, Talmud, Bhagvad Gita, etc.), moderates are just as dangerous as fundamentalists. As leading lights in their communities, religious moderates place their coveted stamps of approval on these dangerous fundamentalist roadmaps.

As the high profile, best-selling author Sam Harris notes, "Religious moderates are, in large part, responsible for the religious conflict in our world, because their beliefs provide the context in which scriptural literalism and religious violence can never be adequately opposed" (Harris 2004: 45). Harris also suggests that religious tolerance is "...one of the principal forces driving us toward the abyss" (Harris 2004: 15).

MOTHER MODEL, THE. "What is it?"

Like the Golden Rule, the Mother Model is a quick and easy way to decide how to behave in any situation. In choosing how to behave, answering the question "In this situation, what would a healthy mother do vis a vis her children?" is always likely to scare up good, moral behavior.

Not just men but all of us need to learn from this mothers-relating-to-their-children model (or "Mother Model" for short). Since I'm a non-mother woman — I've never had children — I need to learn from it too. But even mothers themselves need to learn from the Mother Model. It's easy to love your own children unconditionally. To love someone else's children, though, with the same constant depth of feeling, is something even mothers need to practice and master.

MOTHERS. "A lot of people don't like their mums too much. Could they follow a mother goddess?"

A lot don't like their dads either, but that's not seemed to keep them from worshipping father gods over the past many millennia. In following a Guiding Mother Goddess, it doesn't matter whether you like your mum or not. Most of us, our mothers included, had the misfortune of being born into poisonous environments — starvation cultures headed by war gods. It's amazing any of us is even halfway emotionally healthy.

If your mother was hit harder than most by the war gods, I am very sorry. You've had to pay a big part of the price for that. But you more than most should see the importance of switching to a way of life that doesn't damage mothers (or anyone else). And even though you don't like your own mother, you can probably look around and find a mother who does love her children unconditionally, and well. If not, pop a pot of popcorn and tune in to the nature channel.

POST-MODERNISM. "Isn't your story (about a global Neolithic goddess who gets pummeled by war gods) simply a metanarrative — and therefore not to be taken seriously?"

This book makes no overarching claim that goddess figurines or powerful goddesses were found everywhere around the world before war gods came on the scene around 4000 BC. Neither, however, does it rule out the possibility that in the past, strong peaceful goddesses inhabited many cultures worldwide, and that often it was violent male deities that displaced them. Scientific generalizations are not evil. Since scholars fail to generalize about much of anything anymore, non-scholars are doing it for them — often with sad results. Despite postmodernist claims to the contrary, global sociocultural trends have indeed occurred throughout history. One example: the "rise" of the state, first in the Near East and Egypt, then in China, and later down the west coast of the Americas.

RELIGIOUS APOLOGIA. "This book seems to say it offers the one true religion, and all others are bogus. Isn't that religious apologia?"

If you define "religious apologia" as speaking out in defense of a particular spiritual focus, then this book is religious apologia. But there are striking differences between the way I defend a focus on Mother-Goddess spirituality, and the way Christians and Muslims, for example, defend their religions:

First, as long as "Mother" is its defining principle, I don't care what kind of spirituality you follow. In contrast, "Father" religions have waged vicious war among themselves for millennia, many declaring theirs the Father who knows best — and all others in need of extermination.

Second, I base my defense on rational thinking, scientific reasoning, controlled experimentation, and historical and archaeological recordkeeping — all of which show that throughout history, father gods have lead to death, despair and destruction, and that it's actually Mother who knows best. In contrast, Father followers base their defense of their religions almost totally on "faith."

This is not to say I mind male gods. The problems creep in when Mother deities are replaced by jealous Father deities, who try, but can never really succeed in replacing Mother's overwhelmingly healthy personality, gifts and powers.

SAVING THE WORLD. "Can the world really be saved by imagining different gods? Will it cause the Middle East problem to go away? Territoriality? Tradition?

I believe the world *can* be saved by imagining different gods — as long as we also recognize and deal with the underlying culture that probably helped produce those gods in the first place, and still keeps them humming along, even today. Children are almost infinitely malleable. If your children had been adopted as infants into certain Inuit groups, they'd be eating raw seal blubber marbled with blood and brains — all without batting an eye. They'd think nothing about making red paint by mixing urine and blood — after puncturing the insides of their nostrils to collect the blood (Oswalt 1967: 157).

If your children had been adopted by the Semai of Southeast Asia the thought of hitting people would carry the same horror as the idea of killing them (Dentan 1979: 58). If your children had been adopted by the !Kung of southern Africa, they'd turn down a bushel load of Halloween candy for a handful of roasted caterpillar skins (Shostak 1983: 99). If we could rear our children in places where violent deities had been banished, and mother deities were not only visible everywhere but also pointed to as the quintessential role models, I'm convinced we could save the planet. To a great extent, territoriality and tradition are merely ideas we teach the next generation — or not.

SECULAR HUMANISM. "Why goddesses? Why not secular humanism instead?"

Because secular humanism isn't powerful enough to do the job we need done. Humans need moral and ethical guidance coming from a credible core source powerful enough to move us on deep levels. We also need answers to unanswered questions of enormous importance: where we go when we die, why we're here, where space begins and ends, and other biggies. Secular humanism can't answer these questions, and science probably won't either.

According to anthropologists, all human groups have had religion. Furthermore, that religion has always been based on the supernatural. What makes us think we twenty-first centuryites are somehow so radically "more" that we alone can do what no other time period (to our knowledge) has ever been able to do?

Naturally, many today fear religion — we've just been through six millennia of starvation/war-god hell. But since war-god religion isn't a bona fide sacred system, we can hardly use it to judge the safety or danger of supernatural religion in general.

Also, the proof is in the pudding. Even though secular humanism has been around now for at least thirty years, I don't see it catching fire anywhere.

SEXUAL LICENSE. "Isn't Goddess religion a Pagan religion? And aren't Pagans sexually licentious?"

Originally, "Pagan" was a nasty label tacked onto people by the war god Jehovah so his faithful knew who to take pot shots at. It was like wearing uniforms in a war: you have to have them so you know who to kill and who not to. So a Pagan was simply someone smart enough not to follow Jehovah. Simply put, a Pagan was a non-Christian.

Are non-Christians "sexually licentious"? Of course not. "Licentious," i.e. "pursuing desires aggressively and selfishly, unchecked by morality, especially in sexual matters" (Encarta World English Dictionary 1998-2004), is a word I feel far more comfortable attaching to war-god followers than to Goddess devotees. Just check out the nightly news on the subject of war-god clerics molesting women and children.

On the other hand, the Goddess demands that we all enjoy to the fullest the senses She gave us. So although there are no statistics on the matter (that I know of at least), my guess is that Goddess followers enjoy healthy, loving and delightful sex significantly more often than war-god followers do.

SKY GODS. "When I think of the old Pagan pantheons, I think of sky gods, not war gods. What's up with that?"

The old European pantheons, especially were headed by triads of sky-war-fertility gods. In Rome it was Jupiter, Mars and Quirinus; in Germanic Europe Odin, Thor and Tyr (or Freyr); and among the continental Celts it was Esus, Taranis and Teutates. Among the Slavs it was a combo of Perkuno and various war and fertility gods. University of Connecticut mythographer David Leeming says Jehovah is "triadic within himself," a "warrior-sovereign-storm god who demanded sacrifice" (Leeming 2005: 128-29).

TOLERANCE, RELIGIOUS. "But isn't it best to view all religions as equally valid and worthy of our respect (or at least tolerance)?"

No, not if they're killing us as a species. "Given the link between belief and action," says bestselling, award-winning Stanford University author Sam Harris, "we can no more tolerate a diversity of religious beliefs than a diversity of beliefs about epidemiology and basic hygiene. There are still a number of cultures in which the germ theory of disease has yet to put in an appearance, where people suffer from a debilitating ignorance on most matters relevant to their physical health. Do we 'tolerate' these beliefs? Not if they put our own health in jeopardy" (Harris 2004: 46).

And the primitive desert starvation/war gods are, indeed, putting our own health in jeopardy — not to mention our continued existence as a species. "Tolerating" them is akin to standing back and inviting the plague to enter the castle through the front gates.

UNCONDITIONAL LOVE: MEN HAVE IT TOO? "Men have the desire to protect their families. Isn't that a sort of nurturing?"

When baby's born, unlike mum's, dad's body doesn't shoot him up with the love-hormone oxytocin (see chapter one). How many mothers abandon their families? Now compare that to the number of abandoning dads. So many dads walk out on their families that Americans have a special title for them: "deadbeat dads." Although dads are perfectly capable of unconditional love, it isn't automatic for them. They need to learn it — by watching mothers.

UTOPIA. "How could anyone take seriously a book claiming humans could create utopia?"

By utopia, I don't mean perfect societies, but rather societies that are generally non-violent, egalitarian, democratic, sensual, playful, creative, full of vitality, and free from poverty and repressive rulers. Most world countries today fall far short of this mark, especially on egalitarianism. Even most so-called classless societies — the US comes to mind — have deeply ingrained beliefs that some people are "better than" others, as defined by wealth, age, health status, physical characteristics and so forth. Of course it's true that in the war-god world, some *are* richer, healthier, and prettier than others. But this doesn't make them better. What healthy mother loves her pretty or handsome kid more than the one who's plug ugly?

VIOLENT GODDESSES. "Wouldn't goddesses be as bad as gods? Many seem as violent."

There's no evidence that war goddesses existed before the war gods created them. Before the first war gods appeared around 4000 BC, there's no evidence goddesses were associated with either war or violence. Before 4000 BC, there are no images anywhere of goddesses in war gear. There are no images of goddesses engaged in acts of violence.

WAR SOCIETIES WITHOUT WAR GODS. "Since violence-prone societies like China and Russia have little religion — let alone war gods — how can you say war gods cause war and violence?"

China and Russia do have war gods. And just because their religions have been driven underground, doesn't mean those religions aren't still deeply shaping Chinese and Russian society, culture and behavior.

Most prosperous nations today (and some not so prosperous) have worldviews in which war gods play or played prominent roles in their religions, mythology, or both. In China it's the war god Huangdi, and in Russia and the Slavic nations it's the war gods Svantovit (alias Sventovit, Swiantowid) and Iarovit (Jarovit, Dzarowit, Gerovit, Gerovitus). Ironically, Mao, Pol Pot and Stalin all three held sway over countries outlawing religion (and so had to make gods out of themselves).

Appendix B lists of modern countries and their war gods.

WOMEN: NO BETTER THAN MEN. "I can't quite buy the argument that women are always more nurturing and inclined to protect themselves through bonding. There are just too many women who would stab each other in the back to get what they want."

Not all women prove more nurturing than all men. However, let's face it: Most healthy mothers are more nurturing toward their children than the rest of us are toward the people around us. Logically, then, mothers-relating-to-their-children stand out as the best societal role models we could ask for (this is what I call the "Mother Model").

In addition to the Mother Model, women's "tend and befriend" response to crises situations is also something it would pay us to take a good, hard look at. Not only should women lend a hand in leading the world right now, but men must learn from women how to respond to crises with calm, group-building-instead of fight-or-flight behavior.

After all, the world is in crisis. Who would you elect to lead your family in a crisis? Those who handle trouble by running away or fighting? Or cool heads who stand their ground and problem-solve?

APPENDIX D: Examples of Guiding Goddesses We Can Return To

Country	Goddess
Australia (Arnehmland)	Kunapipi
Canada (Netsilik)	Nuliajuk
China	Kuan Yin
Columbia	Romi Kumu
Egypt	Ma'at, Nut
France (Basques)	Mari
Germanic countries	Holle (Hel etc.)
Greece	Gaia, Mother Rhea (Hera)
India	Devi-Shakti
Iraq	Tiamat
Ireland	Danu, Bridget
Italy	Magna Mater, Cybele
Japan (Ainu)	Fire Goddess
Lebanon	Astarte (Aa-star'-tay)
Nigeria (Ibo)	Ala
Northern Europe	Freya
Peru	Nunkwi
Russian Federation (Siberian Mongols)	Atugan
Scandinavia	Freya
Spain (Basques)	Mari
Turkey (Phrygia)	Cybele
UK	Sovereignty
US	Spider Woman, White Buffalo Woman, Thinking Woman, Okanga Earth Woman

Appendix E: Weblogs in the Closed Countries: Examples of Blogs Authored by African, Russian, Iranian, Iraqi, Islamic and Chinese Bloggers

Nationality of Blogger Name and Address of Weblog
African, Subsaharan Afromusing,
http://www.afromusing.com/blog/2007/07/20/aids-and-the-abstinence-debate-in-uganda-video/
Black Kush (Sudan), <
http://bloggingjuba.blogspot.com/2007/06/south-sudan-rival-for-serengeti.html>
Koranteng's Toli (Ghana), <
http://koranteng.blogspot.com/2007/06/plagiarism-in-plaid.html>
Enanga's POV (Cameroon),
http://www.ekosso.com/2007/06/robert_zoellick.html
Black Looks, < http://www.blacklooks.org>
Chinese Ukjoe (Hong Kong girl),
http://www.ukjoe.com/wordpress/?page_id=2
The ABC, < http://theabc.typepad.com/>
Raymond Zhou (bilingual), <
http://raymondzhou.yculblog.com/>
Angry Chinese Blogger, < http://angrychineseblogger.blog-city.com/>
Amy in a Crazy Hong Kong, < http://amygu.blogspot.com/>
Iranian I Am an Iranian Daughter, <
http://iraniandoughter.blogspot.com/>
The Seven Towns of Love, < http://ebrahimx.blogspot.com/>
Lost for Words: Saleh Ara's Notes, <
http://blog.salehoffline.com/>
Iranian Woman Can't Keep Quiet, <
http://zaneirani.blogspot.com/>
Persian Students in the UK, <
http://www.persianstudents.org/>

Blogs by Iranians, <http://www.blogsbyiranians.com/>
Iraqi   Baghdad Burning, http://riverbendblog.blogspot.com/
Iraq Pundit, http://iraqpundit.blogspot.com/
Iraqi Atheist, http://iraqiatheist.blogspot.com/
Sunshine's Mom: Mama,
<http://youngmammy.blogspot.com/>
Iraqi Bloggers Central, http://jarrarsupariver.blogspot.com/
Korean, North Found none.
RussianMikhail Khodorkovsky,
http://www.khodorkovsky.info/
Sean's Russia Blog, < http://seansrusskiiblog.blogspot.com/>
Scraps of Moscow, <
http://www.scrapsofmoscow.blogspot.com/>
Gorgien (Georgia), < http://georgien.blogspot.com/>
Neeka's Backlog, < http://vkhokhl.blogspot.com/>

Appendix F: World Religions

Religion	Adherents	Percent of Total
Christians	2,038,905,000	33%
Muslims	1,226,403,000	20%
Hindus	828,130,000	13%
Nonreligious	774,615,000	13%
Chinese Folk Religionists	389,543,000	6%
Buddhists	364,014,000	6%
Ethnic religionists	231,708,000	4%
Atheists	150,434,000	2%
New-Religionists	103,249,000	2%
Sikhs	23,821,000	.4%
Jews	14,535,000	.2%
Spiritists	12,601,000	.2%
Baha'is	7,406,000	.1%
Confucianists	6,327,000	.1%
Jains	4,345,000	>.1%

Shintoists	2,703,000	>.1%
Taoists	2,685,000	>.1%
Zoroastrians	2,659,000	>.1%
Other Religionists	1,096,000	>.1%
TOTAL	6,185,179,000	

Based on data from *World Almanac & Book of Facts*, 2004 ("Totals are enumerated following the methodology of the World Christian Encyclopedia ... and World Christian Trends ..., using recent censuses, polls, literature, and other data. As a result of the varieties of sources used, totals may differ from standard estimates for total populations").

Appendix G: Things You Can Do to Flip the Switch

African People -- Find your ancient guiding goddesses, figure out to the best of your ability who they were and what they stood for, and then return to them.

Americans — Apologize to the indigenous Americans, whose cultures you intentionally tortured away from them — cultures which in ways were superior to your own.

Americans, North, South and Central Indigenous -- Find your ancient guiding goddesses, figure out to the best of your ability who they were and what they stood for, and then return to them.

Anthropologists — Investigate and publish your findings on the relationship between female deity and societal health.

Archaeologists — Uncover the ancient guiding goddesses in every modern country, and put your information in a book updated annually as new information arises; translate this book into all major world languages.

Artists — Create images of the Guiding Goddess to adorn books, other media, people's homes, and certain of our public spaces.

Asian People — Find your ancient guiding goddesses, figure out to the best of your ability who they were and what they stood for, and then return to them.

Atheists — Keep up the good work of explaining how deadly the war gods have been to humans and the rest of the earth; understand, however, that since no human group has ever existed without religion (and religion based on the supernatural at that), you have scant chance of converting the world to atheism.

Blog — Start a blog on the Goddess.

Children's Authors — Write children's books about the Guiding Goddesses. Rewrite our fairy tales so that the Goddess is no longer disguised as a "fairy godmother," "Mother Holde," "Mother Goose," or "Mary Mother of God."

Chinese People -- Find your ancient guiding goddesses and switch back to them.

Christian Congregations -- Switch from Jehovah to your ancient Guiding Goddess; publish and disseminate a manual on how you made the switch.

Christian Moderates — Take responsibility for disbanding your Reconstructionists and others who openly admit they want to replace democracy with war-god theocracy.

Christians — For starters, apologize to the descendants of

millions of people worldwide who, in the name of Christ, you've tortured, murdered and maimed.

College Professors — Teach courses about the guiding goddesses today, and the guiding goddesses throughout history.

Comedians — Write some gentle, sympathetic family sitcoms about goddess-centered families.

Educators — Demand, purchase and use textbooks that include information on both the good and the evil done by the starvation/war-god religions.

European People -- Find your ancient guiding goddesses, figure out to the best of your ability who they were and what they stood for, and then return to them.

E-zine — Start one on the Guiding Goddess.

Film producers — Produce films about bonobos, oxytocin, war gods, starvation culture and guiding goddesses.

Genealogists — Help people find their ancestors who were underground followers of a guiding goddess.

Goddess Community leaders — Organize email and letter-writing campaigns demanding equal representation on panel discussions regarding religion, politics and war.

Goddess Followers — Stand with your heads high! When your religion reigned, the world was a far, far better place than it's been ever since. But do take time to see the difference between the healthy guiding goddesses, and the goddesses who are merely starvation/war-god makeovers.

Historians — Publish books and articles on the history of the guiding goddesses.

Hindus — Switch back to your ancient pantheons centered around Guiding Mother Goddesses -- the ones you followed during the era of your magnificent, peaceful and equalitarian Indus Valley Civilization.

Japanese — Switch from your current gods and goddesses back to the Guiding Goddesses you followed during your stunningly peaceful and egalitarian Jomon Era.

Jewish Religious Moderates — Take responsibility for disbanding your fundamentalists.

Jewish Congregations — switch from Yahweh to your ancient Guiding Goddess; publish and disseminate a manual on how you made the switch.

Middle Easterners -- Find your ancient guiding goddesses, figure out to the best of your ability who they were and what they stood for, and then return to them.

Mothers — Whisper to your children from birth on: "Never follow a war god!"

Musicians — Write and perform songs about the Guiding Mother Goddesses.

Muslim Moderates — Take responsibility for disbanding your fundamentalists.

Muslim Congregations -- Switch from Allah to your ancient Guiding Goddesses; publish and disseminate a manual on how you made the switch.

Parents — Teach your children how societies centered around guiding goddesses blossom and prosper. Teach the extreme dangers of starvation and war-god culture.

Parents — Teach your daughters to become strong and wise enough to help lead the world; teach your sons to become strong and wise enough to move over and give girls an equal place at all tables.

Parents, New — Start from its birth whispering to your baby that it shall never follow a war god or support a war-god's wars.

Peace Organizations — Read, research, and disseminate information on the relationship between the Guiding Goddesses and non-violence.

Philanthropists — Fund think tanks on the way in which the world can switch from war gods to guiding goddesses.

Playwrights — Write plays about the guiding goddesses and the urgent necessity to switch back to them.

Political Activists — Form a Goddess Party focused on the abolition of all status hierarchy and social violence.

Psychologists — Study starvation culture and the range of negative psychological effects it has on people.

Publishers — Publish books, magazines and newspapers on the Guiding Goddesses and the negative impact of the starvation/war gods.

Readers — Read books, magazines and e-zines about the guiding goddesses; if you can't find any, write publishers and ask why they're not publishing on them.

Researchers — Research the guiding goddesses and the starvation/war gods.

Sacred Circles — Start a sacred circle centering on the Guiding Goddess, or on one or more guiding goddesses.

Science Fiction Writers — Hugely important job for you: create a world placed in the near future in which the war gods are gone, and all are following a guiding mother goddess. Of course all your characters will have problems, but no one in the world will experience any of the following problems: war, violence, snooty snobbism, political repression, bully-wimps, me-first scroogism, boot-lickers of the rich, slavery, sexual fear, sexual uptightness, poverty or hunger.

Seminarians — Publish manuals on ways your church, temple, synagogue or mosque can make the switch from God to Goddess.

Seminary Board Members — Begin now converting your seminary to one centering on the Guiding Goddess versus the starvation/war gods.

Sociologists -- Research and disseminate information about the relationship between starvation culture, our subconscious fear of never having enough, and the inability of much of the world to avoid war.

Study Circle — Start a study circle on the Goddess.

Television Producers — Create a television show about the

Guiding Mother Goddess.

Television Watchers — Write to television networks and producers demanding shows about the guiding goddesses.

Website — Start a website on the Goddess.

Writers — Write and publish about the guiding goddesses.

Appendix H: Web Directory

ARCHAEOLOGY
Antiquity Archives. http://antiquity.ac.uk/ant/toc.htm.
Archaeologica.
<http://www.archaeologica.org/NewsPage.htm>.
Archaeology Magazine (Archaeology Institute of America).
<http://www.archaeology.org/>.
Archaeology News. <http://www.archaeologynews.org/>.
Archaeology Webring.
<http://c.webring.com/hub?ring=archeoring>.
Bronze Age in Europe.
<http://www.geocities.com/Athens/Crete/4162/bronze_e.htm
>.
Catalhoyuk Dig Site. < http://www.catalhoyuk.com/>.

BASQUES
Buber's Basque Page. <http://www.buber.net/Basque/>.

CHRISTIAN RECONSTRUCTIONISTS (organizations and websites)
National Reform Association (NRA)
American Vision, group run by Atlanta-area Recon leader Gary DeMar. <www.americanvision.org>.
Reconstructionist Chalcedon Foundation

Chalcedon Report (magazine)

GODDESS
(See Appendix I)

HOPI
Hopi Indian Tribal Website. <http://www.hopi.nsn.us/>.

JOMON
The International Jomon Culture Conference.
<http://www.jomon.or.jp/>.

MOSO
Lugu Lake Mosuo Cultural Development Association.
<http://www.mosuoproject.org/main.html>.

Appendix I: Goddess Reading List

Baring, Anne, and Jules Cashford. *The Myth of the Goddess: Evolution of an Image.* London: Viking-Arkana, 1991.

Bolen, Jean Shinoda, *Urgent Message from Mother: Gather the Women Save the World.* York Beach, Maine: Conari Press, 2005.

Budapest, Zsuzsanna. *The Grandmother of Time: A Women's Book of Celebrations, Spells, and Sacred Objects for Every Month of the Year.* San Francisco: HarperSanFrancisco, 1989.

----------. *The Holy Book of Women's Mysteries.* Weiser Books, 2007.

Christ, Carol. *Rebirth of the Goddess: Finding Meaning in Feminist Spirituality.* Reading, Massachusetts: Addison-Wesley Publishing Co., 1997.

Eisler, Riane. *The Chalice and the Blade.* San Francisco: Harper & Row, 1987.

Gadon, Elinor. *The Once and Future Goddess: A Sweeping Visual Chronicle of the Sacred Female and Her Reemergence in the Cultural Mythology of Our Time.* San Francisco: HarperSanFrancisco. 1989.

Gimbutas, Marija. *The Living Goddesses*. Berkeley and London: University of California Press, 2001.

Gunn Allen, Paula. *The Sacred Hoop: Recovering the Feminine in American Indian Traditions*. Boston: Beacon Press, 1992.

Johnson, Buffie. *Lady of the Beasts: Ancient Images of the Goddess and Her Sacred Animals*. San Francisco: Harper & Row, 1981.

Laura, Judith. *Goddess Spirituality for the 21st Century: From Kabbalah to Quantum Physics*. Research Triangle Pub., 1997.

Monaghan, Patricia. *The Goddess Companion: Daily Meditations on the Feminine Spirit*. St. Paul, Minnesota: Llewellyn Publications, 1999.

Mountainwater, Shekhinah. *Ariadne's Thread: A Workbook of Goddess Magic*. Crossing Press, 1991.

Olson, Carl. *The Book of the Goddess Past and Present: An Introduction to Her Religion*. New York: Crossroad, 1990.

Sjoo, Monica, and Barbara Mor. *The Great Cosmic Mother: Rediscovering the Religion of the Earth*. San Francisco: HarperSanFrancisco, 1991.

Spretnak, Charlene. *The Politics of Women's Spirituality: Essays on the Rise of Spiritual Power within the Feminist Movement*. Garden City NY: Anchor Doubleday, 1982.

Starhawk. *The Spiral Dance: A Rebirth of the Ancient Religion of the Great Goddess*. 10th Anniversary Edition, Revised and Updated. New York: HarperCollins Publishers, 1989.

Stone, Merlin. *When God Was a Woman*. New York: Barnes and Noble Books, 1976.

Stone, Merlin. *Ancient Mirrors of Womanhood: A Treasury of Goddess and Heroine Lore from Around the World*. Boston: Beacon Press, 1979.

Tate, Karen. *Sacred Places of Goddess: 108 Destinations*. San Francisco: Consortium of Collective Consciousness. 2006.

Walker, Barbara G. *The Skeptical Feminist: Discovering the Virgin, Mother and Crone*. San Francisco: Harper & Row, 1988.

Walker, Barbara G. *The Woman's Encyclopedia of Myths and Secrets*.

Edison NJ: Castle Books, 1983.

Wilson, Ian. *Before the Flood.* New York: St. Martin's Press, 2001.

MEN AND THE GODDESS

Ward, Tim. *Savage Breast: One Man's Search for the Goddess.* Winchester, England: O Books, 2006.

WEBSITES

Awakened Woman: The Journal of Women's Spirituality
http://www.awakenedwoman.com/
BBC's site on Paganism.
http://www.bbc.co.uk/religion/religions/paganism/
Belief.net's Pagan/earth-based section.
http://belief.net/index/index_10015.html
Judith Laura: Goddess Spirituality:
http://goddess.judithlaura.com/index.html
Goddess Alive.
<http://www.goddessalive.co.uk/current/current.html>.
Goddess Pages.
<http://www.goddess-pages.co.uk/>
Matrifocus: Cross-Quarterly for the Goddess Woman.
http://matrifocus.com/

WEBLOGS

Aquila ka Hecate. http://aquilakahecate.blogspot.com/.
Evoking the Goddess. < http://goddessevoke.blogspot.com/>.
Goddessing. < http://www.goddessmystic.com/>.
Hecate. < http://www.hecatedemetersdatter.blogspot.com/>.
Medusa Coils. <http://medusacoils.blogspot.com/>.
The-Goddess. < http://the-goddess.org/blog/index.html>.
The Gods Are Bored. < http://godsrbored.blogspot.com/>.
Radical Goddess Thealogy [sic].
<http://godmotherascending.blogspot.com/>.
Spiral Crone. < http://spiralcrone.matrifocus.net/>.

APPENDIX J. Cruelty in the Bible: Short List
Genesis

1.   And he said, Take now thy son, thine only son Isaac, whom thou lovest, and ... offer him there for a burnt offering. -- 22.2

2.   And Abraham stretched forth his hand, and took the knife to slay his son. -- 22.10

3.   And Er, Judah's firstborn, was wicked in the sight of the LORD; and the LORD slew him. -- 38.7

4.   And the thing which he did displeased the LORD: wherefore he slew him also. -- 38.10

Exodus

5.   If thou refuse to let him go, behold, I will slay thy son, even thy firstborn.--4.23

6.   For I will pass through the land of Egypt this night, and will smite all the firstborn in the land of Egypt, both man and beast.--12.12

7.   At midnight the LORD smote all the firstborn in the land of Egypt, from the firstborn of Pharaoh that sat on his throne unto the firstborn of the captive that was in the dungeon; and all the firstborn of cattle.--12.29

8.   The LORD slew all the firstborn in the land of Egypt, both the firstborn of man, and the firstborn of beast.--13.15

9. The LORD is a man of war.--15.3

10.   He that smiteth his father, or his mother, shall be surely put to death.--21.15

11.   Thou shalt not suffer a witch to live.--22.18

12.   He that sacrificeth unto any god, save unto the LORD only, he shall be utterly destroyed.--Ex22.20:

13.   And my wrath shall wax hot, and I will kill you with the sword; and your wives shall be widows, and your children fatherless.--22.24

14.   Then shalt thou kill the ram, and take of his blood, and put it upon the tip of the right ear of Aaron, and upon the tip of the

right ear of his sons, and upon the thumb of their right hand, and upon the great toe of their right foot, and sprinkle the blood upon the altar round about. -- 29.20

15.   Ye shall keep the sabbath ... every one that defileth it shall surely be put to death.--31.14

16.   Thus saith the LORD God of Israel, Put every man his sword by his side ... and slay every man his brother, and every man his companion, and every man his neighbour.--32.27

17.   And the LORD plagued the people, because they made the calf, which Aaron made.--32.35

Leviticus

18.   And Moses took of the blood of it, and put it upon the tip of Aaron's right ear, and upon the thumb of his right hand, and upon the great toe of his right foot.--8.24, 14.14, 14.17, 14.25

19.   And Nadab and Abihu ... offered strange fire before the LORD, which he commanded them not. And there went out fire from the LORD, and devoured them, and they died before the LORD.--10.1-2

20.   For every one that curseth his father or his mother shall be surely put to death.--20.9

21.   And if a man lie with his daughter in law, both of them shall surely be put to death.--20.12

22.   If a man also lie with mankind, as he lieth with a woman, both of them have committed an abomination: they shall surely be put to death; their blood shall be upon them.--20.13

23.   If a man take a wife and her mother, it is wickedness: they shall be burnt with fire, both he and they.--20.14

24.   If a man lie with a beast, he shall surely be put to death: and ye shall slay the beast.--20.15

25.   If a woman approach unto any beast, and lie down thereto thou shalt kill the woman, and the beast: they shall surely be put to death; their blood shall be upon them.--20.16

26.   A man also or woman that hath a familiar spirit, or that is a

wizard, shall surely be put to death: they shall stone them with stones: their blood shall be upon them.--20.27

27.   And the daughter of any priest, if she profane herself by playing the whore, she profaneth her father: she shall be burnt with fire.--21.9

28.   Bring forth him that hath cursed without the camp; and let all that heard him lay their hands upon his head, and let all the congregation stone him.--24.14

29.   He that blasphemeth the name of the LORD, he shall surely be put to death, and all the congregation shall certainly stone him.--24.16

30.   And Moses spake to the children of Israel, that they should bring forth him that had cursed out of the camp, and stone him with stones. And the children of Israel did as the LORD commanded Moses.--24.23

31.   I also will do this unto you; I will even appoint over you terror, consumption, and the burning ague, that shall consume the eyes, and cause sorrow of heart: and ye shall sow your seed in vain, for your enemies shall eat it.--26.16

32.   I will also send wild beasts among you, which shall rob you of your children.--26.22

Numbers

33.   And when the people complained, it displeased the LORD: and the LORD heard it; and his anger was kindled; and the fire of the LORD burnt among them, and consumed them .--11.1

34.   And while the flesh was yet between their teeth, ere it was chewed, the wrath of the LORD was kindled against the people, and the LORD smote the people with a very great plague.--11.33

35.   And while the children of Israel were in the wilderness, they found a man that gathered sticks upon the sabbath day ... And the LORD said unto Moses, The man shall be surely put to death: all the congregation shall stone him with stones.--15.32-36

36.   And there came a fire from the LORD, and consumed

the two hundred and fifty men that offered incense.--16.35

37.   And the LORD sent fiery serpents among the people, and they bit the people; and much people of Israel died.--21.6

38.   Behold, the people shall rise up as a great lion, and lift up himself as a young lion: he shall not lie down until he eat of the prey, and drink the blood of the slain.--23.24

39.   And the LORD said unto Moses, Take all the heads of the people, and hang them up before the LORD against the sun, that the fierce anger of the LORD may be turned away from Israel.--25.4

40.   And Moses said unto them, Have ye saved all the women alive? ... Now therefore kill every male among the little ones, and kill every woman that hath known man by lying with him. But all the women children, that have not known a man by lying with him, keep alive for yourselves.--31.15-19

Deuteronomy

41.   And we took all his cities at that time, and utterly destroyed the men, and the women, and the little ones, of every city, we left none to remain.--2.34

42.   And we utterly destroyed them, ... utterly destroying the men, women, and children, of every city.--3.6

43.   And when the LORD thy God shall deliver them before thee; thou shalt smite them, and utterly destroy them; thou shalt make no covenant with them, nor shew mercy unto them.--7.2

44.   And thou shalt consume all the people which the LORD thy God shall deliver thee; thine eye shall have no pity upon them.--7.16

45.   Thou shalt surely smite the inhabitants of that city with the edge of the sword, destroying it utterly, and all that is therein, and the cattle thereof, with the edge of the sword.--13.15

46.   And the man that ... will not hearken unto the priest ... that man shall die.--17.12

47.   And when the LORD thy God hath delivered it into thine

hands, thou shalt smite every male thereof with the edge of the sword: But the women ... shalt thou take unto thyself.--20.13-14

48.   But of the cities of these people, which the LORD thy God doth give thee for an inheritance, thou shalt save alive nothing that breatheth.--20.16-17

49.   But if this thing be true, and the tokens of virginity be not found for the damsel: Then they shall bring out the damsel to the door of her father's house, and the men of her city shall stone her with stones that she die.--22.20-21

50.   If a man be found lying with a woman married to an husband, then they shall both of them die.--22.22

51.   If a damsel that is a virgin be betrothed unto an husband, and a man find her in the city, and lie with her; Then ye shall bring them both out unto the gate of that city, and ye shall stone them with stones that they die; the damsel, because she cried not, being in the city.--22.23-24

52.   When two men strive together on with another, and the wife of the one ... putteth forth her hand, and taketh him by the secrets: Then thou shalt cut off her hand, thine eye shall not pity her.--25.11-12

53.   The LORD shall make the pestilence cleave unto thee, until he have consumed thee from off the land.--28.21

54.   The LORD shall smite thee with a consumption, and with a fever, and with an inflammation, and with an extreme burning, and with the sword, and with blasting, and with mildew; and they shall pursue thee until thou perish.--28.22

55.   Thy carcase shall be meat unto all fowls of the air, and unto the beasts of the earth, and no man shall fray them away.--28.26

56.   The LORD will smite thee with the botch of Egypt, and with the emerods, and with the scab, and with the itch, whereof thou canst not be healed.--28.27

57.   The LORD shall smite thee with madness, and blindness, and astonishment of heart.--28.28

58.   Thy sons and thy daughters shall be given unto another

people, and thine eyes shall look, and fail with longing for them all the day long.--28.32

59.   The LORD shall smite thee in the knees, and in the legs, with a sore botch that cannot be healed, from the sole of thy foot unto the top of thy head.--28.35

60.   And thou shalt eat the fruit of thine own body, the flesh of thy sons and of thy daughters.--28.53

61.   So that he will not give to any of them of the flesh of his children whom he shall eat.--28.55

62.   The tender and delicate woman among you, which would not adventure to set the sole of her foot upon the ground for delicateness and tenderness, her eye shall be evil toward the husband of her bosom, and toward her son, and toward her daughter, and toward her young one that cometh out from between her feet, and toward her children which she shall bear: for she shall eat them.--28.56-57

63.   I will heap mischiefs upon them. I will spend mine arrows upon them.--32.23

64.   They shall be burnt with hunger, and devoured with burning heat, and with bitter destruction: I will also send the teeth of beasts upon them, with the poison of serpents of the dust.--32.24

65.   The sword without, and terror within, shall destroy both the young man and the virgin, the suckling also with the man of gray hairs.--32.25

66.   If I whet my glittering sword, and mine hand take hold on judgment; I will render vengeance to mine enemies, and will reward them that hate me. I will make mine arrows drunk with blood, and my sword shall devour flesh.--32.41-42

Joshua

67.   And they utterly destroyed all that was in the city, both man and woman, young and old, and ox, and sheep, and ass, with the edge of the sword.-- 6.21

68.   He that is taken with the accursed thing shall be burnt with fire, he and all that he hath.-- 7.15

69.   The LORD shall trouble thee this day. And all Israel stoned him with stones, and burned them with fire, after they had stoned them with stones.-- 7.25

70.   And the LORD discomfited them before Israel, and slew them with a great slaughter at Gibeon, and chased them along the way.-- 10.10

71.   The LORD cast down great stones from heaven upon them ... and they died.-- 10.11

72.   And afterward smote them, and slew them, and hanged them on five trees.-- 10.26

73.   So smote all the country ... he left none remaining, but utterly destroyed all that breathed, as the LORD God of Israel commanded.-- 10.40

74.   The LORD God of Israel fought for Israel.-- 10.42

Judges

75.   But Adonibezek fled; and they pursued after him, and caught him, and cut off his thumbs and his great toes.-- 1.6

76.   Then Jael Heber's wife took a nail of the tent, and took an hammer in her hand, and went softly unto him, and smote the nail into his temples, and fastened it into the ground: for he was fast asleep and weary. So he died.-- 4.21

77.   Blessed above women shall Jael the wife of Heber the Kenite be .... She put her hand to the nail, and her right hand to the workmen's hammer; and with the hammer she smote Sisera, she smote off his head, when she had pierced and stricken through his temples.-- 5.24-26

78.   And the Spirit of the LORD came upon him, and he ... slew thirty men.-- 14.19

79.   And Samson went and caught three hundred foxes, and took firebrands, and turned tail to tail, and put a firebrand in the midst between two tails. And when he had set the brands on fire,

he let them go.-- 15.4-5

80.   And when he was come into his house, he took a knife, and laid hold on his concubine, and divided her, together with her bones, into twelve pieces, and sent her into all the coasts of Israel.-- 19.29

1 Samuel

81.   And he smote the men of Bethshemesh, because they had looked into the ark of the LORD, even he smote of the people fifty thousand and threescore and ten men: and the people lamented, because the LORD had smitten many of the people with a great slaughter.--6.19

82.   Thus saith the LORD of hosts ... go and smite Amalek, and utterly destroy all that they have, and spare them not; but slay both man and woman, infant and suckling, ox and sheep, camel and ass.--1Sam.15.2-3

83.   And Saul said, Thus shall ye say to David, The king desireth not any dowry, but an hundred foreskins of the Philistines, to be avenged of the king's enemies.--18.25

84.   Wherefore David arose and went, he and his men, and slew of the Philistines two hundred men; and David brought their foreskins, and they gave them in full tale to the king, that he might be the king's son in law. And Saul gave him Michal his daughter to wife.--18.27

2 Samuel

85.   David commanded his young men, and they slew them, and cut off their hands and their feet, and hanged them up over the pool in Hebron.--4.12

86.   And David said on that day, Whosoever getteth up to the gutter, and smiteth the Jebusites, and the lame and the blind that are hated of David's soul, he shall be chief and captain.--5.8

87.   Because by this deed thou hast given great occasion to the enemies of the LORD to blaspheme, the child also that is born

unto thee shall surely die. And the LORD struck the child that Uriah's wife bare unto David, and it was very sick.... And it came to pass on the seventh day, that the child died.--12.14-15

88.   And he brought forth the people that were therein, and put them under saws, and under harrows of iron, and under axes of iron, and made them pass through the brick-kiln: and thus did he unto all the cities of the children of Ammon.--12.31

89.   Let seven men of his sons be delivered unto us, and we will hang them up unto the LORD in Gibeah of Saul, whom the Lord did choose.--21.6

1 Kings

90.   He smote all the house of Jeroboam; he left not to Jeroboam any that breathed, until he had destroyed him, according unto the saying of the LORD.--15.29

91.   Him that dieth of Baasha in the city shall the dogs eat; and him that dieth of his in the fields shall the fowls of the air eat.--16.4

92.   He slew all the house of Baasha: he left him not one that pisseth against a wall ... according to the word of the LORD.--16.11-12

93.   He laid the foundation thereof in Abiram his firstborn, and set up the gates thereof in his youngest son Segub, according to the word of the LORD.--16.34

94.   Thus saith the LORD, In the place where dogs licked the blood of Naboth shall dogs lick thy blood, even thine.--21.19

2 Kings

95.   If I be a man of God, let fire come down from heaven, and consume thee and thy fifty. And the fire of God came down from heaven, and consumed him and his fifty.--1.12

96.   As he was going up by the way, there came forth little children out of the city, and mocked him, and said unto him, Go up, thou bald head; go up, thou bald head. And he turned back, and looked on them, and cursed them in the name of the LORD.

And there came forth two she bears out of the wood, and tare forty and two children of them.--2.23-24

97.   The leprosy therefore of Naaman shall cleave unto thee, and unto thy seed for ever.--5.27

98.   Elisha prayed unto the LORD, and said, Smite this people, I pray thee, with blindness. And he smote them with blindness according to the word of Elisha.--6.18

99.   This woman said unto me, Give thy son, that we may eat him to day, and we will eat my son tomorrow. So we boiled my son, and did eat him--6.28-29

100.   For the whole house of Ahab shall perish: and I will cut off from Ahab him that pisseth against the wall--9.8

101.   They took the king's sons, and slew seventy persons, and put their heads in baskets, and sent him them to Jezreel.--10.7

102.   And when he came to Samaria, he slew all that remained unto Ahab in Samaria, till he had destroyed him, according to the saying of the LORD--10.17

103.   And the LORD smote the king, so that he was a leper unto the day of his death.--15.5

104.   Therefore he smote it; and all the women therein that were with child he ripped up.--15.16

105.   The LORD sent lions among them, which slew some of them.--17.25

106.   The angel of the LORD went out, and smote in the camp of the Assyrians an hundred fourscore and five thousand: and when they arose early in the morning, behold, they were all dead corpses.--19.35

1 Chronicles

107.   Uzza put forth his hand to hold the ark; for the oxen stumbled. And the anger of the LORD was kindled against Uzza, and he smote him, because he put his hand to the ark: and there he died before God.--13.9-10

108.   And he brought out the people that were in it, and cut them

with saws, and with harrows of iron, and with axes. Even so dealt David with all the cities of the children of Ammon.--20.3

109.   So the LORD sent pestilence upon Israel: and there fell of Israel seventy thousand men.--21.14

2 Chronicles

110.   And king Solomon offered a sacrifice of twenty and two thousand oxen, and an hundred and twenty thousand sheep.--7.5

111.   Whosoever would not seek the LORD God of Israel should be put to death, whether small or great, whether man or woman.--15.13

112.   Behold, with a great plague will the LORD smite thy people, and thy children, and thy wives, and all thy goods. And thou shalt have great sickness by disease of thy bowels, until thy bowels fall out.--21.14

113.   And after all this the LORD smote him in his bowels with an incurable disease.--21.18

114.   Behold, he was leprous in his forehead ... because the LORD had smitten him.--26.20

115.   Thus saith the LORD, Behold, I will bring evil upon this place, and upon the inhabitants thereof, even all the curses that are written in the book.--34.24

116.   The wrath of the LORD arose against his people, till there was no remedy. He ... had no compassion upon young man or maiden, old man, or him that stooped for age: he gave them all into his hand.--36.16-17

Esther

117.   Then said Esther, If it please the king ... let Haman's ten sons be hanged upon the gallows. And the king commanded it so to be done ... and they hanged Haman's ten sons--9.13

Psalms

118.   Thou shalt break them with a rod of iron; thou shalt dash them in pieces.-- 2.9

119. He teacheth my hands to war.-- 18.34

120. Break their teeth, O God, in their mouth.-- 58.6

121. The righteous shall rejoice when he seeth the vengeance: he shall wash his feet in the blood of the wicked.-- 58.10

122. That thy foot may be dipped in the blood of thine enemies, and the tongue of thy dogs in the same.-- 68.23

123. Let their eyes be darkened, that they see not; and make their loins continually to shake.-- 69.23

124. Let his children be continually vagabonds, and beg: let them seek their bread also out of their desolate places.-- 109.10

125. To him that smote Egypt in their firstborn: for his mercy endureth for ever.-- 136.10

126. Happy shall he be, that taketh and dasheth thy little ones against the stones.-- 137.9

Proverbs

127. The blueness of a wound cleanseth away evil: so do stripes the inward parts of the belly.--20.30

128. Foolishness is bound in the heart of a child; but the rod of correction shall drive it far from him.--Pr.22.15

129. Withhold not correction from the child: for if thou beatest him with the rod, he shall not die.--23.13-14

130. The eye that mocketh at his father, and despiseth to obey his mother, the ravens of the valley shall pick it out, and the young eagles shall eat it.--30.17

Isaiah

131. Through the wrath of the LORD of hosts is the land darkened, and the people shall be as the fuel of the fire: no man shall spare his brother.--9.19

132. And he shall snatch on the right hand, and be hungry; and he shall eat on the left hand, and they shall not be satisfied: they shall eat every man the flesh of his own arm.--9.20

133. Their children also shall be dashed to pieces before their

eyes; their houses shall be spoiled, and their wives ravished.--13.16

134. Their bows also shall dash the young men to pieces; and they shall have no pity on the fruit of the womb; their eyes shall not spare children.--13.18

135. Prepare slaughter for his children for the iniquity of their fathers.--14.21

136. He hath utterly destroyed them, he hath delivered them to the slaughter. Their slain also shall be cast out, and their stink shall come up out of their carcases, and the mountains shall be melted with their blood.--34.2-3

137. For my sword shall be bathed in heaven.--34.5

138. The sword of the LORD is filled with blood.--34.6

139. Then the angel of the LORD went forth, and smote in the camp of the Assyrians a hundred and fourscore and five thousand: and when they arose early in the morning, behold, they were all dead corpses.--37.36

140. And I will feed them that oppress thee with their own flesh; and they shall be drunken with their own blood, as with sweet wine.--49.26

141. I have trodden the winepress alone ... for I will tread them in mine anger, and trample them in my fury; and their blood shall be sprinkled upon my garments, and I will stain all my raiment.--63.3

142. For by fire and by his sword will the LORD plead with all flesh: and the slain of the LORD shall be many.--66.16

143. And they shall go forth, and look upon the carcases of the men that have transgressed against me: for their worm shall not die, neither shall their fire be quenched; and they shall be an abhorring unto all flesh.--66.24

Jeremiah

144. They shall not be gathered, nor be buried; they shall be for dung upon the face of the earth.--8.2-3

145. For, behold, I will send serpents, cockatrices, among you,

which will not be charmed, and they shall bite you, saith the LORD.--8.17

146. Therefore thus saith the LORD, Behold, I will bring evil upon them, which they shall not be able to escape; and though they shall cry unto me, I will not hearken unto them.--11.11

147. Therefore thus saith the LORD of hosts, Behold, I will punish them: the young men shall die by the sword; their sons and their daughters shall die by famine.--11.22

148. The sword of the LORD shall devour from the one end of the land even to the other end of the land: no flesh shall have peace.--12.12

149. Thus saith the LORD, Behold, I will fill all the inhabitants of this land ... with drunkenness. And I will dash them one against another, even the fathers and the sons together, saith the LORD: I will not pity, nor spare, nor have mercy, but destroy them.--13.13-14

150. When they fast, I will not hear their cry; and when they offer burnt offering and an oblation, I will not accept them: but I will consume them by the sword, and by the famine, and by the pestilence.--14.12

151. And the people to whom they prophesy shall be cast out in the streets of Jerusalem because of the famine and the sword; and they shall have none to bury them, them, their wives, nor their sons, nor their daughters: for I will pour their wickedness upon them.--14.16

152. And I will appoint over them four kinds, saith the LORD: the sword to slay, and the dogs to tear, and the fowls of the heaven, and the beasts of the earth, to devour and destroy.--15.3

153. They shall die of grievous deaths; they shall not be lamented; neither shall they be buried; but they shall be as dung upon the face of the earth: and they shall be consumed by the sword, and by famine; and their carcases shall be meat for the fowls of heaven, and for the beasts of the earth.--16.4

154. Deliver up their children to the famine, and pour out their

blood by the force of the sword; and let their wives be bereaved of their children, and be widows; and let their men be put to death; let their young men be slain by the sword in battle.--18.21

155.   I will cause them to fall by the sword before their enemies, and by the hands of them that seek their lives: and their carcases will I give to be meat for the fowls of the heaven, and for the beasts of the earth.--19.7

156.   And I will cause them to eat the flesh of their sons and the flesh of their daughters, and they shall eat every one the flesh of his friend.--19.9

157.   And I will smite the inhabitants of this city, both man and beast: they shall die of a great pestilence.--21.6

158.   And I will send the sword, the famine, and the pestilence, among them, till they be consumed from off the land.--24.10

159.   Thus saith the LORD of hosts, the God of Israel; Drink ye, and be drunken, and spue, and fall, and rise no more, because of the sword which I will send among you.--25.27

160.   And the slain of the LORD shall be at that day from one end of the earth even unto the other end of the earth: they shall not be lamented, neither gathered, nor buried; they shall be dung upon the ground.--25.33

161.   Thus saith the LORD of hosts; Behold, I will send upon them the sword, the famine, and the pestilence, and will make them like vile figs, that cannot be eaten, they are so evil.--29.17

162.   They shall die by the sword, by the famine, and by the pestilence: and none of them shall remain or escape from the evil that I will bring upon them.--42.17

163.   Know certainly that ye shall die by the sword, by the famine, and by the pestilence, in the place whither ye desire to go and to sojourn.--42.22

164.   I will bring evil upon all flesh, saith the LORD.--45.5

165.   For this is the day of the Lord GOD of hosts, a day of vengeance, that he may avenge him of his adversaries: and the sword shall devour, and it shall be satiate and made drunk with

their blood.--46.10

166. Cursed be he that keepeth back his sword from blood.--48.10

167. With thee also will I break in pieces man and woman; and with thee will I break in pieces old and young; and with thee will I break in pieces the young man and the maid.--51.22

Lamentations

168. Behold, O LORD, and consider to whom thou hast done this. Shall the women eat their fruit, and children?--2.20

169. The young and the old lie on the ground in the streets: my virgins and my young men are fallen by the sword; thou hast slain them in the day of thine anger; thou hast killed, and not pitied.--2.21

170. The hands of the pitiful women have sodden their own children: they were their meat.--4.10

Ezekiel

171. The fathers shall eat the sons in the midst of thee, and the sons shall eat their fathers.-- 5.10

172. Therefore will I also deal in fury: mine eye shall not spare, neither will I have pity: and though they cry in mine ears with a loud voice, yet will I not hear them.-- 8.18

173. Let not your eye spare, neither have ye pity: Slay utterly old and young, both maids, and little children, and women: but come not near any man upon whom is the mark.-- 9.5-6

174. Thus saith the LORD; Behold, I am against thee, and will draw forth my sword out of his sheath, and will cut off from thee the righteous and the wicked.-- 21.3

175. And I will set my jealousy against thee, and they shall deal furiously with thee: they shall take away thy nose and thine ears; and thy remnant shall fall by the sword: they shall take thy sons and thy daughters; and thy residue shall be devoured by the fire.-- 23.25

176. Thou shalt even drink it and suck it out, and thou shalt break the sherds thereof, and pluck off thine own breasts: for I have spoken it, saith the Lord GOD.-- 23.34

177. And the company shall stone them with stones, and dispatch them with their swords; they shall slay their sons and their daughters.-- 23.47

178. Heap on wood, kindle the fire, consume the flesh, and spice it well, and let the bones be burned.-- 24.10

179. And her daughters which are in the field shall be slain by the sword; and they shall know that I am the LORD.-- 26.6

180. For I will send into her pestilence, and blood into her streets ... and they shall know that I am the LORD.-- 28.23

181. And I will call for a sword against him throughout all my mountains, saith the Lord GOD: every man's sword shall be against his brother.-- 38.21

182. Ye shall eat the flesh of the mighty, and drink the blood of the princes of the earth.-- 39.18

183. Ye shall eat fat till ye be full, and drink blood till ye be drunken, of my sacrifice which I have sacrificed for you.-- 39.19

Hosea

184. Yea, though they bring forth, yet will I slay even the beloved fruit of their womb.-- 9.16

185. I will meet them as a bear that is bereaved of her whelps, and will rend the caul of their heart, and there will I devour them like a lion: the wild beast shall tear them.-- 13.8

186. Their infants shall be dashed in pieces, and their women with child shall be ripped up.-- 13.16

Amos

187. I have sent among you the pestilence ... your young men have I slain with the sword, ... and I have made the stink of your camps to come up unto your nostrils.--4.10

188. I saw the LORD standing upon the altar: and he said ... I will

slay the last of them with the sword.--9.1

189.   Though they be hid from my sight in the bottom of the sea, thence will I command the serpent, and he shall bite them.--9.3

190.   And though they go into captivity before their enemies, thence will I command the sword, and it shall slay them: and I will set mine eyes upon them for evil, and not for good.--9.4

Habakkuk

191.   God came from Teman .... He had horns coming out of his hand .... Before him went the pestilence, and burning coals went forth at his feet.--3.3-5

Zephaniah

192.   I will utterly consume all things from off the land, saith the LORD. I will consume man and beast; I will consume the fowls of the heaven, and the fishes of the sea.--1.2-3

193.   And I will bring distress upon men, that they shall walk like blind men, ... and their blood shall be poured out as dust, and their flesh as the dung.--1.17

194.   All the earth shall be devoured with the fire of my jealousy.--3.8

Zechariah

195.   I will not feed you: that that dieth, let it die; and that that is to be cut off, let it be cut off; and let the rest eat every one the flesh of another.--11.9

196.   And it shall come to pass, that when any shall yet prophesy, then his father and his mother that begat him shall say unto him, Thou shalt not live; for thou speakest lies in the name of the LORD: and his father and his mother that begat him shall thrust him through when he prophesieth.--13.3

197.   Their flesh shall consume away while they stand upon their feet, and their eyes shall consume away in their holes, and their tongue shall consume away in their mouth.--14.12

Matthew

198.   If thy right eye offend thee, pluck it out, and cast it from thee .... And if thy right hand offend thee, cut it off, and cast it from thee: for it is profitable for thee that one of thy members should perish, and not that thy whole body should be cast into Hell.--5.29-30

199.   And he said unto them, Go. And when they were come out, they went into the herd of swine: and, behold, the whole herd of swine ran violently down a steep place into the sea, and perished in the waters.--8.32

200.   God commanded, saying, Honour thy father and mother: and, He that curseth father or mother, let him die the death.--15.4

201.   If thy hand or thy foot offend thee, cut them off, and cast them from thee .... And if thine eye offend thee, pluck it out, and cast it from thee: it is better for thee to enter into life with one eye, rather than having two eyes to be cast into Hell fire.--18.8-9

202. Friend, how camest thou in hither not having a wedding garment? And he was speechless. Then said the king to the servants, Bind him hand and foot, and take him away, and cast him into outer darkness, there shall be weeping and gnashing of teeth.--22.12-13

203.   Ye serpents, ye generation of vipers, how can ye escape the damnation of Hell?--23.33

Mark

204.   And forthwith Jesus gave them leave. And the unclean spirits went out, and entered into the swine: and the herd ran violently down a steep place into the sea, (they were about two thousand;) and were choked in the sea.-- 5.13

205.   For Moses said, Honour thy father and thy mother; and, Whoso curseth father or mother, let him die the death.-- 7.10

206.   And if thy hand offend thee, cut it off: it is better for thee to enter into life maimed, than having two hands to go into Hell, into the fire that never shall be quenched. Where their worm dieth not,

and the fire is not quenched.-- 9.43-44

207. And if thy foot offend thee, cut it off: it is better for thee to enter halt into life, than having two feet to be cast into Hell, into the fire that never shall be quenched: Where their worm dieth not, and the fire is not quenched..-- 9.45-46

208. And if thine eye offend thee, pluck it out: it is better for thee to enter into the kingdom of God with one eye, than having two eyes to be cast into Hell fire: Where their worm dieth not, and the fire is not quenched.-- 9.47-48

209. He that believeth not shall be damned.-- 16.16

Luke

210. Then went the Devils out of the man, and entered into the swine: and the herd ran violently down a steep place into the lake, and were choked.--8.33

211. Fear him, which after he hath killed hath power to cast into Hell.--12.5

212. But those mine enemies, which would not that I should reign over them, bring hither, and slay them before me.--19.27

John

213. He that believeth not the Son shall not see life; but the wrath of God abideth on him.--3.36

214. If a man abide not in me, he is cast forth as a branch, and is withered; and men gather them, and cast them into the fire, and they are burned.--15.6

Acts

215. Then Peter said unto her, How is it that ye have agreed together to tempt the Spirit of the Lord? behold, the feet of them which have buried thy husband are at the door, and shall carry thee out. Then fell she down straightway at his feet, and yielded up the ghost.--5.9-10

2 Thessalonians

216. The Lord Jesus ... In flaming fire taking vengeance on them that know not God ... Who shall be punished with everlasting destruction.--1.7-9

217. God shall send them strong delusion, that they should believe a lie: That they all might be damned.--2.11-12

Hebrews

218. Almost all things are by the law purged with blood; and without shedding of blood is no remission.--9.22

Revelation

219. I will kill her children with death.--2.23

220. And there went out another horse that was red: and power was given to him that sat thereon to take peace from the earth, and that they should kill one another.--6.4

221. And to them it was given that they should not kill them, but that they should be tormented five months: and their torment was as the torment of a scorpion.--9.5

222. And in those days shall men seek death, and shall not find it; and shall desire to die, and death shall flee from them.--9.6

223. And they had tails like unto scorpions, and there were stings in their tails: and their power was to hurt men five months.--9.10

224. The four angels were loosed to slay the third part of men.--9.15

225. The people ... shall see their dead bodies three days and an half, and shall not suffer their dead bodies to be put in graves. And they that dwell upon the earth shall rejoice over them, and make merry, and shall send gifts one to another because these two prophets tormented them that dwelt on the earth.--11.9-10

226. And the smoke of their torment ascendeth up for ever and ever.--14.11

227. The great winepress of the wrath of God ... was trodden without the city, and blood came out of the winepress, even unto

the horse bridles.--14.19-20

228. The second angel poured out his vial upon the sea; and it became as the blood of a dead man: and every living soul died in the sea.--16.3

229. Thou hast given them blood to drink; for they are worthy.--16.6

230. The fifth angel poured out his vial upon the seat of the beast; and his kingdom was full of darkness; and they gnawed their tongues for pain.--16.10

231. And the ten horns which thou sawest upon the beast, these shall hate the whore, and shall make her desolate and naked, and shall eat her flesh, and burn her with fire.--17.16

232. He was clothed with a vesture dipped in blood: and his name is called The Word of God.--19.13

233. And out of his mouth goeth a sharp sword, ... he treadeth the winepress of the fierceness and wrath of Almighty God.--19.15

234. I saw an angel standing in the sun; and he cried with a loud voice, saying to all the fowls that fly in the midst of heaven, Come and gather yourselves together unto the supper of the great God; That ye may eat the flesh of kings, and the flesh of captains, and the flesh of mighty men.--19.17-18

235. And the remnant were slain with the sword of him that sat upon the horse, which sword proceeded out of his mouth: and all the fowls were filled with their flesh.--19.21

236. And whosoever was not found written in the book of life was cast into the lake of fire.--20.15

237. The fearful, and unbelieving ... shall have their part in the lake which burneth with fire and brimstone. — 2.8

From SkepticsAnnotatedBible.com. See them for their "Long List" of cruelty in the Bible.

BIBLIOGRAPHY

Aman, Catherine. "Can Nutrition Come in a Can?" Natural Health [online]. March 1999 [cited 1 February 2007]. Available from:
<http://www.findarticles.com/p/articles/mi_m0NAH/is_2_29/ai_53929978>.

Amico, J.A., R.C. Mantella, R.R. Vollmer and X. Li. "Anxiety and Stress Responses in Female Oxytocin Deficient Mice." Journal of Neuroendocrinology 16 (2004): 319-324.

Anderson, Alun [sic] and Lucy Middleton. "What Is This Thing Called Love?" New Scientist 190, issue 2549 (2006): 32-34.

Anthony, David W. "Nazi and Eco-feminist Prehistories: Ideology and Empiricism in Indo-European Archaeology." In Nationalism, Politics and the Practice of Archaeology, edited by Phillip Kohl and Clare Fawcett, 82-98. New York and London: Cambridge University Press, 1995.

Armstrong, Karen. "A God for Both Sexes." Economist 341, issue 7997 (1996).

Atwood, Roger. "A Monumental Feud." Archaeology 58, issue 4 (2005): 18-25.

Axe, David. "Back from the Brink." Archaeology 59, issue 4 (2006): 59-65.

Azar, Beth. "A New Stress Paradigm for Women." Monitor on Psychology (American Psychological Association) [online]. July/August 2000, vol. 31, no. 7 [cited 16 February 2007]. Available from:
<http://www.apa.org/monitor/julaug00/stress.html Copied 1/10/07>.

Bailey, Douglass W. Prehistoric Figurines: Representations and Corporeality in the Neolithic. Oxford and New York: Routledge, 2005.

Balikci [sic], Asen. The Netsilik Eskimo. Garden City, New York: the Natural History Press, 1970.

Balter, Michael. "Search for the Indo-Europeans." Science 303, issue 5662 (2004): 1323-1326.

----------. The Goddess and the Bull: Catalhoyuk: An Archaeological Journey to the Dawn of Civilization. New York, London: Free Press, 2005.

Bamshad, Michael, Toomas Kivisild, W. Scott Watkins, Mary E. Dixon, Chris E. Ricer, Baskara B. Rao, J. Mastan Naidu, B.V. Ravi Prasad, P. Govinda Reddy, Arani Rasanayagam, Surinder S. Papiha, Richard Villems, Alan J. Redd, Michael F. Hammer, Son V. Nyuyen, Marion L. Carroll, Mark A Batzer, and Lynn B. Jorde. "Genetic Evidence on the Origins of Indian Caste Populations." Genome Research [online]. June 2001, vol.11, issue 6 [cited 7 October 2007]. Available from: http://www.genome.org/cgi/content/full/11/6/994.

Barandiaran, Jose Miguel De. Diccionario Ilustrado de Mitologia Vasca y Algunas de Sus Fuentes. Vol. 1 of Obras Completas. Bilbao: Editorial la Gran Enciclopedia Vasca, 1972.

Baring, Anne, and Jules Cashford. The Myth of the Goddess: Evolution of an Image. London: Viking Arkana, 1991.

Benitez-Bribiesca, Luis, Irma Dela Rosa-Alvarez, and Armando Mansilla-Olivares. "Dendritic Spine Pathology in Infants with Severe Protein-Calorie Malnutrition." Pediatrics 104, no. 2 (1999).

Berreman, G. "The Evolutionary Status of Caste in India." In Social Anthropology of Peasantry, edited by J.P. Mencher, 237-250. Bombay: Somaiya Publishers, 1983.

Betzig, Laura and Santus Wichimai. "A Not So Perfect Peace: A History of Conflict on Ifaluk." Oceania 61 (1991): 240-56.

Biaggi, Cristina. The Rule of Mars: Readings on the Origins, History and Impact of Patriarchy. Manchester, Connecticut: Knowledge, Ideas & Trends (KIT), 2005.

BibleGateway.com [online]. [cited 18 August 2007]. Available from: <http://www.biblegateway.com/>.

Billard, Jules B. The World of the American Indian. Washington, D.C.: National Geographic Society, 1979.

Birley, Anthony. Life in Roman Britain. London: B.T. Batsford LTD, 1968.

Bloom, Paul and Deena Skolnick Weisberg. "Why Do Some People Resist Science?" Edge [online]. May 2007, vol. 29 [cited 29 May 2007]. Available from: <http://www.edge.org/>.

Boardman, John. Early Greek Vase Painting. London: Thames and Hudson, 1998.

Bolen, Jean Shinoda. The Millionth Circle: How to Change Ourselves and the World. Berkeley, California: Conari Press, 1999.

----------. Urgent Message from Mother: Gather the Women, Save the World. York Beach, Maine: Conari Press, 2005.

Bolger, Diane. "Figurines, Fertility, and the Emergence of Complex Society in Prehistoric Cyprus." Current Anthropology 37, no. 2 (1996): 365-3.

Bonta, Bruce D. Peaceful Peoples. Metuchen, New Jersey: The Scarecrow Press, Inc., 1993.

Boston, Rob. "Operation Potomac." Church & State 54 (Oct. 2001): 4-6.

----------. "The End of the Line for Pat Robertson?" Humanist 66, issue 3 (May/June 2006): 37-38.

Bower, Bruce. "Civilization and Its Discontents." Science News 137, issue 9 (1990): 136-139.

Briffault, Robert. The Mothers: A Study of the Origins of Sentiments and Institutions. Holiday House, 1977.

"Bronze Age." Encyclopedia Britannica [online]. 2007 [cited 30 August 2007]. Available from: <http://www.search.eb.com.prxy1.ursus.maine.edu/eb/article-9016618>.

Brown, Dan. The DaVinci Code. New York: Doubleday, 2006.

Brownlee, Shannon. "Can't Do without Love." US News & World

Report 122, issue 6 (1997): 58-60.

Buber's Basque Page [online]. [cited 3 March 2007]. Available from <http://www.buber.net/Basque/>.

Budapest, Zsuzsanna. The Holy Book of Women's Mysteries Part II. Los Angeles: Susan B. Anthony Coven Number one, 1980.

----------. The Grandmother of Time: A Women's Book of Celebrations, Spells, and Sacred Objects for Every Month of the Year. San Francisco: HarperSanFrancisco, 1989.

Caldwell, Richard S. "Introduction." Hesiod's Theogony. Newburyport, MA: Focus Information Group, 1987.

Campbell, Joseph. The Masks of God: Oriental Mythology. New York: The Viking Press, 1962.

----------. The Masks of God: Occidental Mythology. New York, London: Penguin Books, 1964.

Carlson, D. "Famine in History: With a Comparison of Two Modern Ethiopian Disasters." In Famine, edited by Kevin Cahill. Maryknoll, NY: Orbis Books, 1982.

Carpenter, John. "Ascend to the Realm of the Gods." Lancet 358 (2001): 1651.

Carpenter, Tom. "Does Archaeology Prove the Bible?" [online]. [cited 25 May 2007]. Available from: <http://www.creation-defense.org/53.htm>. Originally published in Rockdale/ Newton Citizen [online]. Available from: <http://www.rockdalecitizen.com/>.

Carter, Elizabeth. "At the Dawn of Tyranny" (Review of the Book Uruk Mesopotamia and Its Neighbors, edited by Mitchell S. Rothman). Science 296, issue 5574 (2002): 1809-10.

Cauvin, Jacques. The Birth of the Gods and the Origins of Agriculture. Cambridge: Cambridge University Press, 2002.

"Censorship 'Changes Face of Net.'" BBC News [online]. 6 June 2007 [cited 2 August 2007]. Available from: <http://news.bbc.co.uk/2/hi/technology/6724531.stm>.

"CH06 On-Site Blog 2006." CH07: Archaeological Illustration at

Catalhoyuk [online]. 23 July 2006 1:30 pm [cited 30 April 2007]. Available from: <http://myweb.tiscali.co.uk/jghsillustration/06/blog.htm>.

Chan, Kim-Kwong. "Religion in China in the Twenty-first Century: Some Scenarios." Religion, State & Society 33, issue 2 (2005): 87-119.

Cheilik, Michael S. "Bronze Age." Funk & Wagnalls New World Encyclopedia, 2002. Accession Number: BR181800.

Childe, Gordon. What Happened in History. Baltimore, Maryland: Penguin Books, 1954.

----------. The Dawn of European Civilization. New York: Alfred Knopf, 1958.

"Chinese Bloggers Debate Google." BBC News [online]. 26 January 2006 [cited 1 August 2007]. Available from: <http://news.bbc.co.uk/2/hi/asia-pacific/4650158.stm>.

Christ, Carol. Laughter of Aphrodite: Reflections on a Journey to the Goddess. San Francisco: Harper & Row, 1987.

----------. Rebirth of the Goddess. Reading, MA, and Harlow, UK: Addison-Wesley Publishing Company, 1997.

CIA Factbook [online]. [cited 2 August 2007]. Available from: https://www.cia.gov/library/publications/the-world-factbook/index.html.

City Population [online]. [Cited 15 November 2007]. Available from: http://www.citypopulation.de/UK-England.html.

Coleman, Alexander. "Life in Basqueland." New Criterion 18, issue 8 (2000): 85-88.

Collon, Dominique. Near Eastern Seals. Berkeley CA: University of California Press/British Museum, 1990.

Condren, Mary. The Serpent and the Goddess: Women, Religion, and Power in Celtic Ireland. San Francisco, London: Harper & Row, 1989.

Craven, Roy C. A Concise History of Indian Art. New York and Toronto: Oxford University Press, n.d.

Dashu, Max. "The Meanings of Goddess Part 2: Goddess Heresies: The Legacies of Stigma in Academia." Goddess Pages: An Online Journal of Goddess Spirituality in the 21st Century [online]. Spring 2007, issue 3 [cited 22 May 2007]. Available from: http://www.goddess-pages.co.uk/.

Dawkins, Richard. The God Delusion. Boston: Houghton Mifflin Company, 2006.

----------. "Is Science a Religion?" The Humanist (January/February 1997).

de Waal, Frans B. M. "Bonobo, Sex and Society." Scientific American Special Edition 16, issue 2 (2006): 14-21.

---------- and Frans Lanting. Bonobo: The Forgotten Ape. Berkeley: University of California Press, 1997.

Delleur, Jacques W., "The Evolution of Urban Hydrology: Past, Present, and Future," Journal of Hydraulic Engineering, August 2003.

DeMeo, James. Saharasia: The 4000 BCE Origins of Child Abuse, Sex-Repression, Warfare and Social Violence in the Deserts of the Old World. Greensprings, Oregon: Orgone Biophysical Research Lab, 1998.

----------. "Shredding Saharasia: A Response to Richard Morrock's 'Review.'" Journal of Psychohistory [online]. Spring 1999, vol. 26, no. 4. Available from: http://www.geocities.com/kidhistory/ja/shreddin.htm.

----------. "The Saharasian Origins of Patriarchal Authoritarian Culture." In The Rule of Mars: Readings on the Origins, History and Impact of Patriarchy, edited by Cristina Biaggi, 43-52. Manchester, CT: Knowledge, Ideas & Trends (KIT), 2005.

Dentan, Robert Knox. The Semai: A Nonviolent People of Malaya. Fieldwork Edition. New York, London: Holt, Rinehart and Winston, 1979.

Dess, Nancy K. "Tend and Befriend." Psychology Today 33, issue 5 (2000): 22-23.

Dexter, Miriam Robbins. "The Roots of Indo-European Patriarchy: Indo-European Female Figures and the Principles of Energy." In The Rule of Mars: Readings on the Origins, History and Impact of Patriarchy, edited by Cristina Biaggi, 143-154. Manchester, CT: Knowledge, Ideas & Trends (KIT), 2005.

Diamond, Jared. "Japanese Roots." Discover: Science, Technology, and the Future [online]. 1 June 1998. Available from: http://discovermagazine.com/1998/jun/japaneseroots1455/.

Dickinson, Oliver. The Aegean Bronze Age. Cambridge: Cambridge University Press, 1994.

Dingfelder, S. "What Lies Behind the Female Habit of 'Tending and Befriending' During Stress." Monitor on Psychology [online]. January 2004, vol. 35, no. 1 [cited February 2007]. Available from:
<http://www.apa.org/monitor/jan04/habit.html>.

Dozier, Edward. The Pueblo Indians of North America. Case Studies in Anthropology. New York: Holt, Rinehart and Winston, Inc., 1970.

Driver, Harold. Indians of North America. Chicago: The University of Chicago Press, 1964.

Durkheim, Emil. The Elementary Forms of Religious Life. New York: Free Press, 1995.

Ehlers, C.L., K.C. Rickler, and J.E. Hovey. "A Possible Relationship Between Plasma Testosterone and Aggressive Behavior in a Female Outpatient Population." In Limber Epilepsy and the Dyscontrol Syndrome, edited by M. Girfis and L.G. Kiloh, 183-194. New York: Elsevier, 1988.

Eisler, Riane. The Chalice and the Blade. San Francisco: Harper & Row, 1987.

Elgood, Heather. "Exploring the Roots of Village Hinduism in South Asia." World Archaeology 36, issue 3 (2004): 326-342.

Eller, Cynthia. The Myth of Matriarchal Prehistory. Boston: Beacon Press, 2000.

Emerson, Shirley, and Yvonne Syron. "Adolescent Satanism: Rebellion Masquerading as Religion." Counseling & Values 39, Issue 2 (1995): 145-59.

Encarta World English Dictionary. Microsoft Corporation. 1998-2004.

Evans, Arthur. The Palace of Minos. London: Macmillan, 1921.

Everson, Michael. "Tenacity in Religion, Myth, and Folklore: the Neolithic Goddess of Old Europe Preserved in a Non-Indo-European Setting." Paper given at the Second Conference on the Transformation of European and Anatolian Culture 4500-2500 B.C., Dublin, 15-19 September 1989. Journal of Indo-European Studies [online]. Fall/Winter 1989, vol. 17, no. 3 & 4 [cited 10 February 2007]. Available from: <http://www.evertype.com/misc/basque-jies/basque-jies.html>.

Fagan, Brian M. People of the Earth: An Introduction to World Prehistory. Upper Saddle River, NJ: Prentice Hall, 2004.

Finegan, Jack. An Archaeological History of Religions of Indian Asia. New York: Paragon House, 1989.

Fishman, Ted C. China Inc.: How the Rise of the Next Superpower Challenges America and the World. New York, London: Scribner, 2005.

Fitton, J. Lesley. Minoans. London: The British Museum Press, 2002.

Frankfort, Henri. Cylinder Seals: A Documentary Essay on the Art and Religion of the Ancient Near East. London: Macmillan and Co., 1939.

Freeman, Derek. Margaret Mead and Samoa: The Making and Unmaking of an Anthropological Myth. Cambridge: Harvard University Press, 1983.

Fry, Douglas P. "Conclusion: Learning from Peaceful Societies." In Keeping the Peace: Conflict Resolution and Peaceful Societies around the World, edited by Graham Kemp and

Douglas P. Fry, 185-204. New York and London: Routledge, 2004.

----------. Beyond War: The Human Potential for Peace. Oxford: Oxford University Press, 2007.

Frymer-Kensky, Tikva. In the Wake of the Goddesses: Women, Culture, and the Biblical Transformation of Pagan Myth. New York: The Free Press, 1992.

Gabler, Neal. "Disney: Man or Mouse?" Los Angeles Times [online]. 17 December 2006 [cited 30 July 2007]. Available from: <http://www.latimes.com/news/opinion/la-op-gabler17dec17,0,1578644.story?coll=la-opinion-rightrail>.

----------. Walt Disney: The Triumph of the American Imagination. New York: Vintage, 2007.

Gadon, Elinor. The Once & Future Goddess: A Symbol for Our Time. San Francisco: Harper & Row, 1989.

Gallessich, Gail. "Gas Escaping from Ocean Floor May Drive Global Warming." University of California Newsroom [online]. 19 July 2006 [cited 18 November 2007]. Available from: < http://www.universityofcalifornia.edu/news/article/8333>.

Geary, D.C., and M.V. Flinn. "Sex Differences in Behavioral and Hormonal Response to Social Threat: Commentary on Taylor et al. 2000." Psychological Review 109 (2002): 745-750.

Geertz, Clifford. The Interpretation of Cultures. New York: Basic Books, 1973.

"Gender Equity Means Social Justice for All." Heifer International [online]. [cited 2 August 2007]. Available from: http://www.heifer.org/site/c.edJRKQNiFiG/b.1467545/.

Ghiglieri, Michael. The Dark Side of Man: Tracing the Origins of Male Violence. Reading, Massachusetts: Perseus, 1999.

Gigerenzer, Gerd. Gut Feelings: The Intelligence of the Unconscious. New York: Viking, 2007.

Gimbutas, Marija. "Women and Culture in Goddess-Oriented Old

Europe." In The Politics of Women's Spirituality, edited by Charlene Spretnak, 22-31. Garden City, New York: Anchor Books, 1982.

----------. The Language of the Goddess. San Francisco: Harper & Row, 1989.

----------. The Civilization of the Goddess. New York: HarperCollins Publishers, 1991.

----------. The Living Goddesses. Berkeley: University of California Press, 2001.

Gladwell, Malcolm. Blink: The Power of Thinking Without Thinking. Boston: Back Bay Books, 2007.

Gledhill, Ruth. "Societies Worse Off 'When They Have God on Their Side.'" The London Times [online]. 27 September 2005. Available from: <http://www.timesonline.co.uk/tol/news/uk/article571206.ece>.

Goettner-Abendroth, Heide. "Notes on the Rise and Development of Patriarchy." In The Rule of Mars: Readings on the Origins, History and Impact of Patriarchy, edited by Cristina Biaggi, 27-42. Manchester, CT: Knowledge, Ideas & Trends (KIT), 2005.

Goldfine, Rebecca. "Farms, Churches Link up Through Local Agriculture." Lewiston, Maine, Sun Journal [online]. 29 January 2007. Available from: <http://www.sunjournal.com/story/196875-3/OxfordHills/Farms_churches_link_up_through_local_agriculture/>.

Goodison, Lucy, and Christine Morris. Ancient Goddesses: The Myths and the Evidence. London: British Museum Press, 1998.

Gordon, Cyrus H. Ugarit and Minoan Crete: The Bearing of Their Texts on the Origins of Western Culture. New York: W. W. Norton & Company, 1966.

Graves, Robert. The White Goddess: A Historical Grammar of Poetic Myth. New York: The Noonday Press; Farrar, Straus and Giroux, 1991.

Grimm, Jacob, and Wilhelm Grimm. "Mother Holle." In The Complete Grimm's Fairy Tales. New York: Pantheon Books, 1972.

Gunn Allen, Paula. The Sacred Hoop. Boston: Beacon Press, 1992.

Haarmann, Harald. "Why Did Patriarchy Supersede Egalitarianism?" In The Rule of Mars: Readings on the Origins, History and Impact of Patriarchy, edited by Cristina Biaggi, 163-174. Manchester, CT: Knowledge, Ideas & Trends (KIT), 2005.

Hadingham, Evan. "Europe's Mystery People." World Monitor 5, issue 9 (1992).

Hafner, German. Art of Crete, Mycenae, and Greece. New York: Harry N. Abrams, 1968.

Hamid, Tawfik. "How to End 'Islamophobia.'" Wall Street Journal Opinion Journal [online]. 25 May 2007. [cited 1 August 2007]. Available from: <http://www.opinionjournal.com/editorial/feature.html?id=110010123>.

Hamilton, Carrie. "Re-membering the Basque Nationalist Family: Daughters, Fathers and the Reproduction of the Radical Nationalist Community." Journal of Spanish Cultural Studies 1, no. 2 (2000).

Hardon, John A. Religions of the World. Garden City, New York: Image Books, 1968.

Harris, Sam. The End of Faith: Religion, Terror, and the Future of Reason. New York, London: W. W. Norton & Company, 2004.

Hassan, Fekri A. "The Earliest Goddesses of Egypt." In Ancient Goddesses: The Myths and the Evidence, edited by Lucy Goodison and Christine Morris, 98-112. London: British Museum Press, 1998.

Hausman, Gerald, and Bob Kapoun. Prayer to the Great Mystery: The Uncollected Writings and Photography of Edward S.

Curtis. New York: St. Martin's Press, 1995.

Haviland, William A. Human Evolution and Prehistory. Fort Worth, TX: Harcourt Brace, 1997.

Hawken, Paul. Blessed Unrest: How the Largest Movement in the World Came into Being and Why No One Saw It Coming. New York, London, Toronto: Viking, 2007.

Hawkes, Jaquetta. Atlas of Ancient Archaeology. New York: McGraw-Hill Book Company 1974.

Hedges, Chris. American Fascists: The Christian Right and the War on America. New York, London, Toronto, Sydney: Free Press, 2006.

Heifer International website [online]. [cited November 2007]. Available from: <http://www.heifer.org/>.

Hendelman-Baavur, Liora. "Promises and Perils of Weblogistan: Online Personal Journals and the Islamic Republic of Iran." The Middle East Review of International Affairs [online]. June 2007, vol. 11, no. 2, article 6/8 [cited 1 August 2007]. Available from: http://meria.idc.ac.il/journal/2007/issue2/jv11no2a6.html.

Hijjara, Ismail. The Halaf Period in Northern Mesopotamia. London: NABU Publications, 1997.

Hitchens, Christopher. God Is Not Great: How Religion Poisons Everything. New York: Twelve, 2007.

Hopi Indian Tribal Website [online]. [cited 1 March 2007]. Available from: http://www.hopi.nsn.us/.

Howell, Signe, and Roy Willis. Societies at Peace: Anthropological Perspectives. London: Routledge, 1990.

Hua, Cai. A Society Without Fathers or Husbands: The Na of China. New York: Zone Books, 2001.

Hulbert, Ann. "Boy Problems." New York Times Magazine 154, issue 53173 (2005): 13-14.

Hultkrantz, Ake. "The Religion of the Goddess in North America." In The Book of the Goddess Past and Present: An Introduction to Her Religion, edited by Carl Olson, 202-216.

New York: Crossroad Publishing Co., 1990.

Hunter, Jennifer. "The New North." Maclean's 111, issue 31 (1998): 14-19.

Hyde, Lewis. The Gift: Imagination and the Erotic Life of Property. New York: Vintage Books, 1983.

Internet World Stats [online]. 2007 [cited 1 August 2007]. Available from: http://www.internetworldstats.com.

Jackson, Peter. "Light from Distant Asterisks: Towards a Description of the Indo-European Religious Heritage." Numen: International Review for the History of Religions 49, issue 1 (2002): 61-102.

Jacob, Alexander. "Cosmology and Ethics in the Religions of the Peoples of the Ancient Near East." Mankind Quarterly 40 issue 1 (1999): 95-119.

Jacobsen, Thorkild. The Treasures of Darkness: A History of Mesopotamian Religion. New Haven and London: Yale University Press, 1976.

Jaffee, Kim D., John W. Epling, William Grant, Reem M. Ghandour, and Elizabeth Callendar. "Physician-Identified Barriers to Intimate Partner Violence Screening." Journal of Women's Health 14, issue 8 (2005): 713-720.

James, E.O. The Ancient Gods: The History and Diffusion of Religion in the Ancient Near East and the Eastern Mediterranean. New York: G. P. Putnam's Sons, 1960.

Johnson, Buffie. Lady of the Beasts: Ancient Images of the Goddess and Her Sacred Animals. San Francisco: Harper & Row, 1981.

Joyce, Kathryn. "The Quiverfull Conviction: Christian Mothers Breed 'Arrows for the War.'" The Nation (November 27, 2006): 11-18.

Kagan, Robert. "End of Dreams, Return of History." Hoover

Institution Policy Review [online]. June & July 2007, vol. 143 [cited 30 July 2007]. Available from: <http://www.hoover.org/publications/policyreview>.

Kak, Subhash C. "The Indus Tradition and the Indo-Aryans." Mankind Quarterly 32, issue 3 (1992): 195-213.

Kazuaki, Yoshimura. "Appendix II: Iron Armor and Weapons in Protohistoric Japan." Journal of East Asian Archaeology 2, issue 3-4 (2000): 104-111.

Keeley, Lawrence. War before Civilization: The Myth of the Peaceful Savage. New York: Henry Holt, 1996.

Kelly, Raymond C. Warless Societies and the Origin of War. Ann Arbor: The University of Michigan Press, 2003.

Kemp, Graham and Douglas P. Fry. Keeping the Peace: Conflict Resolution and Peaceful Societies around the World. New York and London: Routledge, 2004.

Kendrick, Keith M. "The Neurobiology of Social Bonds." British Society for Neuroendocrinology [online]. 2007 [cited 10 January 2007]. Available from: <http://neuroendo.org.uk/index.php/content/view/34/11/>.

Kenoyer, Jonathan Mark. "Birth of a Civilization." Archaeology 51, no. 1 (1998): 54-61.

----------. "Uncovering the Keys to the Lost Indus Cities." Scientific American Special Edition 15, issue 1 (2005): 25-33.

Kipnis, Andrew B. "The Flourishing of Religion in Post-Mao China and the Anthropological Category of Religion." Australian Journal of Anthropology 12, issue 1 (2001): 32-46.

Kobayashi, Tatsuo. Jomon Reflections: Forager Life and Culture in the Prehistoric Japanese Archipelago. Park End Place, Oxford, UK: Oxbow Books, 2004.

Koji, Mizoguchi. "Time and Genealogical Consciousness in the Mortuary Practices of the Yayoi Period, Japan." Journal of East Asian Archaeology 3, issue 3-4 (2001): 173-197.

Kovarnik, Jaromir, Radan Kvet and Vladimir Podborsky.

"Europe's Oldest Civilization and Its Rondels: The Real Story." Antiquity 80, no. 310 (2006).

Kramer, Samuel Noah. Sumerian Mythology: A Study of Spiritual and Literary Achievement in the Third Millennium B. C. Philadelphia: University of Pennsylvania Press, 1998.

Kristiansen, Kristian. "What Language Did Neolithic Pots Speak? Colin Renfrew's European Farming-Language-Dispersal Model Challenged." Antiquity 79, issue 305 (2005): 679-691.

Kugler, R. Anthony. "Overlooked 'Jewels.'" Dig 4, issue 4 (2002): 6-8.

Lamberg-Karlovsky, C. "Review of Rethinking World-Systems: Diasporas, Colonies, and Interaction in Uruk Mesopotamia." American Historical Review 107, issue 3 (2002): 975-76.

Langdon, Susan. "Figurines and Social Change: Visualizing Gender in Dark Age Greece." In From the Ground Up: Beyond Gender Theory in Archaeology, edited by Nancy L. Wicker. Oxford: BAR, 1999.

Leeming, David. The Oxford Companion to World Mythology. Oxford: Oxford University Press, 2005.

--------- and Jake Page. Goddess: Myths of the Female Divine. Oxford and New York: Oxford University Press, 1994.

Legrain, Leon. Terra-cottas from Nippur: University of Pennsylvania, The University Museum Publications of the Babylonian Section Vol. XVI. Philadelphia: The University of Pennsylvania Press, 1930.

Lesure, Richard G. "The Goddess Diffracted: Thinking about the Figurines of Early Villages." Current Anthropology 43, no. 4 (2002).

Levinson, David. Religion: A Cross-Cultural Encyclopedia. New York, Oxford: Oxford University Press, 1998.

Lietaer, Bernard and Pamela Gerloff. "Creating a Giving Culture: An Interview with Bernard Lietaer." More Than Money Journal 34 (2003): 28-33.

Lovett, Richard A. "Methane Belches in Lakes Supercharge Global Warming, Study Says." National Geographic News [online]. 6 September 2006 [cited 18 November 2007]. Available from: <http://news.nationalgeographic.com/news/2006/09/06090 6-methane.html>.

Maisels, Charles Keith. Early Civilizations of the Old World: The Formative Histories of Egypt, the Levant, Mesopotamia, India and China. London and New York: Routledge, 2001.

"Man's Best Friends [sic]." Archaeology Magazine 57, issue 4 (2004).

Marinatos, Nanno. Minoan Religion: Ritual, Image, and Symbol. Columbia: University of South Carolina Press, 1993.

----------. The Goddess and the Warrior: The Naked Goddess and Mistress of Animals in Early Greek Religion. London and New York: Routledge, 2000.

Marinatos, Spyridon. Crete and Mycenae. London: Thames and Hudson, 1960.

Marler, Joan. "Cultures of the Goddess." ReVision 20, issue 3 (1998): 44-48.

Mathieu, Christine. "The Moso Daba Religious Specialists." In Naxi and Moso Ethnography: Kin, Rites, Pictographs, edited by Michael Oppitz and Elisabeth Hsu, 209-236. Zurich: Volkerkundemuseum Zurich, 1998.

----------. A History and Anthropological Study of the Ancient Kingdoms of the Sino-Tibetan Borderland — Naxi and Mosuo. Mellen Studies in Anthropology 11. Lewiston, NY: The Edwin Mellen Press, 2003.

Matthews, Caitlin. King Arthur and the Goddess of the Land: The Divine Feminine in the Mabinogion. Rochester, Vermont: Inner Traditions International, 2002.

Maxwell, James A. America's Fascinating Indian Heritage. Pleasantville, NY: The Reader's Digest Association, Inc., 1978.

McCargo, Duncan. "Buddhism, Democracy and Identity in Thailand." In Democratization 11, issue 4 (2004): 155-170.

McCarthy, Lauren A. "Evolutionary and Biochemical Explanations for a Unique Female Stress Response: Tend-and-Befriend." Rochester Institute of Technology [online]. 2005. Available from: <http://www.personalityresearch.org/papers/mccarthy.html>.

McElroy, Damien. "Chinese Men Threaten 'Lake of Free Love' Where Women Rule." London Daily Telegraph [online]. 27 June 2001 [cited 19 February 2007]. Available from: <http://www.telegraph.co.uk/news/main.jhtml?xml=/news/2001/03/25/wmosuo25.xml>.

McIntosh, Jane R. A Peaceful Realm: The Rise and Fall of the Indus Civilization. Boulder, Colorado and Oxford, UK: Westview Press, 2002.

Mellersh, H.E.L. The Destruction of Knossos: The Rise and Fall of Minoan Crete. New York: Barnes & Noble Books, 1993.

Melleuish, Gregory. "The State in World History: Perspectives and Problems." Australian Journal of Politics and History 48, no. 3 (2002): 322-335.

Meltzer, Milton. Slavery: A World History. USA: Da Capo Press, 1993.

Meskell, Lynn. "Twin Peaks: The Archaeologies of Catalhoyuk." In Ancient Goddesses: The Myths and the Evidence, edited by Lucy Goodison and Christine Morris, 46-62. London: British Museum Press, 1998.

Miles, Clement. Christmas Customs and Traditions. New York: Dover, 1976.

Minako, Togawa. "Jomon Clay Figurines of the Kaminabe Site, Kumamoto." Bulletin of the International Jomon Culture Conference [online]. 2004, vol. 1 [cited 24 November 2007]. Available from: <http://www.jomon.or.jp/ebulletin15.html>.

Moberg, Kerstin Uvnas. The Oxytocin Factor: Tapping the Hormone of Calm, Love, and Healing. Cambridge, MA:

Perseus Books Group, 2003.

Montagu, Ashley. Learning Non-Aggression: The Experience of Non-Literate Societies. New York: Oxford University Press, 1978.

Morrock, Richard. "The World in an Orgone Box." Journal of Psychohistory [online]. 1999, vol. 26, no. 4 [cited February 2007]. Available from:

<http://www.geocities.com/kidhistory/ja/worldin.htm>.

Moulton, Susan. "Cultures of the Goddess, Part 2, Introduction." ReVision (1-1-1999).

Muhly, J.D. Review of Knossos: Palace, City, State, by Gerald Cadogan, Eleni Hatzaki, and Adonis Vasilakis. Bryn Mawr Classical Review 2006.09.17.

Murdoch, George Peter. Ethnographic Atlas. Pittsburgh, Pennsylvania: University of Pittsburgh Press, 1967.

Namu, Yang Erche and Christine Mathieu. Leaving Mother Lake: A Girlhood at the Edge of the World. Boston: Little, Brown, 2003.

"Natural Born Heroes." BBC News [online]. 13 November 2002. [Cited 10 February 2007]. Available from:

http://www.bbc.co.uk/science/humanbody/tv/humanin-stinct/programme4.shtml.

Neumann, Eric. The Great Mother: An Analysis of the Archetype. Princeton, NJ: Princeton University Press, 1991.

Nilsson, Martin P. The Minoan-Mycenaean Religion. New York: Biblo and Tannen, 1949.

Oldenburg, Ann, and Edna Gundersen. "God's 'Punk,' Jay Bakker, Opens Doors to His Church." USA Today (8 September 2006).

Oliver, Leonard P. Study Circles: Coming Together for Personal Growth and Social Change. Washington, DC: Seven Locks Press Publishers, 1987.

Olson, Walter. "Invitation to a Stoning." Reason 30, issue 6 (1998): 62-64.

O'Neill, Eugene. Strange Interlude. Kessinger Publishing, 2004.

Oppenheimer, Stephen. "Myths of British Ancestry." Prospect Magazine [online]. October 2006 [cited 10 February 2007]. Available from: <http://www.prospect-magazine.co.uk/article_details.php?id=7817>.

Osborne, Roger. "Digging Up the Origins of Civilization." History Today 56 (Jan 2006): 70-71.

Oswalt, Wendell. Alaskan Eskimos. Chandler Publications in Anthropology and Sociology. San Francisco: Chandler Publishing Company, 1967.

Otterbein, Keith. How War Began. Texas A&M Anthropology Series No. 10. College Station, TX: Texas A&M University Press, 2004.

Page, Jake. "Spider Coming Down." Journal of Religion and Health 42, no. 2 (2003): 111-116.

Palmer, Rose A. The North American Indians: An Account of the American Indians North of Mexico, Compiled from Original Sources. Smithsonian Scientific Series, Vol. 4. Washington, DC: Smithsonian Institution Series, Inc., 1929.

Palubeckaite, Zydrune. "Patterns of Linear Enamel Hypoplasia in Lithuanian Iron Age Population." Variability and Evolution [online]. 2001, vol. 9. Available from: http://var-and-evo.biol.uni.torun.pl/07_9.pdf.

Paoli, T., E. Palagi, and S. Borgognini Tarli. "How Does Agonistic Dominance Relate to Individual Attributes and Social Interactions in Bonobos?" International Journal of Primatology 27 (2006): 252.

Parker, Ian. "Swingers." The New Yorker [online]. 30 July 2007 [cited 30 July 2007]. Available from: <http://www.newyorker.com/reporting/2007/07/30/07073

0fa_fact_parker?currentPage=all>.

Paul, Gregory S. "Cross-National Correlations of Quantifiable Societal Health with Popular Religiosity and Secularism in the Prosperous Democracies: A First Look." Journal of Religion & Society [online]. 2005, vol. 7. Available from: http://moses.creighton.edu/JRS/2005/2005-11.html.

Pearce, Fred. "Stern Words." New Scientist 192, issue 2583/2584 (2006): 43.

Pearson, Richard. "New Perspectives on Jomon Society." Bulletin of the International Jomon Culture Conference [online]. 2004, vol. 1 [cited 9 September 2007]. Available from: < http://www.jomon.or.jp/ebulletin14.html>.

Pinker, Steven. "The Mystery of Consciousness." Time 169, issue 5 (29 January 2007): 58-70.

Pitman, Gayle E. "Evolution, But No Revolution: The 'Tend and Befriend' Theory of Stress and Coping." A review of The Tending Instinct: How Nurturing Is Essential to Who We Are and How We Live. Psychology of Women Quarterly 27, issue 2 (2003): 194-95.

Popova, T.A. "Unique Iconographic Images of Anthropomorphic Sculpture from the Tripolye-Cucenten Culture." Anthropology & Archeology of Eurasia 43, no. 4 (2005): 58-69.

Pritchard, James B. The Ancient Near East: A New Anthology of Texts and Pictures. Vol. 2. Princeton and London: Princeton University Press, 1975.

Radical Goddess The[a]logy Weblog [online]. Available from: <http://godmotherascending.blogspot.com/>.

Raffaele, Paul. "The Smart and Swinging Bonobo." Smithsonian 37, issue 8 (2006): 66-75.

Rahman, Tariq. "Languages of the Proto-historic Indus Valley." Mankind Quarterly 36, issue 3-4 (1996): 221-46.

Reider, Noriko T. "Shuten Dōji 'Drunken Demon.'" Asian Folklore Studies 64, issue 2 (2005): 207-231.

Reimer, Katherine. "Ancient Archetypes of the Jomon." PanGaia: A Pagan Journal for Thinking People 38 (2004): 29-31.

Renfrew, Colin. Archaeology and Language: The Puzzle of Indo-European Origins. New York: Cambridge University Press, 1987.

Reuther, Rosemary Radford. Goddesses and the Divine Feminine: A Western Religious History. Berkeley, Los Angeles, London: University of California Press, 2005.

Roberts, J. M. The Penguin History of Europe. London: Penguin Books, 1997.

Rothman, Mitchell S. "Studying the Development of Complex Society: Mesopotamia in the Late Fifth and Fourth Millennia BC." Journal of Archaeological Research 12, no. 1 (2004): 75-119.

Saggs, H.W.F. The Greatness That Was Babylon. New York: Mentor, 1968.

Sakellarakis, J.A. Herakleion Museum: Illustrated Guide. Athens: Ekdotike Athenon S.A., 2000.

Saner, Reg. "Spirit Root." Southwest Review 82, issue 3 (1997): 443-67.

Sarkar, Tanika. "Women in South Asia: The Raj and After." History Today 47, issue 9 (1997): 54-59.

Scarre, Chris. Smithsonian Timelines of the Ancient World. New York & London: Dorling Kindersley, 1993.

Schlegel, Alice. "Contentious but Not Violent: The Hopi." In Keeping the Peace: Conflict Resolution and Peaceful Societies around the World, edited by Graham Kemp and Douglas P. Fry, 19-34. New York and London: Routledge, 2004.

Shearer, James F. "Basques." Funk & Wagnalls New World Encyclopedia. World Almanac Education Group, Inc., 2002.

Shostak, Marjorie. Nisa: The Life and Words of a !Kung Woman. New York: Random House, 1983.

Sifry, Dave. "The State of the Live Web." Technorati.com [online].

5 April 2007. [cited 1 August 2007]. Available from: <http://technorati.com/weblog/2007/04/328.html>.

Sjoo, Monica and Barbara Mor. The Great Cosmic Mother: Rediscovering the Religion of the Earth. San Francisco: HarperSanFrancisco, 1991.

Skeptic's Annotated Bible [online][cited 19 November 2007]. Available from: <http://skepticsannotatedbible.com/cruelty/short.html>.

Sponsel, Leslie. "The Natural History of Peace: A Positive View of Human Nature and Its Potential." In A Natural History of Peace, edited by Thomas Gregor. Nashville, Tennessee: Vanderbilt University Press, 1996.

Sponsel, Leslie, and Thomas Gregor. The Anthropology of Peace and Nonviolence. Boulder, Colorado: L. Rienner Publishers, 1994.

Stanley-Baker, Joan. Japanese Art. London: Thames and Hudson, 1986.

Stone, Merlin. When God Was a Woman. B & N Books, 1993.

Strong, James. The New Strong's Exhaustive Concordance of the Bible. Nashville Tennessee: Thomas Nelson Publishers, 1996.

Studebaker, Jeri. "A Millennia Without War?" PanGaia: A Pagan Journal for Thinking People 38 (2004): 26-33.

Sugg, John. "Warped Worldview: Christian Reconstructionists Believe Democracy Is Heresy, Public Schools Are Satanic And Stoning Isn't Just For The Taliban Anymore -- And They've Got More Influence Than You Think." Church & State 59 (2006): 11-13.

Tate, Karen. Sacred Places of Goddess: 108 Destinations. San Francisco, California: Consortium of Collective Consciousness, 2006.

Taylor, Shelley E., Laura Cousino Klein, Brian P. Lewis, Tara L. Gruenewald, Regan A. R. Gurung, and John A. Updegraff. "Biobehavioral Responses to Stress in Females: Tend-and-

Befriend, not Fight-or-Flight." Psychological Review [online]. 2000, vol. 107, no. 3 [cited 21 January 2007]. Available from: <http://www.johnupdegraff.net/pdf/TKLGGU-00.pdf>.

Taylor, Steve. The Fall: Evidence for a Golden Age, 6000 years of Insanity, and the Dawning of a New Era. Winchester UK, New York USA: O Books, 2005.

Terrell, John Upton. American Indian Almanac. New York : Barnes & Noble, 1998

Trevor-Roper, Hugh. The Rise of Christian Europe. London: Thames & Hudson, 1989.

Tribollet, E. "Oxytocin in Reproductive Biology." Department of Physiology, Geneva University Medical Centre, Geneva Foundation for Medical Education and Research, Edited by Aldo Campana [online]. 13 August 2003 [cited 10 January 2007]. Available from:
<http://www.gfmer.ch/Endo/Lectures_08/oxytocin_in_repr oductive_biology.htm>.

Tringham, Ruth and Margaret Conkey. "Rethinking Figurines: A Critical View from Archaeology of Gimbutas, the 'Goddess' and Popular Culture." In Ancient Goddesses: The Myths and the Evidence, edited by Lucy Goodison and Christine Morris, 22-45. London: British Museum Press, 1998.

Ucko, Peter. Anthropomorphic Figurines of Predynastic Egypt and Neolithic Crete with Comparative Material from the Prehistoric Near East and Mainland Greece. Royal Anthropological Institute Occasional Paper No. 24. London: Andrew Szmidla [sic], 1968.

"UN Secretary General Kofi Annan Calls for Girls' Access to Education." Women's International Network News 26, issue 2 (Spring 2000): 4.

Van Biema, David, Richard N. Ostling, and Tim McGirk. "Monks vs Monks." Time Magazine 151, issue 18 (1998): 70.

Vasilakis, Andonis. Minoan Crete from Myth to History. Athens, Greece: Adams Editions, 2001.

Vaughan, Genevieve. For-Giving: A Feminist Criticism of Exchange. Austin, Texas: Plain View Press, 1997.

Voyatzis, Mary E. "From Athena to Zeus: An A-Z Guide to the Origins of Greek Goddesses." In Ancient Goddesses: The Myths and the Evidence, edited by Lucy Goodison and Christine Morris, 133-47. London: British Museum Press, 1998.

Walker, Andrew. "The Last Person Killed at Pamplona." BBC News [online]. 14 July 2005. Available from: http://news.bbc.co.uk/1/hi/magazine/4679751.stm.

Walker, Barbara G. The Woman's Encyclopedia of Myths and Secrets. Edison, New Jersey: Castle Books, 1983.

----------. The Woman's Dictionary of Symbols & Sacred Objects. San Francisco: Harper & Row, 1988.

----------. Restoring the Goddess: Equal Rites for Modern Women. Amherst, New York: Prometheus Books, 2000.

Walker, Williston, Richard A. Norris, David W. Lotz, and Robert T. Handy. A History of the Christian Church. New York: Scribner, 1985.

Wall, Dennis, and Virgil Masayesva. "People of the Corn: Teachings in Hopi Traditional Agriculture, Spirituality, and Sustainability." American Indian Quarterly 28, issue 3-4 (2004): 435-53.

Wallace, Foy E. "There Will Be No Such Secession." Bible Banner [online]. June 1941, vol. 3, no. 11 [cited 8 November 2007]. Available from: http://www.wordsfitlyspoken.org/bible_banner/v3/v3n11p3.html.

Ward, Tim. Savage Breast: One Man's Search for the Goddess. Winchester, UK: O Books, 2006.

Weatherford, Jack. Indian Givers: How the Indians of the Americas Transformed the World. New York: Fawcett

Columbine, 1989.

Westenholz, Joan Goodnick. "Goddesses of the Ancient Near East 3000-1000 BC." In Ancient Goddesses: The Myths and the Evidence, edited by Lucy Goodison and Christine Morris, 63-82. London: British Museum Press, 1998.

Wheeler, Mortimer. Civilizations of the Indus Valley and Beyond. New York: McGraw-Hill, 1966.

Widell, Magnus. "Reflections on Some Households and Their Receiving Officials in the City of Ur in the Ur III Period." in Journal of Near Eastern Studies 63, issue 4 (2004): 283-90.

"Women's Response to Stress." Harvard Women's Health Watch 9, issue 9 (2002): 6.

Woolley, Sir Leonard. Excavations at Ur: A Record of Twelve Years' Work. New York: Thomas Y. Crowell, 1965.

World Almanac & Book of Facts, 2004, s.v. "Adherents of All Religions by Six Continental Areas, Mid-2002."

Wrangham, Richard and Dale Peterson. Demonic Males: Apes and the Origins of Human Violence. Boston: Houghton Mifflin, 1996.

Wright, Quincy. A Study of War. Chicago: University of Chicago Press, 1942.

Younger, John G. "The Spectacle-Eyes Group: Continuity and Innovation for the First Mycenaean Administration at Knossos." In Corpus der Minoischen und Mykenischen Siegel: V. Internationales Siegel-Symposium, Marburg, 23.-25. September 1999, edited by Friedrich Matz, 347-60. Berlin: Gebr. Mann Verlag, 2000.

Yuan, Lu and Sam Mitchell. "Land of the Walking Marriage." In Natural History 109, issue 9 (2000): 58-65.

Zwingle, Erla. "Pamplona, No Bull." Smithsonian 37, issue 4 (2006): 88-94.

INDEX

change, 197; ethnocentrism, 196; importance of, 195; and instincts, lack of human, 196; wiggle room in, 195
Cybele, Roman, 87, 89, 91
Cyclopean walls, 126, 187

daddy gods. *See* father gods; God the Father; gods; gods, Abrahamaic; war gods; YAJ; *specific gods*
Dark Ages: Christian civil crimes and, 227-29; Christianity a cause of, 227-30; "darkness" of, 272-73; ended as Goddess revived, 320-31; science decline, 229; suppression of learning, 228; technological regression, 229; widespread literacy disappearance, 229
daughters: need to strengthen, 115, 257; as part of trinity, 219
DaVinci Code, 56
death: Goddess and, 95-96, 215, 216, 280, 285; of Jesus, 13; war gods and, 20, 114, 123, 202, 229, 232, 250, 283, 284
death penalty, 8, 14-15, 18, 278
deities: human behavior, effects on, 265, 276, 299; as human creations, 276; and the unconscious, 7, 299

Desmond Tutu, 244-45
Deuteronomy: child cannibalism in, 333; cruelty in, 20
development organizations, 237-38, 257, 269-70
Devil, 227; Christian not Pagan deity, 233
Devil worship, 233
Diana Triformis, 220
Dieus: incested his daughter, 171; and Indo-Aryans, 183; progenitor of Zeus, 171, 185
disarmament of war gods, 37-38, 257, 305
disciples, Christ's, 221
Disney films, 256-57
Dobson, James, 15
dogu. *See* Japan, Neolithic: female figurines
dolphins, 125
Dominionists. *See* Christian Reconstructionists
Dorje Shugden, 14, 301
dove symbol, 221
drugs, illegal, 39
Durkheim, Emile, 23
dystopia, 10, 165-67, 188, 192, 205, 237, 253, 267, 276; defined, 166; in modern world, 10; the state as, 165

Earth, the, 8, 31, 35, 49, 229, 230, 244, 286; Eastern religion's view of, 22;

BOOKS

O books
O is a symbol of the world, of oneness and unity. In
different cultures it also means the "eye", symbolizing
knowledge and insight, and in Old English it means "place
of love or home". O books explores the many paths of
understanding which different traditions have developed
down the ages, particularly those today that express
respect for the planet and all of life.

For more information on the full list of over 300 titles
please visit our website
www.O-books.net

SOME RECENT O BOOKS

Walking An Ancient Path
Rebirthing Goddess on Planet Earth
Karen Tate

At last, a book about The Goddess for those of us who happily dwell in the twenty first century! This is a thoroughly modern and practical look at the different aspects of goddess worship and how it can be integrated into the modern world. It could bring about a major change in our understanding of the Goddess. Karen Tate's book is a must have. It deserves an important place on the bookshelves of anyone with a curiosity about the world's oldest religion. A truly stunning effort.
Dharma Windham, author of *Reluctant Goddess*

9781846941115 416pp £11.99 $24.95

A Pagan Testament
The literary heritage of the world's oldest new religion
Brendan Myers

A remarkable resource for anyone following the Wicca/Pagan path. It gives an insight equally into wiccan philosophy, as well as history and practise. We highly recommend it. A useful book for the individual witch; but an essential book on any covens bookshelf. **Janet Farrar** and **Gavin Bone,** authors of *A Witches Bible, The Witches Goddess, Progressive Witchcraft*

9781846941290 384pp £11.99 $24.95

The Celtic Wheel of the Year
Celtic and Christian Seasonal Prayers
Tess Ward

This book is highly recommended. It will make a perfect gift at any time of the year. There is no better way to conclude than by quoting the cover endorsement by Diarmuid O'Murchu MSC, "Tess Ward writes like a mystic. A gem for all seasons!" It is a gem indeed. **Revd. John Churcher**, Progressive Christian Network

1905047959 304pp £11.99 $21.95

Coyote Goes Global
A Modern Journey of Forgotten Ways
Star Blanket and Dream Weaver

Coyote Goes Global is a true tale of continuous discovery of Nature's mysteries. Star Blanket, a Shaman and ex-farmer, and Dream Weaver, a high tech guru of metropolitan origin, meet under the chaos and pressures of broken dreams. Together they embark on an adventure facing personal challenges of weaving their stories to rebuild the dream. Coyote is a legendary "Trickster" and spirit guide that assists to illuminate the Illusions and Fantasy's that humans experience, often taking forms that are perfectly acceptable in today's modern world.

978-1-84694-178-8 160pp £9.99 $19.95

Daughters of the Earth
Goddess Wisdom for a Modern Age
Cheryl Straffon

Cheryl combines legend, landscape and women's ceremonies to create a wonderful mixture of Goddess experience in the present day. A feast of information, ideas, facts and visions. **Kathy Jones**, co-founder of the Glastonbury Goddess Conference and author of *The Ancient British Goddess*

1846940163 240pp £11.99 $21.95

Forbidden Rites
Your Complete Introduction to Traditional Witchcraft
Jeanette Ellis

It gives me great pleasure to endorse this book. It manages to be at the same time practical, lucid, helpful, responsible, honest, and at times very moving. **Ronald Hutton**, Professor of Historical Studies, Bristol University

978-1-84694-138-2 624pp £19.99 $39.95

The Gods Within
An interactive guide to archetypal therapy
Peter Lemesurier

When I saw "The Gods Within", I had to pick up the book. This text includes a personality diagnostic, made up of keywords describing various personality traits. Using this easy to use system, the reader then finds out which Greek God or Goddess archetype that he or she most needs to explore. Ten main personality types are thoroughly described with a number of subcategories slightly modifying each. The reader is then encouraged to explore and embrace this archetype through a series of exercise: self-enquiry, invocation, meditation, and remedial activities. **Dr Tami Brady**, TCM Reviews

1905047991 416pp £14.99 $29.95

Kissing the Hag
The Dark Goddess and the Unacceptable Nature of Women
Emma Restall Orr

"Kissing the Hag" is a wonderfully intelligent, earthy, cosmic diary of the feminine life. I love the way it walks the edge between personal and collective, physical and poetic, highly ethical and thick in the uncertainties. While many writers fall into spiritualizing and intellectualizing "the feminine," this life-soaked book remains close to the fluids of body and soul, even as it gives birth to one trusted insight after another. It's an obvious gift-book for women going through a life passage, but it could also be important for men, who are closer to the mysteries presented here than they might wish to be. **Thomas Moore**, author of *Care of the Soul*

978-1-84694-157-3 304pp **£11.99 $24.95**

Medicine Dance
One woman's healing journey into the world of Native...
Marsha Scarbrough

Beautifully told, breathtakingly honest, clear as a diamond and potentially transformative. **Marian Van Eyk McCain**, author of *Transformation Through Menopause*

9781846940484 208pp **£9.99 $16.95**

Plant Spirit Wisdom
Sin Eaters and Shamans: The Power of Nature in Celtic Healing for the Soul
Ross Heaven

"The Joseph Campbell of our times". **James Shreeve**, Guardian journalist

9781846941238 224pp £9.99 $19.95

Shamanic Reiki
Expanded Ways of Workling with Universal Life Force Energy
Llyn Roberts and Robert Levy

The alchemy of shamanism and Reiki is nothing less than pure gold in the hands of Llyn Roberts and Robert Levy. Shamanic Reiki brings the concept of energy healing to a whole new level. More than a how-to-book, it speaks to the health of the human spirit, a journey we must all complete. **Brian Luke Seaward, Ph.D.**, author of *Stand Like Mountain, Flow Like Water, Quiet Mind, Fearless Heart*

9781846940378 208pp £9.99 $19.95

Tales of the Celtic Bards
Claire Hamilton

An original and compelling retelling of some wonderful stories by an accomplished mistress of the bardic art. Unusual and refreshing, the book provides within its covers the variety and colour of a complete bardic festival. **Ronald Hutton**, Professor of History, University of Bristol

9781846941016 320pp £12.99 $24.95

The Heart of All Knowing
Awakening Your Inner Seer
Barbara Meiklejohn-Free

A 'spell' binding trip back in time. It's a rediscovery of things we already knew deep down in our collective consciousness. A simple-to-understand, enjoyable journey that wakes you up to all that was and all that will be. **Becky Walsh** LBC 97.3 Radio

9781846940705 176pp **£9.99 $24.95**

The Last of the Shor Shamans
Alexander and Luba Arbachakov

The publication of Alexander and Luba Arbachakov's 2004 study of Shamanism in their own community in Siberia is an important addition to the study of the anthropology and sociology of the peoples of Russia. Joanna Dobson's excellent English translation of the Arbachakov's work brings to a wider international audience a fascinating glimpse into the rapidly disappearing traditional world of the Shor Mountain people. That the few and very elderly Shortsi Shamans were willing to share their beliefs and experiences with the Arbachakov's has enabled us all to peer into this mysterious and mystic world. **Frederick Lundahl,** retired American Diplomat and specialist on Central Asia

9781846941276 96pp **£9.99 $19.95**

The Other Side of Virtue
Where our virtues really came from, what they really mean, and where they might be taking us
Brendan Myers

This is one of the most important books you can read. 'The Other Side of Virtue' explores territory that is vitally important to understand at this critical time in our history. Reading it will deepen your soul. It might seem strange to recommend cheating when discussing a book on virtues and ethics, but let me say this: this is one of the most important books you can read, but if you doubt this, turn to the very last two pages of the book and read the final passage marked 'The Messenger'. Better still, start at the beginning and let the book deepen your soul and broaden your understanding. **Philip Carr-Gomm**, author of *Sacred Places, Chief of the Order of Bards, Ovates and Druids*

9781846941153 272pp £11.99 $24.95

The Way Beyond the Shaman
Birthing a New Earth Consciousness
Barry Cottrell

"The Way Beyond The Shaman" is a call for sanity in a world unhinged, and a template for regaining a sacred regard for our only home. This is a superb work, an inspired vision by a master artist and wordsmith. **Larry Dossey, MD**, author of *The Extraordinary Healing Power Of Ordinary Things*

9781846941214 208pp £11.99 $24.95

A Global Guide to Interfaith
Reflections From Around the World
Sandy Bharat

This amazing book gives a wonderful picture of the variety and excitement of this journey of discovery. **Rev Dr. Marcus Braybrooke,** President of the World Congress of Faiths

1905047975 336pp £19.99 $34.95

Helena's Voyage
A mystic adventure
Paul Harbridge

A beautiful little book, utterly charming in its simplicity. **Rabbi Harold Kushner,** author of *When Bad Things Happen to Good People*

9781846941146 48pp £9.99 $19.95

Living With Honour
A Pagan Ethics
Emma Restall Orr

This is an excellent pioneering work, erudite, courageous and imaginative, that provides a new kind of ethics, linked to a newly appeared complex of religions, which are founded on some very old human truths. **Professor Ronald Hutton,** world expert on paganism and author of *The Triumph of the Moon*

9781846940941 368pp £11.99 $24.95

Peace Prayers
From the World's Faiths
Roger Grainger

Deeply humbling. This is a precious little book for those interested in building bridges and doing something practical about peace. **Odyssey**

1905047665 144pp £11.99 $19.95

The Good Remembering
A Message for our Times
Llyn Roberts

Llyn's work changed my life. "The Good Remembering" is the most important book I've ever read. **John Perkins**, *NY Times* best selling author of *Confessions of an Economic Hit Man*

1846940389 96pp £7.99 $16.95

The Thoughtful Guide to Religion
Why it began, how it works, and where it's going
Ivor Morrish

A massive amount of material, clearly written, readable and never dry. the fruit of a lifetime's study, a splendid book. It is a major achievement to cover so much background in a volume compact enough to read on the bus. Morris is particularly good on illustrating the inter-relationships betwen religions. I found it hard to put down. **Faith and Freedom**

190504769X 384pp £24.99 $34.95

Bringing God Back to Earth
John Hunt

Knowledgeable in theology, philosophy, science and history. Time and again it is remarkable how he brings the important issues into relation with one another... thought provoking in almost every sentence, difficult to put down. **Faith and Freedom**

1903816815 320pp **£9.99 $14.95**

From the Bottom of the Pond
The forgotten art of experiencing God in the depths of the present moment
Simon Small

Don't just pick this book up, read it and read it again. It's the best Christian book I have read in years. This is a book that will inform, delight, and teach. It needs to be heard. It has the potential to light up Christianity. This is what happens when God is happening. It's a brave book, expressing what it feels like to feel God. It shines a light on God in the midst of life, in the detail and the dirt, and it should be on every Christian's reading list. **Revd Peter Owen-Jones**, Anglican Priest, author and BBC TV presenter of *The Lost Gospels* and *The Battle for Britain's Soul.*

978-1-84694-0 96pp **£7.99 $16.95**